TECHNOLOGY IN CONSTRUCTION LAW

A LEGAL GUIDE

LESLIE KING O'NEAL, EDITOR

AMERICAN BAR ASSOCIATION
Forum on Construction Law

Cover design by Sara Wadford/ABA Design

Printed in the United States of America.

27 26 25 24 23   5 4 3 2 1

A catalog record for this book is available from the Library of Congress.

CONTENTS

About the Editor ix
About the Authors xi
Acknowledgments xvii
Introduction xix

CHAPTER 1
Construction Technology: Past and Future 1
Russ Gibbs, Author
Anoop Sattenini, PhD, Author
Hala Nassereddine, PhD, Contributor

I. Introduction 1
A. Software 5
B. BIM 5
C. Construction Document Control 9
D. Construction Project Management Software 10
E. Big Data and Artificial Intelligence 11
F. Artificial Intelligence (AI) 11
G. Hardware/Computers 12
II. Infrastructure: Internet, Connectivity, Security 13
A. Drones (Unmanned Aircraft Systems—UAS) 14
B. Laser Scanning 16
C. Control/GPS/Positioning 18
D. 360-Degree Photographs 19
E. Robotics 19
F. Internet of Things (IoT) Tags and Devices 20
G. 3D Printing 21
H. Prefabrication 21
I. Summary 22

CHAPTER 2
Lawyer's Duty of Technological Competence 23
Sanjay Kurian and Benjamin T. Johnson, Authors

I. ABA Model Rule 1.1 24
II. Continuing Legal-Technology Education 25

III. Case Law 28
A. Electronic Communication Is the New Normal 28
B. Preservation of Electronic Evidence 29
C. Lawyer's Duty to Investigate Information Obtained from the Internet 30
D. Lawyer's Duty to Identify and Verify Electronic Documents Admitted into Evidence 31
E. Local Counsel Obligations for Pro Hac Vice Counsel's Technological Competence 32
F. Lawyer's Duty to Understand and Comply with Court E-Filing Requirements 33
G. Attorneys Must Have Adequate Systems in Place to Monitor Electronic Court Filings and Dockets 34
H. Lawyer's Duty to Understand ESI Discovery 37
I. Compelled Technology Training 38
IV. Ethics Opinions 39
A. Working Remotely 39
B. Virtual Practice 40
C. ChatGPT 41
V. Conclusion 42

CHAPTER 3
Data/Cybersecurity and Insurance 45
Reggie Jones and Kristen Broz, Authors
Sarah Glover, Contributor
Maynard Nexsen, Shareholder

I. Department of Defense (DOD) Regulations re: Cybersecurity 47
A. National Institute of Standards and Technology (NIST) 48
B. FAR/DFARS 49
II. Who Pays for Certification? 68
III. Potential Consequences for Noncompliance 69
IV. May 12, 2021, Executive Order Regarding Cybersecurity 69
A. Zero Trust Architecture 71
V. Private Sector Cybersecurity Risks and Solutions 72
A. Risk Assessments 73
B. Best Practices 75
C. Training 77
VI. Insurance for Cyber Risks 78
VII. Conclusion 79

CHAPTER 4
Dealing with Construction Technology in Law Practice 81
Rebecca Sherman and Megan George, Authors
Chris Harnett and Sarah Glover, Contributors
Maynard Nexsen, Shareholders

I. Introducing Emerging Technology and Its Legal Concerns, Impacts on Existing Practices, and Vetting the New Technology 81
A. Core Issues Regarding Construction Technology (BIM Technology) 82
B. The Rise of Drones and Wearable Technology 83
C. Technology's Impact on Insurance 86
D. Vetting New Technology 89
II. Contract Drafting, Risk Allocation, and Intellectual Property Concerns 93
A. Allocation of Risk for Technology-Impacted Contracts 93
B. Design and Construction Contract Templates 94
C. Addressing Data Security in Contracts 103
III. Ransomware, Law Firm Considerations, and Cybersecurity Best Practices 104
A. Ransomware Attacks in Construction Businesses and Law Firms 105
B. Best Practices for Mitigating Cybersecurity Risks 108

APPENDIX TO CHAPTER 4
Sample Cybersecurity Clauses 113

CHAPTER 5
Overview of Electronic Discovery in Construction Law Cases 115
Brett Lamb and Elisabeth Malsch, PhD, PE, Authors
Thornton Tomasetti, Principal
Leslie King O'Neal, Mediator, Arbitrator, Project Neutral, JAMS

I. Introduction 115
A. E-Discovery in Construction Litigation 115
B. Electronically Stored Information on Construction Projects 116
C. Data Retention Policies and Preservation 118
II. Locating ESI in Construction Projects 119
A. Discovery Planning 124
B. eDiscovery Budget 130
C. eDiscovery Protocols 130

APPENDIX A TO CHAPTER 5 133

APPENDIX B TO CHAPTER 5
Sample Litigation Hold and Data Preservation Notice 137

CHAPTER 6
Gathering ESI from Construction Projects 139
Brett Lamb and Elisabeth Malsch, PhD, PE, Authors
Thornton Tomasetti, Principal
Leslie King O'Neal, Mediator, Arbitrator, Project Neutral, JAMS

I. ESI Collection and Review 139
A. Who Should Perform Data Collection? 139
II. Discovery and Production of Different Types of ESI Used in Construction Projects 149
A. Construction Design and Management Software 149
B. Email 150
C. Photos, Video, Drone Data 151
D. IoT Sensors 152
E. Wearable Technology and Robots 153
F. Enterprise Video Meeting Recordings 153
G. Texts and IM, and Other Collaboration Applications 153
H. Social Media 154
I. Proprietary Software and Databases 155
J. Contract Documents, Plans, Specifications, and Shop Drawings 156
K. Device and Cloud Backup Systems 157
III. Inspecting Opposing Party Devices 157
IV. Cost Shifting 159
V. Protecting Client Confidences 161
A. Duty of Confidentiality 161
B. Protective Orders 162
C. Privilege Logs and Clawback Agreements or Orders 163
D. Protecting Trade Secrets 164
E. Managing What Goes in the Court File and Sealing Court Records 165
VI. Conclusion 167

APPENDIX TO CHAPTER 6
Sample ESI Protocol for Construction Matters #1 169

CHAPTER 7
Presenting ESI Evidence at Trial, Arbitration Hearings, and Mediation 177
Elisabeth Malsch, PhD, PE, Author
Thornton Tomasetti, Principal
Leslie King O'Neal, Contributor, Mediator, Arbitrator, Project Neutral

I. Summaries of Electronically Stored Evidence 179
A. Summary by Rule 180
II. The Consultant's Role in Preparing and Authenticating ESI for Use at Trial, Arbitration, or Mediation 196
A. Planning for Use of Demonstrative Exhibits 197
B. Big Data and Use of Analytics 198
C. Developing Demonstrative and Evidentiary Exhibits 201
III. Conclusion 204

CHAPTER 8
Technology Tools for the Construction Litigator 205
Joseph T. Imperiale, John J. Gazzola, and Chris G. Haley, CISSP, Authors

I. Using Artificial Intelligence to Identify the Sentiment Behind Written Records 206
II. Extraction Tools That Compile Data from a Large Volume of Documents 208
III. Depicting Complex Projects and Technical Concepts in Easily Digestible Ways 209
IV. Effectively Preparing and Presenting the Case 211
V. Litigation Technology on the Horizon—What's to Come? 212
VI. Recommendations and Best Practices 213
V. Conclusion 215

ABOUT THE EDITOR

Leslie King O'Neal is a neutral with JAMS, handling construction-related disputes as a mediator, arbitrator, and project neutral. From 2007 to 2022, she was associate general counsel for Brasfield & Gorrie, L.L.C., an ENR top 25 commercial general contractor, where she advised the company on contracts, insurance and disputes. Previously, she was a partner in and practiced construction and commercial litigation with Markel, McDonough & O'Neal, Holland & Knight, LLP and Greenberg Traurig LLC in Orlando, Florida. While in private practice and as in-house counsel, she managed and litigated a variety of construction and surety disputes in mediation, arbitration, and litigation and on appeal throughout the United States.

She has been active in the ABA Forum on Construction Law throughout her career, serving as Chair of Division One (Dispute Resolution) and on the Governing Committee before serving as Forum Chair from 1996–97. She is a Fellow in the American College of Construction Lawyers, where she served on the Board of Governors. She has written numerous articles on construction-related topics and has been a contributing author in several books. Ms. O'Neal is a frequent speaker to industry and legal groups. In 2019, she received the Lifetime Achievement Award from the Construction Law Committee of the Florida Bar Real Property Probate and Trust Law Section. In 2023, she received the Cornerstone Award from the ABA Forum on Construction Law. She received her BA from the University of Florida and her JD from the University of Florida College of Law.

ABOUT THE AUTHORS

Kristen W. Broz is a partner in the Washington D.C. office of Fox Rothschild LLP and an experienced litigator with a national practice focused on class actions, data privacy, and federal government contracts. Kristen defends clients in data breach class actions and works closely with businesses on investigating and responding to data loss or breach incidents. She also advises clients on regulatory compliance with existing and emerging regulations, including the Cybersecurity Maturity Model Certification (CMMC) and federal and state data breach notification regulations. Kristen teaches courses on legal and ethical issues in cybersecurity and information assurance at the University of Virginia and at Capitol Technology University in Washington D.C. She also serves on the board of directors for Wildlife SOS, a not-for-profit organization committed to protecting wildlife in India. Kristen is a graduate of George Washington University Law School and the University of Virginia.

John Gazzola is an associate in the Philadelphia office of the law firm Troutman Pepper. John's practice focuses on litigation and arbitration associated with construction projects. He represents project owners, EPC contractors, construction managers, general contractors, subcontractors, and material suppliers in disputes arising from a wide array of construction projects, including mass transit systems, pipelines, colleges and universities, medical facilities, senior living facilities, museums, quarries, hotels, and other large commercial buildings. John frequently contributes to the firm's construction litigation blog and is a member of the American Bar Association's Forum on Construction Law. John graduated from Harvard University in 2011. He graduated from Rutgers Law School–Camden, summa cum laude, in 2016, where he was executive editor of the *Rutgers University Law Review.*

Megan George is a member of Stites & Harbison's Construction Service Group. She counsels clients on construction matters and regularly drafts, negotiates, and reviews contracts for clients. Her clients include public and private project owners, general contractors, and subcontractors, whom she guides through all stages of project development and execution. She regularly advises national clients on design, construction, commissioning, consulting, vendor agreements, and other contracts. Locally, Megan helps both public and private clients navigate state and federal procurement laws. Megan is also experienced in federal grant administration, offering clients an integrated approach to federally funded public project delivery.

Russ Gibbs is the vice president of VDC, Innovation, and Operational Technology and oversees Brasfield & Gorrie's Virtual Design + Construction and Innovation Departments, serving as a thought leader and mentor while managing the use of innovation- and construction-related technologies. He's naturally curious, and he collects and shares forward-thinking ideas from across the company for the benefit of the entire workforce. Russ also works with personnel at all levels to understand their daily needs and develop creative solutions to streamline those day-to-day processes, often introducing inventive methods that become standard practice. He received his bachelor of architecture from Auburn University in 2007.

Sarah Glover is a shareholder in Maynard's Cybersecurity & Privacy Practice, where she heads up cybersecurity risk assessments, data breach response, and cybersecurity compliance and training initiatives. Sarah has gained prominence as a cyber expert, earning the ANSI-Accredited Certified Information Privacy Professional/United States (CIPP/US) from the International Association of Privacy Professionals (IAPP) while also serving as the vice chair of the Alabama State Bar Cybersecurity Task Force and an adjunct cybersecurity law professor at the University of Alabama School of Law. She is a graduate of the University of Alabama and of the University of Alabama School of Law.

Chris Haley is the director of legal technology in the Atlanta office of the law firm of Troutman Pepper and its legal technology subsidiary Troutman Pepper eMerge. He has been practicing in the areas of eDiscovery, litigation, and legal technology for over 25 years at both law firms and service providers. He has testified and been acknowledged as an expert in legal technology in state and federal courts. He is a frequent speaker on legal technology issues to attorneys and other technologists. Chris is a Certified Information Systems Security Professional (CISSP). He has won multiple industry awards and was recognized by the International Legal Technology Association as the Litigation Technology Professional of the Year in 2016.

Chris Harnett, a shareholder in Maynard's New York office, focuses his practice on the litigation of intellectual property matters. Over the past three decades, Chris has litigated cases in more than 35 jurisdictions around the country. After graduating from the Georgetown University Law Center in 1990, Chris began his career at the preeminent intellectual property law firm, Fish & Neave, where he was a partner for many years.

Joseph Imperiale is a partner in the Philadelphia office of the law firm Troutman Pepper. Joe has dedicated his practice exclusively to the construction and manufacturing industries for more than 18 years. He represents owners, EPC contractors, construction managers, general contractors, and subcontractors in disputes on a wide array of construction projects, including power plants, mass transit systems, highways, high-voltage electric transmission lines, pipelines, and heavy industrial and commercial construction projects. Joe currently serves on the Steering Committee for the Dispute Resolution Division of the ABA Forum on Construction Law. He lectures and writes on construction-related topics. Joe graduated from Dickinson College, cum laude, in 2001. He graduated from Villanova University Charles Widger School of Law, magna cum laude, in 2004, where he was managing editor of the *Villanova Law Review*; Order of the Coif.

Benjamin Johnson is an in house attorney with American Express. Previously, he was with the law firm Becker & Poliakoff, P.A. and was a member of the firm's Construction Law & Litigation practice group. Mr. Johnson is an active member of the Florida Bar and is a member of the Florida Bar's Construction Law Committee. He has frequently presented on Florida's construction defect statutes and has authored several publications relating to construction and condominium law.

Reginald ("Reggie") Jones is a partner in the Washington D.C. office of Fox Rothschild LLP and chair of the firm's Federal Government

Contracts Group. He centers his practice on federal compliance and litigation with an emphasis on large, complex claims prosecution and defense. He has significant experience overseeing internal investigations with civil and criminal False Claims Act implications. Reggie speaks and writes frequently on topics relevant to federal contractors, including the litigation of bid protests, enforcement of the Foreign Corrupt Practices Act, and navigating the requirements of the Defense Federal Acquisition Regulation Supplement (DFARS) and Cybersecurity Maturity Model Certification (CMMC). Reggie served as a captain in the U.S. Army from 1991 to 1996, including four years in Germany, Hungary, Croatia, and Bosnia-Herzegovina. He serves on the board of directors Washington Building Congress and is the board liaison for the Diversity Task Force. Reggie is a graduate of the University of Georgia School of Law and The College of William and Mary.

Sanjay Kurian is a shareholder with the law firm of Becker & Poliakoff, P.A., is the Managing Shareholder of the Fort Myers office, and is a member of the Firm's Construction Law and Litigation group. He is Board Certified in Construction Law by the Florida Bar, is ranked by Chambers USA, and rated AV Preeminent by Martindale-Hubbell. Mr. Kurian is active in the Florida Bar and is Chair of the Florida Bar's Construction Law Committee, serves on the steering committee for Division 12 (Owners and Lenders) of the ABA Forum on Construction Law, chairs Florida's 20th Circuit Judicial Nomination Commission, and serves on the Florida Bar's Professional Ethics Committee. He has presented and written frequently on the topics of construction defects, construction contracts, and insurance claims.

Brett Lamb is the CEO of an eDiscovery technology provider and consulting firm, Construction Discovery Experts (CDE), which specializes in supporting construction litigants and their outside counsel. Prior to leading CDE, Brett served as a partner in the law firm of Gardere Wynne Sewell (now Foley Lardner) and later served as general counsel at Austin Industries in Dallas, Texas. Brett has been a frequent lecturer on construction law and eDiscovery topics to both professional associations and industry groups. He has also authored numerous articles in the area of construction law. Brett graduated from the University of Colorado and Baylor University School of Law.

Elisabeth Malsch is an expert in structural analysis and design, with specializations in investigative projects. She is proficient in static, dynamic, and nonlinear analysis and the evaluation of buildings, temporary structures, and mechanical systems under the effects of typical to extreme loads. Her work includes emergency response, litigation support, construction defect cases, structural collapse investigation, and mechanical systems failure analysis. In addition to serving on Thornton Tomasetti's board of directors and as co-leader of their forensics practice, Elisabeth is a member of the leadership team that oversees the firm's research and development program. Elisabeth is a frequent lecturer, speaking on topics that range from technical innovation to improving diversity in the field of engineering. She received her BS in civil engineering, her MS in engineering mechanics, her MPhil in engineering mechanics and her PhD in engineering mechanics from Columbia University.

Hala Nassereddine, PhD, is an assistant professor in construction engineering and project management at the University of Kentucky in Lexington, Kentucky. She received her BS from Rafik Hariri University–Lebanon, and her PhD from the University of Wisconsin–Madison. Her research focuses on addressing the past and present of the construction industry while maintaining a positive vision for the future. She studies organizational change, workforce shortages, Construction 4.0 (with a focus on Digital Twins and Augmented Reality), Lean Construction, digital delivery, and process reengineering.

Dr. Anoop Sattineni is the William A. Hunt Endowed Associate Professor in the McWhorter School of Building Science at Auburn University. He has a PhD from the University of Salford in built environment, a master of science in civil engineering from Auburn University, and a bachelor of civil engineering from Osmania University in India. His areas of research include the use of advanced information and communication technologies to improve construction industry practices. He has been contributing to this field since 1998 and has published his work at numerous national and international conferences, as well as journals. He is a current board member of the International Association for Automation and Robotics in Construction (IAARC).

Rebecca Sherman is a partner in the Lexington, Kentucky, office of Stites & Harbison, PLLC, where she is a member the Construction Practice Group. Her practice focuses on advising clients throughout all phases of construction projects including planning, contracting, project administration, and disputes. She represents owners, contractors, and subcontractors, with a particular focus on commercial construction contract drafting and negotiation. Admitted to practice in both Kentucky and Ohio, she earned her JD from the University of Kentucky College of Law, cum laude and Order of the Coif, and was production editor for the *Kentucky Law Journal*.

ACKNOWLEDGMENTS

Many people contributed their time and talent to this project; it takes a village to write a book such as this. In addition to the authors, a host of others assisted with cite checking and reviewing, providing helpful comments, and other assistance. The book would not have been possible without their contributions. I am very grateful to Asha Echeverria (BernsteinShur) and Sarah ("Sam") Orwig (ABA Publishing) for their continued support and assistance. Thanks also to Andy Ness for the book idea and his continuing support for this effort. Special thanks to the Hon. Ralph Artigliere (retired) for his leadership and contributions, especially to the chapters on eDiscovery and presentation of evidence. Also many thanks to Amy Phillips for her support.

Many thanks to Gregg Bundschuh, Sarah Glover, Chris Haley, and Hala Nassereddine for contributing to several chapters as authors and providing helpful comments. Thanks also to Angelo DiBartolomeo, Sarah Glover, Peter Hahn, Liz Kraengel, Nicole Lentini, Joanne Noel, and Andrea Woods for cite checking and reviewing the chapters.

Leslie O'Neal

INTRODUCTION

This book arose from two personal experiences I had: first, I was asked to introduce James Benham, a well-known speaker on construction technology, at the ABA Forum on Construction Law 2022 Annual Meeting. Also, I edited the excellent paper that Rebecca Sherman and Megan George of Stites & Harbison wrote for that program. Around the same time, I attended a meeting at my former employer, Brasfield & Gorrie, L.L.C., where I heard a report from the virtual design and construction department about a robot dog the company was using on some projects. This fascinated me. These two incidents piqued my interest in learning more about new construction technology and the legal issues it raises. When I told my friend, Andy Ness, about the paper for the Annual Meeting, he said, "That would make a great book. You should suggest it to the Forum Publications Committee." I took this advice and, as they say, the rest is history.

Since I am not an expert in construction technology or all the related legal issues, it was important to recruit experts who could clearly explain and advise on these topics. With the help of the inimitable Amy Phillips, I was very fortunate to recruit an extremely talented and experienced group of authors. Russ Gibbs, head of innovation at Brasfield & Gorrie, L.L.C., and Dr. Anoop Sattenini, professor at Auburn University's McWhorter School of Building Science, wrote the first chapter discussing the history of and the current and future uses of design and construction technology. Sanjay Kurian of Becker Poliakoff and Benjamin Johnson of American Express wrote about the lawyer's ethical duty of technological competence. Reggie Jones and Kristen Broz of Fox Rothschild authored the chapter on cybersecurity and government regulation, with contributions from Sarah Glover of Maynard Nexsen. Rebecca Sherman and Megan George of Stites & Harbison expanded their Annual Meeting paper explaining how construction technology affects lawyers in contracts, insurance, data security, and other areas in the chapter on technology and law practice; Maynard Nexsen partners Sarah Glover and Chris Hartnett contributed the explanation of intellectual property and other issues to this chapter. Brett Lamb, CEO of Construction Discovery Experts wrote about the important topic of eDiscovery and construction technology. Dr. Elisabeth Malsch of Thornton Tomasetti used her expertise in authoring the chapter on presentation of electronic evidence derived from construction technology and the expert's role in assisting counsel with such evidence. Finally, Joseph Imperiale, John Gazzola, and Chris Haley of Pepper Troutman authored the chapter discussing various technology tools available for construction litigators use in managing and organizing the massive amount of data generated on construction projects by new technology.

This book is intended as a resource and a practical reference for construction lawyers looking for information about the various types of technology now being used in design and construction, or who want guidance on how to gather and manage the vast quantities of data these technologies generate. While technology is evolving so rapidly that this book may need updating soon after publication, I hope it will give construction lawyers useful information and references to assist them in representing their clients and managing their cases.

CHAPTER 1

Construction Technology: Past and Future

Anoop Sattenini, PhD and Russ Gibbs, *Authors*
Hala Nassereddine, PhD, *Contributor*

1. Introduction

The design and construction industry has adapted to technological innovations since the beginning of time. However, since 2010 use of digital technologies in design and construction has increased substantially, pushing the industry to adopt changes. A digital revolution has been underway since the 1950s; however, it accelerated in the late 1990s when personal computers became affordable for nearly every household. The advent of the internet and popular web browsers such as Netscape and search engines like Yahoo and Google further propelled the use of computers in everyday life and for most industries.[1] Prior to the advent of these digital tools information in the design and construction industry was conveyed primarily using two-dimensional drawings and in text through contracts and specifications. Communication

1. Leiner, B.M., Cerf, V.G., Clark, D.D., Kahn, R.E., Kleinrock, L., Lynch, D.C., Postel, J., Roberts, L.G., & Wolff, S. (1997). *Brief History of the Internet.* Retrieved from Internet Society: https://www.internetsociety.org/internet/history-internet/brief-history-internet/.

occurring after design completion was through regular mail and later through fax machines. Design and construction firms were slow to adopt technology advances compared to other industries. In the year 2000, "Most construction companies were still largely using paper for their operations—from paper plans, to paper spec books to paper records for project schedules, requests for information, submittals and more. A contractor using Excel would have been considered advanced."[2]

The advent of email brought about massive change in how design and construction professionals communicated with each other. Introduction of smartphones in 2007, allowing people to connect and to replay and consume information remotely, was a catalyst for construction companies to use this and other technology on job sites. "Next to the migration of computing resources to the cloud and delivering tech through the web browser, which had a huge impact on project management and enterprise resource planning (ERP) software, the second big impact [to construction] from technology was definitely mobility through the 2007 popularization of smartphones."[3] Computer-aided design (CAD) came on the market in the 1960s. At first, CAD was only two dimensional (2D) and not much faster than hand drawing. By the 1970s 3D CAD was introduced; in the late 1980s use of CAD exploded. "It has totally changed how engineering design is practiced and has been a major element in the increase in industrial productivity we have seen during the past decade."[4]

In today's construction landscape, many digital changes focus on adoption of construction specific software to help communicate among the major trade partners throughout the design and construction process. Early versions of digital platforms were primarily designed to enable and document communication among the stakeholders. These platforms have evolved to comprehensive software solutions including

---

2. Crosby, R. (2020, January). *The Evolution of Construction Tech: 20 Years in Review.* Retrieved from Construction Business Owner Magazine: https://www.constructionbusinessowner.com/technology/evolution-construction-tech-20-years-review.

3. *Id.*

4. Weisberg, D. (2008). *A Brief Overview of the History of CAD.* Retrieved from The Engineering Design Revolution (p. 21). Cyon Research: http://images.designworldonline.com.s3.amazonaws.com/CADhistory/85739614-The-Engineering-Design-Revolution-CAD-History.pdf.

all stakeholders and including all aspects of the construction process. An inherent problem created by the outdated design and construction process is "silos" of information. Construction contractors can be compared to the automobile industry in the sense that the car manufacturer does not manufacture every single part that goes in the car but instead relies on suppliers for parts that, in many instances, are sourced globally. Similarly, the general contractor (GC) relies on information from the design team and on trade partners (subcontractors) to complete the project. Every entity is separate and has its own ways of going about the construction process. Large trade partners on a project, such as subcontractors for the structure, HVAC, plumbing, and electrical systems, rely on accurate and complete information from their respective design partners. However, each trade contractor and design firm is an independent business entity. The software they use is often unique and customized for their operations. This creates "silos" of information throughout the design and construction industry. The GC is often required to coordinate between all the stakeholders—owner, design team, and trade partners.

Compared to the integrated nature of other businesses such as Amazon or Walmart where supply chains are comprehensively connected, the construction industry struggles with far too many cases of inaccurate and/or incomplete information because of these information silos. These silos play a major role in the loss of productivity, but more importantly contribute to misinformation and miscommunication throughout project design and construction. These "digital silos" of information have confused the construction process, while the complexity of buildings and systems continues to increase. Complexities created by the information passed from the architects/engineers, through the GC, and ultimately to the major subcontractor trade partners sometimes grind construction projects to a halt. The method of project organization in design and construction where each temporary project is a unique combination of numerous different specialist disciplines makes it difficult for the industry to adopt widespread innovation quickly.[5] The multitude of separate, bilateral contracts between project stakeholders that created the industry's traditional adversarial contractual culture is

5. Cornick, T., & Mather, J. (1999). *Construction Project Teams: Making Them Work Profitably* (Thomas Telford Publishing).

another factor adding to the communication gap.[6] This lack of communication can result in parties not fully understanding who owns the risk throughout both design and construction. This situation forced the industry to look to technology to improve processes and communication.[7] As Industry 4.0—the fourth industrial revolution—continues to evolve, the construction industry is playing catchup with more innovative industries. The term Construction 4.0 was coined as the construction industry grapples with these changes. Although there is no universally accepted definition of Construction 4.0 and the technologies it encompasses,[8] there are three broad themes: (1) industrial production—examples include prefabrication, offsite manufacturing, and 3D printing; (2) cyber-physical systems—examples include robotics and drones; and (3) digital technologies—examples include building information modeling, augmented reality, artificial analysis, and big data and data analytics.

This chapter deals with two forms of technological tools available in the marketplace to improve the design and construction process. Broadly, the authors describe them under the labels "software" and "hardware." Specifically, this chapter addresses recent disruptive technologies that have vastly reshaped construction industry practices. The authors acknowledge that items listed under these labels are a loose classification and, as such, are generalized only for the purpose of discussion in this chapter.

---

6. Eschenbruch, K., Bodden, J., Borrmann, A., König, M., Koch, C., & Beetz, J. (2018). *Building Information Modeling: Technology Foundations and Industry Practice* (Springer International Publishing AG, part of Springer Nature).

7. Al Hattab, M., & Hamzeh, F. (2013, July). *Information Flow Comparison between Traditional and BIM-Based Projects in the Design Phase.* International Group for Lean Construction, Fortaleza, Brazil (v.21). Retrieved from ResearchGate: https://www.researchgate.net/publication/258885932.

8. Sawhney, A., Riley, M., Irizarry, J., Toca Perez, C., & Leathem, T. (ed.). (2020, September). *A Proposed Framework for Construction 4.0 Based on a Review of Literature.* EPiC Series in Built Environment (vol. 1, pp. 301–09). 56th Annual International Conference, Associated Schools of Construction (ASC). Retrieved from ResearchGate: https://www.researchgate.net/publication/344242586_A_proposed_framework_for_Construction_40_based_on_a_review_of_Literature.

A. Software

Numerous specialized types of software exist that are designed for specific processes such as cost estimating and project scheduling. This chapter explores recent software that the authors considered disruptive[9] to traditional construction industry practices, which are fast becoming the norm. Disruptions include creation of a new industry practice or process or transferring a process or practice from one party to another.

B. BIM

Building Information Modeling (BIM) is the next generation of Computer-Aided Design (CAD). The National Institute of Building Science defines it as, "A BIM is a digital representation of physical and functional characteristics of a facility. As such, it serves as a shared knowledge resource for information about a facility forming a reliable basis for decisions during its lifecycle from inception onward."[10] Evidence suggests some owners are taking advantage of BIM's full potential and using these models throughout the facility's life cycle. However, in practice, it is used primarily by designers to collaborate with one another and produce printable construction drawings. Often the models are passed on to the GC with "hold-harmless" signoffs stating that the model is not to supplant the 2D drawings; however, the GC uses the models for various construction-related functions. The trade partners generally use the design models to produce shop-drawing quality models for the coordination process. There is much room for improvement in the workflow related to how these models are produced and used in

---

9. A "disruptive technology" is a specific technology that can fundamentally change not only established technologies but also the rules and business models of a given market, and often business and society overall. The internet is the best-known example in recent times; the personal computer and telephone in previous generations. The term was coined by Clay Christensen, a Harvard Business School professor, in his 1997 book *The Innovator's Dilemma.* Disruptive technology often has problems because it is new, appeals to a limited audience, and may not yet have a proven practical application.

10. National Institute of Building Sciences (nibs.org) is an independent nonprofit, nongovernmental organization that supports advances in building science and technology. It was established in the Housing and Community Development Act of 1974 (P.L. 93-383).

the industry. However, credit is due to the architecture/engineering/construction (AEC) sector for the remarkable achievement of making BIM mainstream within the short span of a decade or so.[11]

Developing construction drawings is the process of designers visualizing a building in 3D space, but then having to communicate that space downstream through a series of 2D drawings bound together so they can be printed, held by a person, and rolled out on a table to be read and understood. BIM disrupted the process of having to think in 3D, communicate in 2D, and then build in 3D. BIM enabled designers to construct their thoughts in 3D and maintain the 3D information to share with their design partners. This new, improved sharing and communication increased the level of understanding by all design partners, resulting in the ability to spatially merge information into one digital model, increasing visualization and understanding. This new workflow is a disruptive technology that allows major advancements in technology to emerge throughout the industry. However, the disruption was so significant that it sometimes caused confusion and contradictions for established processes within the industry. The ability to simulate the construction process in a digital environment forced the industry to relearn, adapt, and evolve. Entities that could not do this were left behind. This disruption brought about new project delivery methods such as "integrated project design" (IPD)[12] at a stunning speed.

"Can I trust the 3D model?" is a question one often hears from construction professionals. The design and construction community has been on a 15-year-long journey to understand better when to use the 3D

11. In 2022, the AIA issued a suite of documents focused on BIM and digital data. The suite includes four BIM exhibits (E201-2022, E202-2022, E401-2022, E402-2022), each specific to how the model is used and the parties with whom the model is shared. *See* AIA Digital Documents Guide, https://zdassets.aiacontracts.org/ctrzdweb02/zdpdfs/digital-practice-docs_guide.pdf (last accessed on Feb. 20, 2023). *See* Chapter 4 for further discussion of contract language regarding BIM models.

12. Integrated Project Delivery (IPD) is a project delivery approach that integrates people, systems, business structures and practices into a process that collaboratively harnesses the talents and insights of all participants to optimize project results, increase value to the owner, reduce waste, and maximize efficiency through all phases of design, fabrication, and construction. Integrated Project Delivery: A Guide, American Institute of Architects, AIA California Council (AIA 2007).

model and when to use the 2D drawings. Even in 2022, 2D drawings take priority over the 3D model as the governing documents that all parties legally agree to use, although the design team uses the 3D model to develop the design, and the general contractor and subcontractors interpret the 3D model for construction purposes. Sometimes 2D drawings are extracted from the 3D models. The more interesting conversation is, what processes led to creation of those 2D drawings that were approved and accepted by legal contracts? In the last 15 years there has been more communication between trade subcontractors, more partnership between contractors and designers, and more visibility for owners than ever before in the AEC industry. However, sadly, there are companies, or employees within companies, that have no idea what is happening. The 15-year debate of whether to trust the 3D model or the 2D drawings is yielding a high level of confidence by asking the question, "What process did you have in place when using the 3D model to create your 2D drawings?" It is not about one versus the other; it is about the process and the people involved in it while decisions were being made. Early communication between designers, contractors, and subcontractors is the key for the successful use of BIM on a construction project. In projects using "negotiated" and "design build" project delivery methods, this can be accomplished better, as all parties can be communicating during the earliest phases of design and construction. Ideally, design documents referenced in contracts should include 2D drawings and 3D models, but the industry as a whole is not ready to accept this yet.

Several tools known as "BIM execution plans"[13] are available to include BIM in the contractual agreements and help to clearly define expectations with all major trade partners before they are brought on board the project.

---

13. A BIM Execution Plan (BEP) is a comprehensive document that assists project participants by outlining clear roles and expectations. A BEP should be created before beginning any construction project, especially large or complex projects with many collaborators. In July 2022, AIA issued a template for a BIM Execution Plan (G203-2022).

1. *BIM for Construction Coordination*

The most significant change BIM has provided for general contractors is its ability to aid in coordinating the construction process. Professionals often describe construction as a "problem-solving" business. The use of BIM models to optimize coordination and collaboration between trade partners and the various stake holders epitomizes this saying. Combining accurate 3D models from trade partners and using them to detect and fix clashes between physical elements, such as between a beam and a pipe, months or weeks before actual construction has been one of the most consequential uses of BIM for the construction industry. The models are also probed to ensure that all elements are code compliant. Equipment clearances can be checked to ensure serviceability issues. The phrase "a picture is worth a thousand words" is apt when thinking of BIM for coordination. One major benefit in the coordination process is all stakeholders having the ability to have a 3D visual representation of issues related to a proposed course of action.

2. *BIM for Cost Estimation*

An accurate count of all materials needed is an important step in developing accurate cost estimates for a construction project. The "parametric" nature of BIM models can be used to develop an accurate materials count. The parameters inherent to model objects in a BIM are key features that allow software to extract exact quantities. However, the first step in using a BIM for construction-related issues is to "scrub" the model. To use the model for quantity survey, it must be explored thoroughly to ensure it is an accurate representation of what is to be installed on the site. An example is to ensure that an exterior wall model object includes the components such as insulation, brick, block, and so on. Once quantities are extracted, estimators can use proposed means and methods of construction to develop an estimated cost for the project. In today's construction industry, several project delivery methods are available to allow early collaboration between the construction and design teams. The automation of quantity extraction can allow the construction team to collaborate effectively with the design team in early phases. This can ensure that the design team stays informed about the costs of construction and impact of design decisions on the overall project budget in a timely manner.

3. *BIM for Facility Management*

Owners can use facility data generated during the design and construction phase of a project to manage the facility during its lifetime. The digital tools needed to manage a facility are traditionally separate from the ones used for developing a BIM. However, with proper initial planning, BIM data can be imported into facility management software to optimize interoperability. Parameters within a BIM can be developed to include maintenance data for equipment in the project. The ability to visualize using a BIM is an important benefit for facility managers to collaborate with others.[14]

4. *BIM for Field Management*

Construction site personnel must have the latest construction drawings (or BIM), as designers and subcontractors modify the design through the coordination process. The use of tablet devices and digital tools allowing field personnel to view and probe the model enable such personnel to keep track of design changes. The model can be used as the basis to communicate with subcontractors to resolve site-related issues. It is fairly common practice for designers on a fast-track project to develop design drawings and release them for construction. Later, the design team may go back and update or provide additional detailed section views of these drawings that field personnel can examine. Site personnel can also add parametric attributes to the model in the form of raster images[15] that can help document as-built conditions.

C. Construction Document Control

How was information created and shared throughout the design and construction process before 2010? A series of design professionals created a set of drawings to be printed to a size small enough to be carried, held by a person, and rolled out on a desk or table to be read by a team. The physical size of the paper determined how the project would be

---

14. This can be done through use of a "digital twin," which can be part of a BIM process.

15. A CAD drawing or a BIM model has x/y or x/y/z coordinates for everything shown on the drawing or model. Even though it may look the same, a scanned in PDF or JPEG picture has only digital pixels and is referred to as a raster image.

communicated to all others downstream (including specifications and submittals). If that information was revised or changed, someone had to physically print the changed sheets and distribute them to field personnel on the construction site, updating the paper plan sets. Designing and construction using outdated information was, and still is, a constant problem for construction productivity.

This questioning resulted in the widespread adoption of centralized data in the construction industry. Autodesk's PlanGrid was among the first products that forced the industry to think differently about storing and distributing design information. By using this tool, drawing sets could be stored in a central location, updated by one person, but then sent out to everyone participating on the project at the same time. This forced the entire industry to rethink how information is shared and received. The concept of printing plans and specifications is now outdated. If information is extracted from the centralized location, then is your information no longer current? All sorts of new questions emerged, and many limitations had to be overcome. However, the construction industry was not slowing down; general contractors saw the power of centralized data and knew the potential risks did not outweigh the reward. In December 2018, Autodesk purchased PlanGrid for $875 million. Today several commercial solutions such as Procore, e-Builder, Kahua, ProjectSight, and more allow construction documents to be centrally managed and distributed via online portals.

D. Construction Project Management Software

Given that commercial construction projects can span multiple years, a vast amount of information is generated on a project during its construction phase. Over the past two decades, with the surge of internet usage in all aspects of business operations, most of this data has been digitized and made available online. The data generated includes information such as requests for information, schedules, submittals, daily reports, change management, safety reports, pay applications, punch lists, and so on. Many of these items are generated by one party such as the general contractor and approved by another party such as the architect, owner, or other members of the design team. Present-day construction project management software developed by companies such as Autodesk, Trimble, Procore, and many others track all communication, approvals, and tasks in a central portal, allowing all parties to track information relevant to their needs. Each project participant has permissions set up so only information relevant for their domain is visible and/or editable. Most or all of this software also can provide companywide status information on all projects via a dashboard. These dashboards allow senior executives to watch the health of the company from a macro level, as well as providing a quick summary of each project's status.

E. Big Data and Artificial Intelligence

One of the major concerns around the increased use in technology in construction is the fact that we are adding more complex layers that might produce data that cannot be turned into a quick, accurate decision-making tool. Too much technology and too much data can be bad if they do not serve a purpose. Companies must understand the problems first and then explore specific technologies to solve them. Companies must also capture the information necessary to communicate results. "Big data" is a term that means bringing all the information together into a single location to help leverage machine learning and artificial intelligence. We can no longer silo information so that it cannot be leveraged by computing power. We must think through an approach to capture data, connect data, store data, and leverage data. Factoring business intelligence into data sets will be key to a company's success. When the data sets become so large that people can longer sift through all the information, we must leverage computing power to help in decision-making.

F. Artificial Intelligence (AI)

Artificial Intelligence (AI) is the discipline of machines demonstrating humanlike intelligence to make complex decisions. Examples of AI can be found in all business disciplines, including use of robots for manufacturing, autonomous driving vehicles, analyzing health care data, and more. There are several AI uses in the construction industry; however, they are still at their nascent stage. Regardless, construction is ripe for a large-scale infusion of AI due to several converging factors. A tremendous amount of data is generated in the life of a construction project, which is archived in various digital formats such as text, databases, and photographs. This data can be analyzed and used to make future predictions regarding a project or a company to further enable the construction team to make better decisions during the project and enable company management to make better decisions company-wide. Given the scarcity of skilled labor, the use of robots and construction methods such as prefabrication are on the rise. The use of robots, drones, laser scanners, and the like are no longer novelties in the construction industry. Several of these hardware and software technologies already use AI to optimize workflow and processes. Construction is full of repeatable tasks across all phases of a project. Many of these tasks can be automated by AI. Some examples include inspections, planning, checks for gaps in information, schedule analysis, image processing for safety checks, and so on. Use of AI also creates risks for the construction industry. The use of data inherently exposes the owner of the data to cybersecurity risks.[16] Most data in the modern construction industry is stored in third-party cloud software and is accessible by multiple parties, further exposing the risk to the owner of the data. Questions regarding who owns the data and how the data may be used in the future, for purposes not intended during the collection phase, and consequences of these issues remain to be answered.

G. Hardware/Computers

The construction industry's ability to embrace technology is directly tied to its ability to invest in the types of computers and hardware necessary to handle the changes in information. Emerging software always pushes against the limitations of computers. This is nothing new to industry giants such as IBM, Apple, and Google. However, for a construction company, it is a major shift in overhead spending and liability. If a construction company decides to switch from a paper-based workflow, where all the drawings must be printed and distributed to a centralized digital-based workflow, where all information is now viewed on computers and iPads, then the company must make a large investment in the hardware and in training its people to ensure a seamless transition. For most companies that investment requires an overlap in both cost and resources, because no company is willing to go all in on a new workflow for the first time on a "live" project. Centralizing information

16. Cybersecurity is discussed in detail in Chapter 3.

is such a major improvement for the design and construction community that Information Technology (IT) departments in both design firms and construction firms now equal the size and importance as other support groups within those firms. These IT groups must understand and constantly evolve to meet companies' needs around the following questions:

- Where is the data being stored?
- Is the data secure?
- How can a project team's information be recovered if lost?
- Is my iPad connected to the internet?
- Does my iPad have enough storage for this project?
- Does the construction project have internet?
- Do I have access to the design team's information?

Computers, tablets, smartphones, servers, render farms,[17] virtual reality (VR) headsets, augmented reality (AR) headsets, unmanned aircraft systems (UAS or drones), laser scanners, robotic total stations,[18] base stations, rovers, grade-controlled enabled construction equipment, IoT wearables, robotics, and so on; these are all technology hardware that construction firms are using today, and there are many more on the horizon.

II. Infrastructure: Internet, Connectivity, Security

As construction information migrates from paper based to digital, and from "siloed" to centralized, companies must understand the risks associated with the infrastructure required to store, transmit, and access the required information to keep projects running. What happens when the internet goes out? Does everyone go home? As construction information becomes digital, projects are 100 percent reliant on these systems to stay up and running. Connectivity must be maintained from office to office,

17. A "render farm" is a cloud-based rendering firm where computers generate a 2D picture from 3D design drawings.

18. Base Stations are Site Positioning/Layout Solutions for construction projects. Base Stations receive signals from GPS System satellites and create a correction factor. Robotic Total Stations are electronic/optical instruments used to measure both vertical and horizontal angles and the slope distance between the RTS and a particular topographical point.

as well as from project to office. Using the PlanGrid example, imagine an office in Dallas updating the drawing set at the same time a project manager is walking the job site performing his or her quality inspections. The complexities around that scenario are daunting; the amount of storage on a tablet device such as an iPad can be a limiting factor. The information added by the office team with high-speed internet, and the information added by that project manager while walking the project site offline with no internet, can lead to confusion and improper documentation, which may not come to light in a timely manner. How can all this information come together and be correct? Even if the information is correct, will it be trusted? As construction information for each project migrates more and more to the Cloud, who owns this data? Will owners begin requiring a data strategy from everyone on the project? None of these questions has a straightforward answer yet, but all stakeholders in the industry need to be engaged in developing answers.

A. Drones (Unmanned Aircraft Systems—UAS)

In 2011, a construction company needed to inspect the caulk joints on a 14-story façade that had been completed ten years previously. The team decided to fly an unmanned aircraft systems (UAS) made by a drone company called DJI vertically along the façade of the building and take a series of images and videos that could be viewed at a high resolution back at the office. Using the UAS rather than the traditional inspection methods seemed safer for the project team, quicker, and was substantially less expensive than manual inspection. The UAS data pointed out key areas of the façade that needed manual inspection. This was more efficient than manually inspecting all areas by lowering an employee on a swing stage. The test proved successful. However, the FAA grounded all commercial use of UASs until it could promulgate rules and regulations. It was over a year later that the FAA announced the "333 Airman Waiver,"[19] which requires the pilot in command of an UAS to have an actual pilot's license. Companies wishing to use drones

19. The 2018 FAA Reauthorization Act (P.L. 115-254) repealed section 333 and replaced it with section 44807: Special Authority for Certain Unmanned Aircraft Systems. Federal Aviation Administration. Retrieved from: https://www.faa.gov/uas/advanced_operations/certification/section_44807.

then purchased the craft, insured the craft for potential damages caused, developed internal procedures, and developed a UAS pilot training plan. While it was obvious that UASs had a future in construction, at that point it was impossible to determine the return on investment. In the early days UASs were overpriced drones with hard-to-use software. Initially the purpose was to allow for safer project inspections, but that changed when another company, Leica, created a 3D photogrammetric model of a project from the imagery the UAS created. Using this tool, the general contractor could overlay the 3D model over the existing site to verify that existing site conditions matched the design, which was previously possible only through traditional survey practices. This new process enabled an entirely new avenue in the BIM process. However, there were still three major limiting factors:

- The pilot in command had to be a licensed pilot.
- The UAS was very expensive.
- 3D photogrammetry was not scalable.

In 2017, the FAA made policy changes, allowing UAS pilots to operate under a much less-extensive 107 permit.[20] Insurance coverage allowing multiple craft under one umbrella policy became available, DJI products became very affordable and reliable and DroneDeploy™ hit the market, allowing easy-to-use 3D photogrammetry data to capture large existing conditions. Photogrammetry relies on cameras to measure real-world objects and turn 3D space into 2D maps. This requires photogrammetry software to identify the location, orientation, and movement of the camera to circulate the position of three-dimensional points.[21] The internal UAS program expanded and UASs are now a consistent tool used on projects to help monitor quality control, inspections, as-built documentation, and for site contour mapping.

---

20. *Part 107—Small Unmanned Aircraft Systems.* Title 14 (2022, June). ch. I/ sub F. Code of Federal Regulations. National Archives and Records Administration. Retrieved from: https://www.ecfr.gov/current/title-14/chapter-I/subchapter-F/part-107

21. Putch, A. *Linear Measurement Accuracy of DJI Drone Platforms and Photogrammetry.* Drone Deploy. Retrieved from: https://dronedeploy-www.cdn.prismic.io/dronedeploy-www%2F46e720cd-fb03-41ec-a6a3-09b424d674b8_linear+measurement+accuracy+of+dji+drone+platforms+and+cloud-based+photogrammetry-v11.pdf.

The information collected from UAS devices pose some risks, including the following:

- Privacy issues of neighboring building owners.
- Where is the drone manufacturer storing the imagery and location data?
- What happens if the UAS captures a defect, but that image is not seen by a project member?
- Is the UAS survey information aligned to the correct coordinate system?
- Is 3D photogrammetry data stitched properly?[22]

The UAS's hardware in flight also poses risks, enumerated here:

- Is the hardware calibrated and maintained properly?
- Is the construction site secure; are all employees aware of the flight?
- If the flight is over people, does the UAS require a parachute?
- Does a 107.39 apply for a particular flight (107.39 regulation provides that only authorized personnel are allowed under flight path)?
- If a UAS crashes, what is the general contractor's crash investigation and reporting process?

B. Laser Scanning

One of the greatest challenges in design and construction is capturing the existing conditions of an existing space. The traditional method was to verify by hand with pencil and paper and take this back to the office to draw in 2D and 3D. Most renovation projects require a general contractor to "field verify" existing conditions to limit the designer's liability for errors in capturing the existing conditions. If the design is based on bad information, it will be wrong; however, the contractor must build from the approved design. Field verification makes the contractor responsible for catching erroneous field information and bringing it to the design team's attention before starting construction or even

---

22. Often 3D photogrammetry involves taking multiple pictures and "stitching" the pictures together as one image.

ordering material. This is the paralyzing information loop that dissolves trust in the team. Is there a better way? There is, and it is called laser scanning. Laser scanning is a process/technology that sets up at a fixed place and rotates while shooting thousands of lasers into the existing conditions of that space. The actual activity is not harmful; the risks are around the data and how it is used. Each laser creates a point in space when it hits an existing object. With thousands of lasers being shot per second, the result is a data set of points so dense that it can capture a 3D point cloud of the space with millimeter accuracy. Each setup is line of sight and takes about three minutes to capture; however, as it moves throughout the existing conditions, the software registers the individual 3D point clouds into a unified 3D model of the existing conditions that can be linked into the BIM process. This process captures the existing conditions directly into 3D and maintains the information in a format that can be easily shared and understood. The drawback to this process is that the file sizes are extremely large and require costly computers to manipulate the information. It also requires knowledge and experience to register the information into a trusted unified 3D point cloud.

Some general contractors were quick to adopt this technology without fully understanding the overall risks associated with the workflows. The small window a contractor has between receiving the design from the design team and starting construction was enough make improving the existing condition documentation process with laser scanning a useful tool; however, what if contractors used laser scanning as a process to dictate design? What if architects and engineers ask general contractors to laser scan for them? Traditionally, a civil engineer provides a stamped as-built documentation drawing. However, the civil engineer usually has a contract limiting its liability from the laser scan. Who is willing to assume the risk? What qualifies someone as an expert of a specific technology? The data generated by the technology is equally important as the skill of the individual making measurements from the extracted scan data. Some general contractors are becoming experts in laser scanning but use the information only for their own internal quality control measures to avoid taking on additional risk.

Laser scanning can also be used to verify the quality of constructed items. Where vertical walls or large flat slabs need to be within a specific tolerance, laser scanning can be done once the forms are stripped and a quality control report can be generated with millimeter accuracy before equipment is delivered, glazing is installed, precast is flown, or shafts are inspected. If the desired items to be scanned are visible and accessible, laser scanning can be performed and turned around to the project team without slowing down construction.

C. Control/GPS/Positioning

The digitization of construction information is forcing all parties to focus on the correct positioning of their digital files. This does not refer to where files are stored, but to the ability of the lines and objects within the file to know their exact location in real space. Very few design and construction experts understand the principles of orienting CAD or BIM files correctly. The civil engineer can perform this step early in the project and share it with the entire design team, or all files can be manipulated to match the project control once it is established on-site. Nonetheless, control must be established and communicated to the entire team. Digital control and physical site control must be aligned and checked for accuracy. CAD files, Revit files, UAS data, and laser-scanning data, all can be locked into a control network to ensure the proper alignment of information. This is important for the following activities:

- Back checking grade elevations;
- Cut/Fill analysis—pay apps;
- Building placement;
- Interior layout:
  - Floor plate[23]
  - Hangers
  - Penetrations

Latitude/longitude references are replacing field dimensions. With advancements in automation and robotics, more and more layout is performed with coordinates. Establishing a control network and then reporting through a base station is becoming more common throughout the industry. Dozers, excavators, and trucks are guided by positioning devices and cutting the earth based on a CAD file or 3D model. Most

23. A single floor in a multistory structure is sometimes called a "floor plate."

construction materials are required to be placed within 1/16th of an inch accuracy. Therefore, correctly modeled files correctly aligned to the project coordinates will be a major factor in the rapidly growing area of automation, specifically in an automated fabrication environment.

D. 360-Degree Photographs

A new phenomenon in construction is the capture of 360-degree photographs on the job site. A member of the construction management staff (or a robot) walks the job site with a camera capable of capturing photographs that can be uploaded and overlaid on a set of digital drawings. Over a period, these photos document how the site has evolved in that time span. This allows the construction team to document project progress over the span of the project. These photographs can also supplement as-built drawings and can assist future design teams with renovation or refurbishment issues. The photos can also update project progress to various stakeholders who are not present on the construction site daily. For these photos to be used effectively, a robust software component is needed to allow easy access and uploading processes.[24] These photos can be used for simulating future construction, schedule predictions and so on. However, as with all data, these photographs can also be used against a party in claims related to quality, schedule, safety incidents review, or other issues.

E. Robotics

The term "robotics" causes a lot of confusion in the construction industry because it is difficult to understand what can be automated. The constantly changing environment of a construction site poses many challenges for robotics. However, the industry should ask: "What would we like to automate if we could?" and "Can we increase the production hours of a job site from eight hours a day to 24 hours a day with robotics?" These are questions with answers just several years away. In 2019, Boston Dynamics released a robotic dog named SPOT that is fully capable of navigating a construction site.[25] It has nearly solved

---

24. Some examples: PTGui, Autopano Pro/Giga. Adobe Photoshop, Hugin, Pano2VR 5.2 Pro, Microsoft Image Composite Editor.

25. https://www.bostondynamics.com/products/spot.

the most challenging variable: a constantly evolving site. Projects will see robotic deliveries, equipment without operators, terrestrial layout vehicles, and many more advancements making sites safer, cleaner, and more productive.[26]

F. Internet of Things (IoT) Tags and Devices

Internet of Things (IoT)[27] tags and devices are sensors capable of capturing real-time information and communicating it over the internet. This data can be used for further analysis to make informed decisions or trigger follow-up actions. Examples of IoT devices in construction include site condition monitors, security monitors, health and safety management, and fleet management. Contractors also install devices within smart buildings that are IoT enabled, such as air-conditioners, temperature sensors, switches, occupancy sensors, and so on. Contractors should assume that IoT-enabled tags, sensors, and devices will be ubiquitous in the future. Consequently, they will need some level of in-house expertise to deal with them on the job site and for owners of smart buildings. IoT devices have been shown to be particularly vulnerable to cybersecurity threats.[28] Contractors must deal with this security threat to ensure a reliable and productive workspace. Often these devices need

---

26. Startup companies are proposing various types of robots for use in construction, for example: "Australia's Fastbrick Robotics, which builds a mobile robot called the Hadrian X that can lay up to 1,000 bricks an hour. Pennsylvania's Advanced Construction Robotics builds robots that can tie up to 1,100 rebar intersections an hour. Canvas, founded in San Francisco, has a mobile robot that finishes drywall." Pranshu Verma, *These Robots May Build Your House*, WASH. POST (Jan. 30, 2023), https://www.washingtonpost.com/technology/2023/01/30/construction-companies-robotic-technology/.

27. The "Internet of Things" (IoT) is the networking capability that allows information to be sent to and received from objects and devices (such as fixtures and kitchen appliances) using the internet. *Merriam-Webster.com Dictionary*, Merriam-Webster, https://www.merriam-webster.com/dictionary/Internet%20of%20Things. Last accessed 27 June 27, 2022.

28. Andrea, A., Chrysostomou, C., Hadjichristofi, G. (2015). *Internet of Things: Security Vulnerabilities and Challenges.* The 3rd IEEE ISCC 2015 International Workshop on Smart City and Ubiquitous Computing Applications. Department of Computer Science and Engineering Frederick University, Cyprus. Retrieved from: https://e-tarjome.com/storage/btn_uploaded/2020-05-19/1589883649_10674-etarjome%20English.pdf. See Chapter 3 for further discussion of cybersecurity.

occasional digital upgrades. Contractors should ensure that facility owners are trained to perform such upgrades, and contracts must use explicit language to indicate the responsible party for such upgrades.[29]

G. 3D Printing

3D printing is also known as additive manufacturing. 3D printing is a powerful tool for rapidly prototyping ideas into physical objects. 3D printing is the construction of physical elements, in three dimensions, by extruding materials such as plastics, concretes, powders, and resins from a machine guided by a CAD-based model.[30] These 3D-printed objects can be strong and be operational immediately upon removal from the printer. In manufacturing, companies now can design a part and then instantly 3D print that part in-house. A replica part can be analyzed, studied, and tested before the company moves forward with making thousands of those parts and starting the assembly process. In construction, scale replicas of projects can be printed to verify how the project will be built or what the finished product will look like. Architectural models can now be 3D printed in a fraction of the time required to make models by hand. However, scale is the limiting factor when 3D printing. Most 3D-printing applications are for parts or objects smaller than 10 feet × 10 feet square. However, several companies are pushing those boundaries with new technologies. Specifically, concrete printers are being debuted to print large-scale structures such as small commercial buildings and houses. The form factor of the machines themselves are revolutionizing the 3D-printing world. The time where a thought can become a reality within days is not too far away.

H. Prefabrication

The term "prefabrication" represents a process where physical components are planned so they can be fabricated in a warehouse in one location, then shipped to their destination and assembled with speed and

---

29. See Chapter 4 for further discussion regarding contract language. See Chapter 6 for discussion of requesting IoT data.

30. Hurtado, K., & Leavitt, J. (2015). *Brave New Extruded World: Legal Issues Arising in the Construction Industry from Using Additive 3D Printing Technology*, 9 J. Am. Coll. Const. Law. 1.

accuracy. No matter the components, companies must maximize what they can control. Prefabrication can be employed for subassemblies with mechanical, electrical, and plumbing systems or entire hotel rooms that can be stacked to make an entire building. Design and construction are moving to more predictable processes, like those used in manufacturing today. This will impact many aspects of design and construction contracts as well as sustainability, labor, and safety.[31] Construction companies are trying to replicate the manufacturing process in the AEC sector. Not all buildings will be candidates for this process, but the designers and contractors should consider the ability to prefabricate components before the design process begins.

I. Summary

The digitization of the design and construction industry is underway. Advances in software and hardware have resulted in the advent of disruptive technologies affecting all industries, including construction. Construction companies have reaped tremendous productivity benefits from these technologies. However, these productivity benefits have not sky-rocketed profits in the industry. At best they have had small but measurable effects on profits. The progression of this evolving digital construction environment has created the need for design and construction companies to take on another area of expertise, which is not their core business. Companies able to achieve this will reap the largest rewards from new technology.

---

31. Colby, K. & Davis, L. (2015). *The Rise of Modular Construction: A Changing Legal Landscape*, 9 J. Am. Coll. Const. Law. 124.

CHAPTER 2

Lawyer's Duty of Technological Competence

Sanjay Kurian and Benjamin T. Johnson, *Authors*

The rapid pace of change in technology impacts all of us. Lawyers, not known for their embrace of technology or innovation, are being dragged along. The ethical duty to stay abreast of technological advancements is now required in most states, and lawyers must maintain the requisite level of competence to practice law.

A broad range of technological tools, services, and platforms are available in the design and construction industry. To be technologically competent lawyers in the construction industry need to stay abreast of industry technologies in addition to legal technology as both may impact the ability to represent design and construction clients competently. These technologies include the basics, such as email and cloud storage, and the more complicated, such as building information modeling (BIM), robotics, construction-progress recordation, image recognition, safety technology, and legal products marketed to construction attorneys, including contract drafting, review, and administration tools, research and forecasting platforms, e-discovery products, and billing software.[1] This chapter reviews the ethical obligations facing attorneys

1. For example, and in the construction context, software applications such as Brainspace by Reveal Data allow attorneys to use artificial intelligence to derive meaningful information from construction project photos, videos and other visual inputs. Other applications, like Relativity One by Ricoh eDiscovery, provide communication

generally and looks at cases where legal professionals failed to carry out their duty to provide competent representation to their clients due to lack of knowledge or understanding of technology.

I. ABA Model Rule 1.1

In 2012, the American Bar Association (ABA) revised the Model Rules of Professional Conduct to incorporate a duty of technology competence alongside the perennial duty to keep abreast of changes in the law. Model Rule 1.1 requires lawyers to provide competent representation for their clients; providing "[c]ompetent representation requires the legal knowledge, skill, thoroughness and preparation reasonably necessary for the representation."[2] This has been the standard for a long time and has not changed due to technology.

However, the ABA amended comment 8 to Model Rule 1.1 to specifically require lawyers to "keep abreast of changes in the law and its practice, *including the benefits and risks associated with relevant technology*, engage in continuing study and education and comply with all continuing legal education requirements to which the lawyer is subject" to maintain the requisite knowledge and skill required of a lawyer.[3] Lawyers are now required to be familiar with not only substantive changes in their practice but also the relevant technology that could impact that practice.

This need for technology training is well recognized in the legal profession. According to the 2021 ABA Legal Technology Survey Report, 68 percent of respondents agreed that lawyers must stay current with the benefits and risks of technology to maintain competency under the rules of professional conduct.[4] Law firms have also taken a

---

analysis through interactive visualization of communications between key individuals on a jobsite.

2. Model Rules of Pro. Conduct r. 1.1 (Am. Bar Ass'n 2020) [hereinafter Model Rules].

3. Model Rule 1.1 cmt. 8 (emphasis added).

4. Sofia Lingos, *ABA TechReport 2021: Technology Training* (Dec. 8, 2021), https://www.americanbar.org/groups/law_practice/publications/techreport/2021/techtraining/.

proactive approach toward technology, as 65 percent of firms consider budgeting and planning for technology to be essential.[5]

Today, 40 states have adopted a statement or comment on technological competence being included in a lawyer's duty to provide competent representation.[6] While many jurisdictions have adopted comment 8 to Model Rule 1.1 verbatim, several states have taken additional measures to ensure that practicing attorneys are continuing to educate themselves about the risk and use of technology.[7]

II. Continuing Legal-Technology Education

Florida has paved the way in legal-technology education and training. In 2016, Florida modified the comments to Rule 4-1.1, Florida Rules of Professional Conduct:[8]

> To maintain the requisite knowledge and skill, a lawyer should keep abreast of changes in the law and its practice, engage in continuing study and education, *including an understanding of the benefits and risks associated with the use of technology,* and comply with all continuing legal education requirements to which the lawyer is subject.

The Florida Supreme Court also directly changed Rule 6-10.3 for minimum continuing legal education standards to require 33 hours of continuing education over each three-year cycle, instead of 30 hours, with three hours specifically dedicated to approved technology programs.[9]

Competent representation requires safeguarding confidential information related to the representation, including electronic transmissions

5. Julie Bays, *ABA TechReport 2021: Budgeting & Planning* (Dec. 1, 2021), https://www.americanbar.org/groups/law_practice/publications/techreport/2021/bp/.

6. Effective January 1, 2022, Hawai'i became the 40th state to add a duty of technological competence to its Rules of Professional Conduct.

7. Chapter 3 and Chapter 5 discuss ABA Model Rule 1.6(c), the lawyer's ethical duty of confidentiality and to make reasonable efforts to prevent unauthorized disclosure of information related to the client.

8. *See In re* Amendments to Rules Regulating the Florida Bar 4-1.1 and 6-10.3, No. SC16-574, 200 So. 3d 1225, 1227–28 (Fla. 2016).

9. *See id.* at 1228.

and communications.[10] The new Florida rules require the additional three hours of continuing education so the lawyer can obtain "an understanding of the risks and benefits associated with the use of technology"[11] or provide sufficient information so the lawyer can elect to "meet this obligation through a lawyer's association with, or retention of, a non-lawyer advisor with established technological competence in the relevant field."[12] While Florida was the first state to require technology continuing education for lawyers, it was not the first state to require technology competence.

Effective in 2019, North Carolina became the second state to require all licensed attorneys to complete two hours of legal ethics and one hour of continuing legal education devoted to technology training; this hour is part of North Carolina's annual 12-hour requirement. North Carolina's Governing Rules of the State Bar defines technology training as "a program, or a segment of a program, devoted to education on information technology (IT) or cybersecurity."[13] The rules further acknowledge that the primary objective of technology training is to enhance a lawyer's proficiency or improve law office management.[14]

Most recently, New York joined the list of states requiring technology education and training for attorneys. In June 2022, the Judicial Departments of the Appellate Division of the New York State Supreme Court formally added technology training to the state's continuing legal education requirements.[15] In fact, New York has taken a focused approach toward its technology training, as the new requirement mandates that practicing attorneys complete at least one credit hour of training in cybersecurity, privacy, and data protection every two years. This narrowly tailored technology training program comes in response to increasing concerns surrounding the disclosure of confidential

---

10. *Id.* at 1226.

11. *Id.*

12. *Id.*

13. 27 N.C. Admin. Code ch. 1D, § .1501.

14. *Id.* § .1602.

15. Joint Order of the Departments of the New York State Supreme Court, Appellate Division (June 10, 2022), https://www.nycourts.gov/LegacyPDFS/RULES/jointappellate/Joint%20Order%20amending%2022%20NYCRR%201200.0%20Rule%20of%20Professional%20Conduct%208.4%20g%20%2006-10-22.pdf.

information, which traces back to 2020 when the New York State Bar Association's Committee on Technology and the Legal Profession first proposed to implement a one-credit continuing legal education requirement in cybersecurity protection, as opposed to a general credit in technology training.[16] The proposal was presented with the intent of focusing on "what the Committee believes to be one of the most pressing and urgent issues facing our legal profession: cybersecurity protection of confidential and proprietary client and law firm electronic information and assets. . . ."[17]

While only three states currently require licensed attorneys to obtain continuing legal education credits in technology training, other states are likely to follow suit. For example, Maine has incorporated an aspirational goal of maintaining technological competence through continuing legal education: "The purpose of minimum continuing legal education (MCLE) requirements is to promote and sustain competence and professionalism and to ensure that attorneys remain current on the law, law practice management, and technology in our rapidly changing society."[18]

In 2015, the California State Bar Association released an ethics opinion that expressly acknowledged a duty of lawyers to be competent in technology.[19] The opinion requires attorneys who represent clients in litigation either to be competent in e-discovery or associate with others who are competent.[20] The opinion cites the ABA's comment 8 and states: "[m]aintaining learning and skill consistent with an attorney's duty of competence includes 'keeping abreast of changes in the law and its practice, including the benefits and risks associated with

---

16. *Report and Recommendations of Committee on Technology and the Legal Profession*, New York State Bar Association, House of Delegates (June 3, 2020), https://nysba.org/app/uploads/2020/06/3.-Report-and-recommendations-of-Committee-on-Technology-and-the-Legal-Profession-Agenda-Item-9-with-comments.pdf.

17. *Id.*

18. Maine Rule of Professional Conduct 5.

19. *See* Cal. Bar Standing Comm. on Prof'l Responsibility and Conduct, Formal Op. 2015-193 (June 30, 2015), https://www.calbar.ca.gov/Portals/0/documents/ethics/Opinions/CAL%202015-193%20%5B11-0004%5D%20(06-30-15)%20-%20FINAL.pdf.

20. *Id.*

technology.'"[21] In February 2021, California became the 39th state to adopt a general duty of technology competence when it added comment 1 to Rule 1.1 of the California Rules of Professional Conduct, which mirrors the language of Model Rule 1.1.

Similarly, at the request of the U.S. Virgin Islands Bar Association, the Supreme Court of the Virgin Islands amended its mandatory continuing legal education requirements in 2019 to require two credit hours per reporting cycle in technology programming.[22] The Virgin Island's rules specifically note that technology programming, defined as "CLE programming designed for lawyers that provides education on safe and effective ways to use technology in one's law practice," assists lawyers in complying with the Virgin Islands Rules of Professional Conduct, requiring lawyers to possess the knowledge and skills necessary for competent representation.[23]

III. Case Law

Technology issues impact all practitioners in a wide area of practices and can result in bar discipline if not taken seriously. The following cases demonstrate the technological issues facing lawyers and potential consequences for failing to deal with them appropriately.

A. Electronic Communication Is the New Normal

By Supreme Court order, dated October 17, 2011, South Carolina required all lawyers admitted to practice law in South Carolina to log-on, verify, and update their contact information on the Attorney Information System (AIS) by November 18, 2011.[24] The order specified attorneys "shall ensure that his or her contact information in the AIS includes a mailing address, an e-mail address, and a telephone or cell phone number, and that this information is current and accurate."[25]

---

21. *Id.*

22. *In re* Amendments to Supreme Court Rule 208, 2019 WL 2051942, *1 (V.I. 2019).

23. *Id.* at *3.

24. *In re* Collie, 406 S.C. 181, 182 (S.C. 2013).

25. *Id.*

In this case, the attorney refused to provide an email address and claimed she was not required to do so because she was "retired."[26] The South Carolina Supreme Court notes that "[a]lthough respondent may consider herself retired from the practice of law since she has not represented clients in many years, she is nevertheless classified as a regular member of the South Carolina Bar and . . . required to provide a valid email address. Even if she were eligible to elect to be a retired member of the Bar, she would still be required to maintain an email address."[27] The court suspended the attorney's license to practice law, noting that the attorney had "repeatedly refused to comply with the explicit directives, orders, and rules of this Court and of requests by the Clerk of Court by refusing to maintain and monitor an operational email account."[28]

This case teaches that an email address is now considered a basic requirement for law practice, as having a telephone number and, later, a fax number became requirements. Email is the preferred method of communication in most commercial and professional settings and all lawyers must be able to communicate in this way.

B. Preservation of Electronic Evidence

The lawyer's duty to instruct clients about preserving electronic evidence was the subject of *Kenneth Paul Reisman*.[29] This is a complicated case involving an employee who, without permission, transferred files from his former employer's laptop to his new employer's laptop.[30] The former employer sued the employee. Unbeknownst to his counsel, the employee used a scrubbing program to delete files from the new laptop.[31] The former employer's attorney sent counsel for the employee a litigation hold letter asking for preservation of all documents relating to the case, but employee's counsel took no action and did not advise employee not to delete files from the laptop.[32]

26. *Id.* at 185.
27. *Id.* at 186.
28. *Id.* at 186–87.
29. *Kenneth Paul Reisman*, 2013 WL 5967131, at *1 (Ma. St. Bar. Disp. Bd. 2013).
30. *Id.*
31. *Id.*
32. *Id.*

The court entered an order allowing a forensic examination of the new laptop. The employee advised counsel that there were files unrelated to the litigation that should not be disclosed.[33] Counsel, without inquiring further as to the specific nature or content of these documents advised employee that he could scrub such confidential information from his laptop.[34] Ultimately, employee's counsel withdrew but there was a referral for attorney discipline filed against employee's counsel.

The board of bar overseers noted that due to a lack of experience in electronic discovery, counsel failed to appreciate that the court's order required the entire hard drive to be preserved for the expert. Counsel's advice to the employee that he should scrub "unrelated" files without first conferring with experienced counsel or conducting research as to his client's legal obligations and without any attempt to confirm that the materials to be deleted were as represented was conduct violating Massachusetts Rule of Professional Conduct 1.1.[35] Counsel was subject to a public reprimand for this conduct.

C. Lawyer's Duty to Investigate Information Obtained from the Internet

While representing a client in a criminal case in 2011, counsel, a 30-year practitioner, was presented with documents purporting to evidence that his client was the beneficiary of a large bequest from his long-lost cousin in Nigeria.[36] The client represented that upon payment of $177,660 in taxes owed on the inheritance in Nigeria, the sum of $18,800,000 would be released to him. He asked counsel to represent him in securing the transfer of the funds from Nigeria. Counsel agreed to do so in consideration for a fee equal to 10 percent of the funds recovered. Counsel then engaged in conduct including borrowing money from other clients, communicating with persons he believed were representatives of the "Central Bank of Nigeria," the "African Union," the President of Nigeria, a purported Nigerian lawyer who had witnessed the decedent's

---

33. *Id.*
34. *Id.*
35. *Id.* at *2.
36. Iowa Supreme Court Attorney Disciplinary Bd. v. Wright, 840 N.W. 2d 295 (Iowa 2013).

will, and a person claiming to be an English lawyer who had traveled to Nigeria and investigated the legitimacy of the inheritance.

In its evaluation and report, the board withdrew the allegation against counsel that he engaged in illegal or fraudulent conduct by noting that counsel "honestly believed—and continues to believe—that one day a trunk full of . . . one hundred dollar bills is going to appear upon his office doorstep," and although such conduct might aptly be described as delusional, it was not fraudulent. The board's evidence established that a cursory internet search "would have revealed evidence that counsel's dream of a Nigerian inheritance was probably based on a scam." The board considered counsel's failure to verify the scam, verify the identity of the people he spoke with, and his conflict of interest with his clients in obtaining the loans and suspended him for 12 months.

While this attorney seemed gullible, this case highlights the need to investigate and verify information found on the internet. Such independent verification would include not relying on client-provided contacts and phone numbers as well as general skepticism of anything that sounds too good to be true.

D. Lawyer's Duty to Identify and Verify Electronic Documents Admitted into Evidence

State v. Ratliff was a criminal case involving surveillance video.[37] The parties viewed the tape pretrial and were aware it contained audio but did not make the court aware of this.[38] The video was admitted into evidence without limitation during the trial and was shown to the jury without sound.[39] During deliberations the jury requested to review the surveillance video and was provided a DVD player and television to watch the video; ultimately, the jury heard the audio that was not provided at trial. The defense did not object or move for a mistrial but agreed with the court's suggestion to poll the jurors.[40] The conviction was affirmed without addressing any technological issues for counsel.

37. State v. Ratliff, 849 N.W. 2d 183 (N.D. 2014).
38. *Id.* at 188.
39. *Id.*
40. *Id.*

In the concurring opinion, Justice Carothers noted many potential issues with electronic evidence as raised by the facts:

> Given our holding in the present case, lawyers and judges increasingly must be vigilant about identifying and knowing precisely what "evidence" is being admitted. . . . When another form of electronic information is introduced—say an electronic document—questions may arise whether they contain metadata. If so, is metadata being admitted along with the information on the face of the document? Knowing the answer will be important to lawyers, who must "provide competent representation to a client."[41]

Justice Carothers noted that knowing and understanding the evidence before the court would be important to judges, but given that judges could not conduct independent investigations, the burden falls on counsel to understand and communicate these issues.[42] Justice Carothers concluded that there were a great number of potential questions, and he sampled a few to "alert the bench and bar of concern as the nature of adjudicative evidence shifts from one-dimensional paper to multidimensional electronic documents."[43]

E. Local Counsel Obligations for Pro Hac Vice Counsel's Technological Competence

James v. National Financial LLC involved a discovery dispute related to data contained in different spreadsheets.[44] The court sanctioned the party for the discovery conduct, and sanctioned counsel including counsel admitted pro hac vice and local Delaware counsel.

Lead counsel appearing pro hac vice, stated to the court: "I have to confess to this Court, I am not computer literate. I have not found presence in the cybernetic revolution. I need a secretary to help me turn on the computer. This was out of my bailiwick."[45] The court showed

41. *Id.* (citing North Dakota Rule of Professional Conduct 1.1 and MODEL RULE 1.1 cmt. 8).

42. *Id.* at 196.

43. *Id.*

44. James v. Nat'l Fin. LLC, 2014 WL 6845560, at *1 (Del. Ch. 2014).

45. *Id.* at *12.

no sympathy and, relying on Delaware's adoption of Model Rule 1.1's comment 8, stated that "[p]rofessed technological incompetence is not an excuse for discovery misconduct."[46] The trial court noted further that Pennsylvania, where the sanctioned attorney was licensed, had a parallel requirement.[47]

The court then addressed local Delaware counsel. The court noted that the "rules make clear that the Delaware lawyer who appears in an action always remains responsible to the Court for the case" and "Delaware lawyers are ultimately responsible for the documents they file with the Court and serve on the [opposing party]."[48] The court concluded by stating: "Delaware counsel are expected to police the behavior of their out-of-state colleagues and ensure that out-of-state counsel understand the standards expected by Delaware courts."[49] The court did not distinguish the technology competency requirements from any other requirements under the rules governing attorney conduct.

It is common for construction attorneys to be admitted pro hac vice in other jurisdictions. Local counsel should discuss the pro hac vice lawyer's technology competence before agreeing to act as local counsel. If, as in this case, the out-of-state counsel professes not to be computer literate, local counsel should suggest hiring another lawyer or consultant to manage the technology requirements or consider declining the assignment.

F. Lawyer's Duty to Understand and Comply with Court E-Filing Requirements

An attorney's lack of computer skills and frustration with following federal court electronic pleading requirements led to his suspension from the U.S. Bankruptcy Court for the Western District of Oklahoma.[50] However, the attorney failed to report this suspension to the Oklahoma Supreme Court, where he was licensed. The attorney had

---

46. *Id.* (citing Delaware Supreme Court amended Comment 8 to Rule 1.1 of the Delaware Lawyers' Rules of Professional Conduct, which addresses competence, to include maintaining technological competence).

47. *Id.*

48. *Id.* (citations omitted).

49. *Id.*

50. State *ex rel.* Oklahoma Bar Ass'n v. Oliver, 369 P.3d 1074 (Okla. 2016).

been admitted to the Oklahoma Bar in 1967, practiced in bankruptcy courts almost 30 years, and had never had any prior complaints or disciplinary actions.[51] No testimony nor any documents showed an insufficiency in the attorney's knowledge of substantive bankruptcy law.[52] The trial tribunal reported that the problem was technological proficiency. These problems led to an initial suspension by the bankruptcy court for 30 days, then 60 days, and finally permanently.[53] Although the technological failures did not disqualify him from practicing law in the courts of Oklahoma, the failure to report his suspensions to the Oklahoma Bar and timely notify his bankruptcy clients of those suspensions warranted public censure.[54] The court concluded with a note that they encouraged the attorney "to continue to improve his computer skills, or better, to hire an adept administrative assistant to do his pleadings."[55]

If a lawyer lacks computer skills, he or she must engage competent staff to assist with these tasks while the lawyer obtains some level of competence. However, as noted in the ABA Model Rules, the attorney must make reasonable efforts to ensure subordinate attorneys and staff conduct is compatible with the attorney's professional obligations.[56]

G. Attorneys Must Have Adequate Systems in Place to Monitor Electronic Court Filings and Dockets

In *Emerald Coast Utilities Authority v. Bear Marcus Pointe, LLC*, the trial court electronically issued an award of attorneys' fees.[57] Counsel for Emerald Coast Utilities Authority (ECUA) did not receive the order for reasons noted below and filed a motion to set aside the award due to excusable neglect. At the trial court level, counsel for ECUA argued that relief was appropriate from the attorneys' fees order because he never received the order in time to file a timely appeal.[58] Opposing party

51. *Id.*.
52. *Id.* at 1075.
53. *Id.*
54. *Id.* at 1077.
55. *Id.*
56. Model Rules 5.2 and 5.3.
57. Emerald Coast Util. Auth. v. Bear Marcus Pointe, LLC, 227 So. 3d 752 (Fla. 1st DCA 2017).
58. *Id.* at 756.

responded that ECUA was not entitled to relief because appellant's ability to file a timely appeal was not hindered by any action attributable to the trial court or the clerk, but attributable to the actions of ECUA's counsel.[59]

Both the trial and appellate court found against ECUA and its counsel. The issue both courts focused on revolved around the decisions made by ECUA's counsel regarding the firm's email spam filter and counsel's failure to monitor the online docket. The firm's IT consultant advised ECUA's counsel that the spam filter was unreliable and that it was better practice to hire a third-party to handle spam filtering on a full-time basis.[60] This was rejected by ECUA's counsel due to cost concerns.[61]

Multiple technological consultants, including ECUA's counsel's IT consultant, reviewed the transaction logs from the clerk's server to the firm's server and concluded that the order assessing attorneys' fees was properly delivered and that it was possible that the server deleted the email as spam.[62] One technological consultant testified that counsel's mail filtering system was set to drop and delete emails identified as spam and that this was inadvisable in any business setting because it resulted in data loss.[63]

The appellate court concluded that, based on the evidence presented, "the trial court could conclude that [ECUA counsel] made a conscious decision to use a defective email system without any safeguards or oversight to save money. Such a decision cannot constitute excusable neglect."[64] The court found a lawyer's failure to meet a case deadline was not excusable neglect where the spam filters on the law firm's email deleted an order sent by the court assessing fees and the lawyer failed to check the online docket.[65] The court stated that counsel had a duty to have sufficient procedures and protocols in place, which included adequate spam filter safeguards and independent monitoring

59. *Id.*

60. *Id.* at 757.

61. *Id.*

62. *Id.* at 754.

63. *Id.* at 755.

64. *Id.* at 757 (citations omitted).

65. *Id.*

of the court's electronic docket.[66] The court further noted that where rendition of an appealable order was delayed for a significant period of time, this duty might also include the filing of a joint motion for a case management conference to ensure that the order has not slipped through the cracks.[67]

Another cautionary tale in the era of e-filing is *Rollins v. Home Depot USA*.[68] Kevin Rollins sued his employer for personal injury. The employer filed a motion for summary judgment on the eve of the parties' agreed deadline for dispositive motions. Rollins's counsel never saw the electronic notification of that motion or the motion because counsel's computer email system placed that notification in a folder not regularly monitored. As in the *Emerald Coast Utility* case in Florida, the lawyer did not check the docket either. As a result, Rollins did not file an opposition to the summary judgment motion, leading the district court to enter judgment against Rollins. Rollins, on appeal to the Fifth Circuit, contended that the district court abused its discretion in denying his Rule 59(e) motion, on the ground that the only reason his counsel did not know about Home Depot's motion for summary judgment was due to a glitch in his email system.

The Fifth Circuit stated that it did not question the good faith of Rollins's counsel but there was "manifest error to deny relief when failure to file was within [Rollins's] counsel's 'reasonable control.'"[69] The Fifth Circuit noted that notice of Home Depot's motion for summary judgment was sent to the email address that Rollins's counsel provided, that under Federal Rule 5(b)(2)(E) that service was complete upon filing or sending, and that rule was satisfied here. "Rollins's counsel was plainly in the best position to ensure that his own email was working properly certainly more so than either the district court or Home Depot. Moreover, Rollins's counsel could have checked the docket after the agreed deadline for dispositive motions had already passed."[70] The

---

66. *Id.* at 758.
67. *Id.*
68. Rollins v. Home Depot USA, 8 F.4th 393 (5th Cir. 2021).
69. *Id.* at *3 (citing Trevino v. City of Fort Worth, 944 F.3d 567, 571 (5th Cir. 2019)).
70. *Id.*

Fifth Circuit found that the district court did not abuse its discretion in denying relief under Rule 59(e).

H. Lawyer's Duty to Understand ESI Discovery

In a complex case involving a manufacturer of prescription medication, alleging breach of contract, racketeering, and violation of various antitrust statutes,[71] counsel had reached extensive agreements about search terms and random sampling of documents and other electronically stored information (ESI) production protocols.[72] The issue before the court dealt with "null set"[73] searches and "elusion."[74] It is important to see what plaintiff proposed:

> The producing party agrees to quality check the data that does not hit on any terms (the Null Set) by selecting a statistically random sample of documents from the Null Set. The size of the statistically random sample shall be calculated using a confidence level of 95 percent and a margin of error of 2 percent. If responsive documents are found during the Null Set review, the producing party agrees to produce the responsive documents separate and apart from the regular production. The parties will then meet and confer to determine if any additional terms, or modifications to existing terms, are needed to ensure substantive, responsive documents are not missed.[75]

To the average practitioner all of this may be technical "mumbo-jumbo"; however, the Model Rule changes make ignoring matters such as the "null set" or "elusion" difficult, if not impossible, for competent counsel.

The magistrate, understanding that readers of the opinion may be panicked, stated:

---

71. City of Rockford v. Mallinckrodt ARD Inc., 326 F.R.D. 489 (N.D. Ill. 2018).

72. *Id.*

73. The "null set" is the set of documents that are not returned as responsive by a search process, or that are identified as not relevant by a review process. *Id.* at 491.

74. The null set can be used to determine "elusion," which is the fraction of documents identified as nonrelevant by a search or review effort that are, in fact, relevant. *Id.* at 492.

75. *Id.* at 492.

> The Court pauses here for a moment to calm down litigators less familiar with ESI. (You know who you are.) In life, there are many things to be scared of, including, but not limited to, spiders, sharks, and clowns—definitely clowns, even Fizbo. ESI is not something to be scared of. The same is true for all the terms and jargon related to ESI. Discovery of ESI is still discovery, governed by the same Federal Rules of Civil Procedure as all other civil discovery. . . . So don't freak out. Having said that, the ethical rules now require attorneys to be competent with technologies such as ESI. ABA Model Rule 1.1, Comment 8 ("To maintain the requisite knowledge and skill, a lawyer should keep abreast of changes in the law and its practice, including the benefits and risks associated with relevant technology. . . .")[76]

Attorneys with reservations about ESI can ease those concerns by following a few simple rules: work to stay abreast of changes to the pertinent technology, undertake appropriate continuing education, engage with others who have appropriate technological knowledge and skills, and read the portion of this book dealing specifically with ESI.

I. Compelled Technology Training

While most states do not require continuing education related to technology, attorneys should be aware that state bar disciplinary boards may order mandatory technology training, in addition to sanctions, for failure to demonstrate technological competence.

For example, in *Disciplinary Counsel v. Valenti*,[77] an Ohio attorney was charged with failing to represent clients competently and diligently in three separate matters. Specifically, the sanctioned attorney failed to submit timely filings and inform the court of scheduling conflicts on multiple occasions. The disciplinary board concluded that counsel's pattern of misconduct surrounding case management was evidence of insufficient technological competence and imposed a six-month suspension. In addition to the suspension, the board ordered counsel to

76. *Id.* at 492 n.2 (citations omitted).

77. Disciplinary Couns. v. Valenti, 175 N.E. 3d 520 (Ohio 2021).

complete six hours of continuing legal education in law-office management and law-office technology.

IV. Ethics Opinions

Ethics opinions from jurisdictions throughout the country shed light on lawyers' ethical obligations to stay abreast of technology. These opinions cover a broad range of technology-related issues that present themselves to lawyers daily, such as cloud computing, email, social media, and even digital currencies such as Bitcoin. These opinions are insightful as to how lawyers may best manage analogous technology issues going forward. Looking back at these opinions and the questions that gave rise to them, it may seem glaringly obvious what the answer should have been. However, the answers may not seem clear when the lawyer faces the issue for the first time.

A. Working Remotely

In a pandemic-driven ethics opinion, the Pennsylvania Bar Association provided practicing attorneys with guidance regarding the ethical implications of working remotely.[78]

The Ethics Opinion focused on a lawyer's duty to provide competent representation through the obligation to understand the risks and benefits of technology pursuant to comment 8 to Rule 1.1 of the Pennsylvania Rules of Professional Conduct: "Consistent with this Rule, attorneys must evaluate, obtain, and utilize the technology necessary to assure that their communications remain confidential."

The opinion further focused on the correlation between understanding the risks and benefits of technology and the obligation to safeguard client information. The Pennsylvania Bar noted some of the many obstacles to maintaining client confidentially, especially when working in a remote environment: "For example, smart devices such as Amazon's Alexa and Google's voice assistants may listen to conversations and record them."[79] Similarly, "when communicating using electronic mail, text messages, and other methods for transmitting confidential

78. Pennsylvania Bar Ethics Opinion 2020-300.
79. Penn. Bar. Ethics Opinion 2020-300 at p. 8.

and sensitive data, attorneys must take reasonable precautions, which may include the use of encryption, to assure that unauthorized persons cannot intercept and read these communications."[80]

The opinion concluded its guidance by reminding attorneys of the many ways to enhance online security, including but not limited to avoiding unsecure public internet hotspots, using virtual private networks (VPNs), using multifactor authentication systems, and using strong passwords.[81]

B. Virtual Practice

The ABA Model Rules of Professional Conduct, which have formed the blueprint for maintaining technology competence, permit the virtual practice of law.[82] However, the ABA has emphasized the importance of considering ethical duties regarding competence, diligence, and communication when using technology to practice virtually. "As lawyers increasingly use technology to practice virtually, they must remain cognizant of their ethical responsibilities."[83]

The ABA opinion not only addresses an attorney's core ethical duties surrounding changes in technology and the practice of law but also focuses on the ethical obligations of supervisory lawyers to establish policies and procedures to ensure ethical compliance by subordinate lawyers and nonlawyer assistants. Practicing virtually does not change or diminish this obligation. Further, this duty to supervise nonlawyers extends to those both within and outside of a law firm.

The duty to practice law virtually with the same professionalism as in-person practice is becoming increasingly important, as courts across

80. Penn. Bar Ethics Opinion 2020-300 at p. 5.

81. The legal profession is aware of the importance of cybersecurity; however, the profession still has many shortcomings when it comes to understanding cyber threats and having the necessary training to protect against them. This point is highlighted by the *2021 ABA Legal Technology Survey Report*, which reported that 25 percent of survey respondents experienced a security breach at some time, yet 17 percent of attorneys stated that their practice or law firm does not have any cybersecurity policies in place. David G Ries, *ABA TechReport 2021: Cybersecurity* (Dec 22, 2021), https://www.americanbar.org/groups/law_practice/publications/techreport/2021/cybersecurity/.

82. ABA Formal Opinion 498.

83. ABA Formal Opinion 498 at p.1

the county are utilizing the convenience and efficiency of virtual proceedings implemented during the pandemic. For example, the Florida Supreme Court recently voted, unanimously, to amend its rules of procedure and adopt permanent authorization for remote court proceedings.[84] The new rules, which take effect October 1, 2022, permit remote proceedings for matters such as depositions, non-evidentiary hearings, jury trials, and mediation conferences.[85] As Florida demonstrates, virtual practice is here to stay and will only continue to play a greater role in the practice of law.

However, virtual practice and technology do have their limits. As the ABA has noted, lawyers practicing virtually must ensure that trust accounting rules, which vary significantly across states and often require brick and mortar capabilities, are followed. Litigators must be able to file and receive pleadings at a physical address. Further, attendance at remote hearings should still comport with the appropriate level of decorum for the serious matters before the court.

C. ChatGPT

Launched in November 2022, ChatGPT is the latest artificial intelligence tool to enter the legal profession. The chatbot, which is a natural language processing tool developed by San Francisco-based startup OpenAI, purports to be capable of having human-like communications, including the ability to provide users with responses to legal inquiries. In theory, attorneys could use ChatGPT to prepare motions, agreements, correspondence, and other legal work-product. Although widely debated, some argue that ChatGPT and similar technology could render the legal profession obsolete. The most pressing questions regarding use of ChatGPT in the legal sector surround the ethical considerations lawyers will face as more and more professionals begin to rely on artificial intelligence to assist in their practice, in whole or in part. For example, an attorney's use of ChatGPT for even a minor or harmless inquiry

---

84. *In re* Amendments to Fla. Rules of Civil Procedure, Fla. Rules of General Practice and Judicial Administration, Fla. Rules of Criminal Procedure, Fla. Probate Rules, Fla. Rules of Traffic Court, Fla. Small Claims Rules, and Fla. Rules of Appellate Procedure, 2022 WL 2721129, at *1 (Fla. 2022).

85. *Id.*

could expose confidential client information to the ChatGPT platform, which records user input to better its responses.[86] Blind reliance on ChatGPT could lead to severe consequences such as attorney malpractice. This is a foreseeable circumstance, as ChatGPT has the potential to provide information and work-product that is not accurate or complete. Therefore, while the temptation to use artificial intelligence such as ChatGPT may be compelling due to its potential ability to short-circuit time-intensive writing tasks, practitioners must tread carefully as blind reliance on artificial technology may not only prejudice the interests of their clients, but also risk their professional license. As with any other technology, ChatGPT may have a place in the practice of law, but the practitioner should understand how it works and its limitations.

V. Conclusion

The duty of technological competence does not require attorneys to become technological wizards, but attorneys must do more than stick their heads in the sand and ignore the changing world and practice around them. As seen from the preceding case law examples and disciplinary proceedings, whether an attorney is managing complicated ESI issues, not searching spam filters, or lacking a valid email address, technological competence (or lack thereof) could significantly impact his or her practice. This is potentially true in all courts, in acting as pro hac counsel, or as local counsel.

Attorneys should understand that they do not have to tackle technology alone. Comment 2 to Model Rule 1.1 encourages the use of third parties to maintain competence: "A lawyer need not necessarily have special training or prior experience to handle legal problems of a type with which the lawyer is unfamiliar. [. . .] Competent representation can also be provided through the association of a lawyer of established competence in the field in question." As noted in the Florida Rules: "Competent representation may also involve the association or retention of a non-lawyer advisor of established technological competence in the field

86. OpenAI, *ChatGPT: Optimizing Language Models for Dialogue* (Nov. 30, 2022), https://openai.com/blog/chatgpt.

in question."[87] Accordingly, attorneys, particularly solo practitioners and small law firms without IT personnel, should turn to consultants when presented with technology concerns or issues.

The construction practice is one where there are many technological aspects, and a competent construction attorney must stay well informed of those technologies, but they are not required to do so on their own. These technological issues are not going away, so become educated, stay educated, and affiliate with someone versed in these matters if needed.

87. Comments, Fla. R. Prof. Cond. 4-1.1.

CHAPTER 3

Data/Cybersecurity and Insurance

Reggie Jones and Kristen Broz, *Authors*
Sarah Glover, *Contributor*

As technology has advanced it has created opportunities for new types of crime and disruption, thus creating the need for means to combat such activities through cybersecurity.

> Cybersecurity began in the 1970s when researcher Bob Thomas created a computer programme called Creeper that could move across ARPANET's network, leaving a breadcrumb trail wherever it went. Ray Tomlinson, the inventor of email, wrote the programme Reaper, which chased and deleted Creeper. Reaper was the very first example of antivirus software and the first self-replicating programme, making it the first-ever computer worm.[1]

In 1987, the first anti-virus program became available. During the 1990s, cybercrime increased as people began putting their personal information online. "By the mid-1990's network security threats had

1. Vikki Davies, "The History of Cybersecurity," *Cyber Magazine*, https://cybermagazine.com/cyber-security/history-cybersecurity, Oct. 4, 2021.

increased exponentially and firewalls and antivirus programmes had to be produced on a mass basis to protect the public."[2]

In the last two decades, cybersecurity threats to individuals, governments, and businesses have exploded, making cybersecurity a major concern and an expanding industry. In a recent Baker McKenzie survey, 62 percent of respondents expected cybersecurity disputes to present a risk to their organization in 2023.[3] Recent news articles highlight cybersecurity incidents ranging from ransomware attacks on hospitals[4] to hackers stealing personal information from a mobile phone network.[5] Federal and state agencies are investigating cyberattacks on military and civilian targets.[6]

The significance of understanding cyber and data security to companies operating in 2023, particularly for government contractors, cannot be overstated. Not only do all companies that handle sensitive information face daily threats from cyber criminals, but, also, companies must ensure constant access to information in a world that is increasingly reliant on remote work and cross-border communications. These issues are front and center for regulators and government agencies that need to protect the national infrastructure from security threats and ensure the continued availability of information. Because the threat landscape changes daily, the regulatory landscape must constantly shift as well. As a result, the cybersecurity rules that apply to contractors are in a state of flux. In this chapter, we discuss recent developments in the cybersecurity landscape for government contractors, recommendations for compliance, and practical insights regarding how companies can manage and mitigate their risks.

---

2. *Id.*

3. https://www.bakermckenzie.com/en/newsroom/2023/01/new-survey-from-baker-mckenzie.

4. https://abcnews.go.com/Business/wireStory/major-florida-hospital-hit-ransomware-attack-96879773; https://abcnews.go.com/Health/wireStory/cyberattack-top-indian-hospital-highlights-security-risk-94684104.

5. https://abcnews.go.com/US/video/hackers-steal-personal-info-37-million-mobile-customers-96561633.

6. https://abcnews.go.com/US/baltimore-schools-failed-fully-act-security-recommendations-cyber/story?id=96671802; https://abcnews.go.com/Politics/fbi-director-sees-threat-chinas-ai-program-talks/story?id=96547649.

I. Department of Defense (DOD) Regulations re: Cybersecurity

The purpose of the current DOD regulations is to ensure that unclassified DOD information residing on a contractor's internal information system (i.e., computers, computer networks, and any third-party-provided cloud-based network) is safeguarded from cyber incidents. Simply stated, a "cyber incident" is any action taken through use of computers or computer networks that compromises or potentially adversely affects an information system or the data residing on that system.[7] The regulations seek to assess and minimize the consequences associated with cyber incidents through reporting and damage assessment processes. While that sounds straightforward, the process to develop coherent regulations has been long and is still evolving. To understand how DOD arrived at its current contract requirements, it helps to understand how the federal government has responded legislatively and regulatorily to increasing cyber threats. The following sections address the efforts by the National Institute of Standards and Technology (NIST), the governing body that produces the detailed technical requirements that DOD later implemented through Federal Acquisition Regulation (FAR) and Defense Federal Acquisition Regulation Supplement (DFARS) contract clauses.

DOD currently regulates nonfederal (i.e., DOD contractors') information systems security primarily through five DFARS contract clauses that govern the contractor's systems and two DFARS contract clauses that address cloud computing services:

- DFARS 252.204-7008 (Compliance with Safeguarding Covered Defense Information Controls)
- DFARS 252.204-7012 (Safeguarding Covered Defense Information and Cyber Incident Reporting)
- DFARS 252.204-7019 (Notice of NIST SP 800-171 DoD Assessment Requirements)
- DFARS 252.204-7020 (NIST SP 800-171 DoD Assessment Requirements)

---

7. DFARS 252.204-7012(a); Cyber Incident Reporting and Cloud Computing, 53 Fed. Reg. 36,905 (July 30, 2019).

- DFARS 252.204-7021 (Cybersecurity Maturity Model Certification Requirements)
- DFARS 252.239-7009 (Representation of Use of Cloud Computing Services)
- DFARS 252.239-7010 (Cloud Computing Services)

In addition to the contract clauses, DOD recently introduced the Cybersecurity Maturity Model Certification (CMMC), a certification process that will largely satisfy the DFARS contract requirements, and which is still a work in progress. CMMC is a verification mechanism under which contractors will have to pass an audit to obtain the level of cybersecurity specified under a specific government contract.

To make sense of the current DFARS requirements, it is helpful to understand three regulatory frameworks—NIST Special Publications, the Federal Acquisition Regulation (FAR), and the Defense Federal Acquisition Regulation Supplement (DFARS)—and how they relate to one another.

A. National Institute of Standards and Technology (NIST)

Congress created NIST (then known as the National Bureau of Standards) in 1901 to create a uniform metric system.[8] Thus, America's powerhouse of uniform standardization was born. NIST is relevant in cybersecurity today because NIST has established the standards contractors must comply with under DFARS, and the standards to which agencies must conform. As to the DFARS contract requirements, there are two NIST special publications (SP) that address privacy of federal information systems specifically:

- NIST SP 800-53 (Security and Privacy Controls for Federal Information Systems and Organizations)
- NIST SP 800-171 (Protecting Controlled Unclassified Information in Nonfederal Systems and Organizations)

The NIST SP 800-53 was created in response to the Federal Information Security Management Act (FISMA) in February 2005 and

8. Nat'l Inst. of Standards and Tech., NIST SP 800-171 Rev. 1, ch. 1, Protecting Controlled Unclassified Information in Nonfederal Information Systems and Organizations (2016) [hereinafter NIST SP 800-171 Rev. 1].

addressed the government's computer systems and networks.[9] The initial version of DFARS contract clause 252.204-7012, first published in 2013, required contractors to comply with certain portions of this NIST manual.[10]

The NIST SP 800-171 governs nonfederal information systems.[11] In other words, it provides guidance for DOD contractors, rather than to DOD itself. DFARS 252.204-7012 (Safeguarding Covered Defense Information and Cyber Incident Reporting) and DFARS 252.204-7008 (Compliance with Safeguarding Covered Defense Information Controls) require DOD contractors to comply with NIST SP 800-171 Revision 2.

B. FAR/DFARS

1. The FAR Requirements

In 2016, DOD, the General Services Administration (GSA), and the National Aeronautics and Space Administration (NASA) issued a final rule amending the FAR to include FAR contract clause 52.204-21 (Basic Safeguarding of Covered Contractor Information Systems).[12] This cybersecurity clause is important for several reasons. First, it was the first contract clause to meaningfully address cybersecurity for information systems across all agencies. Second, it was born out of DOD's early attempts to uniformly safeguard unclassified information itself, not just the information systems through which unclassified information flows or is stored.[13] Third, it does not require any training, penetration testing, cyber incident reporting, or cybersecurity insurance because the rule does not address controlled unclassified information (CUI) or classified federal information systems.[14]

The requirements in FAR 52.204-21 are intended to be "reflective of the actions a prudent businessperson would employ," and they apply to all

---

9. Basic Safeguarding of Contractor Information Systems, 77 Fed. Reg. 51,496 (Aug. 24, 2012).

10. 81 Fed. Reg. at 30,444.

11. *Id.* at 30,440.

12. *Id.*

13. Federal Information Security Management Act of 2002 (FISMA), Pub. L. No. 107-347, 116 Stat. 2946 (Dec. 17, 2002) (formerly 44 U.S.C. §§ 3531–3549 prior to repeal).

14. 81 Fed. Reg. at 30,439.

federal contractors, not only DOD contractors.[15] The clause contains 15 basic requirements to safeguard contractors' information systems. NIST SP 800-171 defines information system as "a discrete set of information resources organized expressly for the collection, processing, maintenance, use, sharing, dissemination, or disposition of information."[16]

2. *The DFARS Contract Requirements*

Compliance with DFARS contract requirements is a salient and often challenging issue. A July 2019 audit by DOD's Inspector General (IG) concluded that, "DOD contractors did not consistently implement DOD-mandated system security controls for safeguarding Defense information."[17] DOD IG cited examples such as failure to use multifactor authentication or strong passwords, failure to protect sensitive data on removable media such as flash drives, failure to oversee network protection services provided by third-party vendors, failure to implement physical security controls, or failure to grant access based on the user's assigned duties.[18] Given that contractors submit applications for payment that certify that they are compliant with the terms of the contract, failure to comply could turn every pay application into a civil false claim. Therefore, it is important to be vigilant about implementing each requirement.

3. *Navigating DFARS 252.204-7012 (Safeguarding Covered Defense Information and Cyber Incident Reporting)*

Since 2013, the main DFARS contract clause addressing cybersecurity is DFARS 252.204-7012 (Safeguarding Covered Defense Information and Cyber Incident Reporting). It is always accompanied by the notice provision found in DFARS 252.204-7008 (Compliance with Safeguarding Covered Defense Information Controls). DFARS 252.204-7012 incorporates NIST SP 800-171 (Protecting Controlled Unclassified

---

15. Inspector Gen., Dep't of Def., Audit of Protection of DoD Controlled Unclassified Information on Contractor-Owned Networks and Systems, Rep. No. DODIG-2019-105, at i (July 23, 2019).

16. *Id.* at i–ii.

17. *Id.*

18. DFARS 252.204-7010 (codified at 80 Fed. Reg. 51,747 (Aug. 26, 2015)), *as amended by* Technical Amendments, 80 Fed. Reg. 74,695 (Nov. 20, 2015).

Information in Nonfederal Systems and Organizations) and requires contractors to implement 110 security requirements.

DFARS 252.204-7012 requires contractors to document in a system security plan (SSP) how compliance has been achieved and if some of the controls are still in progress, it requires contractors to develop plans of action (POA) as to how and when compliance will be achieved. The clause requires contractors to "rapidly report" cyber incidents "within 72 hours of discovery of any cyber incident."[19] As stated earlier, a "cyber incident" is any action taken through use of computers or computer networks that compromises or potentially adversely affects an information system or the data residing on that system.[20]

The 72-hour reporting requirement is one of the most troubling parts of the regulation for contractors because it is much sooner than the disclosures required under FAR 52.203-13 (Contractor Code of Business Ethics and Conduct), which permits time to conduct an internal investigation, which could take weeks. FAR 52.203-13 requires timely disclosure of evidence of a violation of the civil False Claims Act or Title 18 of the U.S. Code but does not require a specific time period, implying that a reasonable time to investigate is allowed.[21] Under the DFARS clause, by contrast, contractors are not only required to report "whatever information is available" within the 72-hour period but also "should submit a follow-on report when additional information becomes available."[22]

It is important for prime contractors and subcontractors to be aware of these requirements because DFARS 252.204-7012 has a mandatory flow-down provision that applies to all subcontracts.[23] This is true for all the DFARS clauses addressed in this chapter.

Failure to comply with these requirements can be costly, and DOD is focusing its attention on penalizing contractors who do not implement these cybersecurity requirements. On June 16, 2022, the Office of Under Secretary of Defense issued a memorandum entitled in relevant part:

---

19. DFARS 252.204-7012(a) (codified at 81 Fed. Reg. 72,986).

20. DFARS 252.204-7012(a); Cyber Incident Reporting and Cloud Computing, 53 Fed. Reg. 36,905 (July 30, 2019).

21. FAR 52.2013-13(c)(2)(ii)(F) (codified at 30 Fed. Reg. 38,293 (July 2, 2015)).

22. *Frequently Asked Questions (FAQs) Regarding the Implementation of DFARS Subpart 204.73*, DEP'T OF DEF. PROCUREMENT TOOLBOX (July 30, 2030).

23. DFARS 252.204-7012 (m).

"Contractual Remedies to Ensure Contractor Compliance with DFARS 252.204-7012 for contracts not subject to Clause 252.204-7020."[24] According to that memo, "[f]ailure to have or make progress on a plan to implement NIST SP 800-171 requirements may be considered a material breach of requirements. Remedies for such a breach may include: withholding progress payments; foregoing remaining contract options; and potentially terminating the contract in part or in whole."[25]

Contractors can effectively and accurately implement DFARS 252.204-7012 into their systems by following three steps. First, identify the information covered under the DFARS. Second, integrate the cyber incident reporting requirements into the FAR 52.203-13–required code of business ethics and compliance. Third, develop and document a system security plan and plans of action, as necessary. The following sections explain each of these steps.

(a) Step 1: What Information Is Covered?

The first step in complying with DFARS 252.204-7012 is to identify its scope. The clause applies to "all *covered contractor information systems*" that hold "*covered defense information.*"[26] A covered contractor information system is an unclassified information system that is owned or operated by or for a contractor and processes, stores, or transmits covered defense information.[27] The clause does not cover information that is lawfully publicly available without restrictions.[28]

---

24. John M. Tenaglia, *Contractual Remedies to Ensure Contractor Compliance with Defense Federal Acquisition Regulation Supplement Clause 252.204-7012, for contracts and orders not subject to Clause 252.204-7020; and Additional Considerations Regarding National Institute of Standards and Technology Special Publication 800-171 Department of Defense Assessments*, https://www.acq.osd.mil/dpap/policy/policyvault/USA000807-22-DPC.pdf.

25. *Id.* at 2.

26. DFARS 204.7301.

27. Susan B. Cassidy, Melinda Lewis & Weiss Nusraty, *DoD Announces the Cybersecurity Maturity Model Certification (CMMC) Initiative*, National Archives, Inside Gov't Contracts (July 16, 2019), https://www.insidegovernmentcontracts.com/2019/07/; https://dodcio.defense.gov/CMMC/About/#:~:text=The%20Cybersecurity%20Maturity%20Model%20Certification%20(CMMC)%20program%20is%20aligned%20to,with%20its%20contractors%20and%20subcontractors (last visited Feb. 22, 2023).

28. 32 C.F.R. § 2002.4(h).

(1) Covered Defense Information

This section explains how to identify covered defense information (CDI). After identifying which systems are covered, contractors must identify what information qualifies as CDI. DFARS 252.204-7012 defines CDI as one of two things: (1) "unclassified controlled technical information" (CTI)" or (2) "other information, as described in the Controlled Unclassified Information (CUI) Registry . . . that requires safeguarding or dissemination controls."[29] In addition, the information (whether CTI or CUI) must (1) be "marked or otherwise identified in the contract, task order, or delivery order and provided to the contractor by or on behalf of DOD in support of the performance of the contract; or" (2) be "[c]ollected, developed, received, transmitted, used, stored by or on behalf of the contractor in support of performance of the contract."[30] To determine whether information should be classified as CDT, one must (1) identify any CTI or CUI; (2) determine if the information requires safeguarding or dissemination controls; and (3) identify information that is marked as CDI and information collected, developed, received, transmitted, used, or stored by or on behalf of the contractor in support of contract performance. The first category of CDI—marked or otherwise identified—is easy to identify because DOD has the burden to tell the contractor that the material is CDT. The second category—collected, developed, or stored—is murkier and hence carries more risk because the contractor must exercise its discretion in identifying the information that requires safeguarding.

Unclassified controlled technical information (CTI). CDI consists of either CTI or CUI. The DFARS defines CTI as:

> Technical information with military or space application that is subject to controls on the access, use, reproduction, modification, performance, display, release, disclosure, or dissemination. . . . The term does not include information that is lawfully publicly available without restrictions.[31]

---

29. *See CUI Registry: CUI Glossary*, NAT'L ARCHIVES, https://www.archives.gov/cui/registry/cui-glossary.html (last visited Dec. 30, 2019).

30. *CUI Registry*, NAT'L ARCHIVES, https://www.archives.gov/cui (last visited Jan. 6, 2020).

31. *CUI Category: Export Controlled*, NAT'L ARCHIVES, https://www.archives.gov/cui/registry/category-detail/export-control.html (last visited Dec. 20, 2019).

Technical information as used in the definition means technical data or computer software, as those terms are defined in DFARS 252.227-7013 (Rights to Technical Data—Noncommercial Items).[32] CTI's complicated definition can be simplified into three parts: (1) technical information that (2) has military/space application and (3) is subject to some form of controls.[33] Examples of such data include research and engineering data, engineering drawings, and associated lists, specifications, standards, process sheets, manuals, technical reports, technical orders, catalog-item identifications, data sets, studies and analyses and related information, and computer software executable code and source code.[34]

Controlled unclassified information (CUI). Turning to controlled unclassified information, or CUI, 32 C.F.R. § 2002.4(h) defines CUI as any information that "a law, regulation, or government-wide policy requires or permits an agency to handle using safeguarding or dissemination controls," but it does not include information formally classified as confidential, secret, top secret, or sensitive compartmentalized information.[35] It can include information marked as "For Official Use Only" (FOUO) or information identified by the Department of Energy as "Unclassified Controlled Nuclear Information" (UCNT). References to CUI go beyond DOD and extend to cybersecurity regulations for other agencies as well. For this reason the FAR references CUI, rather than the specific scope found in the DFARS. The easiest way to identify exactly what constitutes controlled unclassified information is to reference the online CUI registry.[36] The CUI registry applies to all agencies and indicates what information is controlled or sensitive.[37]

---

32. 32 C.F.R. § 236.2.

33. DFARS 204.7301.

34. Susan B. Cassidy, Melinda Lewis & Weiss Nusraty, *DoD Announces the Cybersecurity Maturity Model Certification (CMMC) Initiative National Archives*, Inside Gov't Contracts (July 16, 2019), https://www.insidegovernmentcontracts.com/2019/07/dod-announces-the-cybersecurity-maturity-model-certification-cmmc-initiative/.

35. 32 C.F.R. § 2002.4(h).

36. *See CUI Registry: CUI Glossary*, NAT'L ARCHIVES, https://www.archives.gov/cui/registry/cui-glossary.html (last visited Dec. 30, 2019).

37. *CUI Registry*, NAT'L ARCHIVES, https://www.archives.gov/cui (last visited Jan. 6, 2020).

One particularly common CUI category to watch out for is "export controlled."[38] This category applies to all information marked or identified in the contract as CDI *or* that is collected, developed, and so on, on behalf of the contractor in support of performance on the contract.[39] Information is considered CUI if its "export could reasonably be expected to adversely affect the United States' national security and nonproliferation objectives."[40] It may be difficult to determine what does and does not constitute CUI, especially for contractors who generate business from sources other than DOD. Although only covered contractor information systems are subject to these regulations, businesses may find themselves in the position of needing to create security plans on all their systems if the covered contractor information systems are not separated. DOD regulations only require contractors to protect federal information systems. If the federal systems are separate from commercial ones, contractors can save time and money by implementing the required information systems safeguards on fewer systems and information. Therefore, the authors recommend putting CDI on a separate internal network. This may be difficult in situations where contractors have multiple offices in which they conduct both commercial and federal business, because the requirements apply only to federal systems. However, it will be necessary and can save time and money because contractors can focus on creating a security system plan for CDT alone, without overextending their resources to cover unregulated information.

(2) Is It CTI or CUI?

To complicate matters, the CUI Registry lists CTI as a category of CUI. In other words, CTI is also CUI. DOD has done little to describe how CDI differs from CUI or why the definition of CDI separates CTI from CUI. In many ways, the differences may be negligible. The differing definitions may simply come from DOD's unilateral attempt to regulate information security independently from other agencies. The only language in CDI's definition distinguishing it from CUI is that CDI can

38. *CUI Category: Export Controlled*, NAT'L ARCHIVES, https://www.archives.gov/cui/registry/category-detail/export-control.html (last visited Feb. 22, 2023).

39. *Id.*

40. *Id.*

be, "collected, developed, received, transmitted, used, stored, etc. by the contractor." Generally, CUI must also be marked as such. However, by adding this second clause, DOD expanded CDI to cover not only information marked as CUI but also information collected, developed, received, transmitted, used, or stored by the contractor in relation to the contract. As discussed later in the chapter, the Cybersecurity Maturity Model Certification (CMMC), covering only DOD contractors, applies only to CUI, meaning the difference between CDI and CUI may be trivial.[41]

The question is not whether a DOD contractor has CDI, but whether the information it possesses constitutes CDI. Virtually anyone doing DOD contracting will have CDI. In practice, DOD contractors should keep track of all the information DOD provides to them as well as information developed in connection with a DOD contract and determine if it fits into one of the CUI registry categories, including controlled technical information.[42] Different types of contractors may have most of their information fall into different categories. For example, construction contractors should focus on the "Critical Infrastructure" categories, which are Ammonium Nitrate, Chemical-terrorism Vulnerability Information, Critical Energy Infrastructure Information, Emergency Management, General Critical Infrastructure Information, Information Systems Vulnerability Information, Physical Security, Protected Critical Infrastructure Information, SAFETY Act Information, Toxic Substances, and Water Assessments.[43] On the other hand, IT contractors may want to be aware of the Privacy Information and Sensitive Personally Identifiable Information categories.[44]

(3) Other CDI Requirements

If information is CUI (as opposed to CTI), the contractor must determine whether the information is controlled. CDI is information that

---

41. Carnegie Mellon Univ. & Johns Hopkins Univ. Applied Physics Lab. LLC, Cybersecurity Maturity Model Certification (CMMC) Draft Version 0.7 (2019) [hereinafter CMMC Version 0.7] at app. D.

42. The definition of controlled technical information found in the CUI registry is identical to the one found in the DFARS.

43. *See* CUI Categories, Nat'l Archives, https://www.archives.gov/cui/registry/category-list (last visited Jan. 6, 2020).

44. *Id.*

"requires safeguarding or dissemination controls." DOD expanded on this by saying that CDI is information "that requires safeguarding or dissemination controls *pursuant to and consistent with law, regulations, and Government wide policies*."[45] Essentially, any information that is regulated or controlled meets this part of the definition.

Finally, the contractor must identify whether the information is either (1) marked or otherwise identified or (2) collected, developed, received, transmitted, used, or stored by or on behalf of the contractor in support of performance of the contract. Identifying CDI that is marked is simple. In this case, DOD is simply telling a contractor when information is CDI. It is the second category that confuses many contractors. This second category "recogniz[es] the shared obligation of the contractor to recognize and protect covered defense information that the contractor is developing during contract performance."[46] This second category alerts contractors that they may hold or develop CDI throughout the course of contract performance, even if the CDI was not originally given to them or marked as CDI.

(b) Step 2: What Are the Cyber Incident Reporting Requirements?

Once a contractor determines what information is covered, it should create a system to report cyber incidents to DOD. DFARS 252.204-7012 defines a "cyber incident" as "actions taken through the use of computer networks that result in a compromise or an actual or potential adverse effect on an information system and/or the information residing therein."[47] For example, discovering malware on its system or discovering that information has been "exfiltrated" (taken from your system) are both reportable cyber incidents.[48]

45. Network Penetration Reporting and Contracting for Cloud Services, 81 Fed. Reg. 72,986 (Oct. 21, 2016) (emphasis added).

46. *Id.*

47. DFARS 252.204-7012(a)(2) (codified at 81 Fed. Reg. 72,986 (Oct. 21, 2016)).

48. Frequently Asked Questions (FAQs) Regarding the Implementation of DFARS Subpart 204.73, Dep't of Def. Procurement Tool-box (Apr. 2, 2018), https://dodprocurementtoolbox.com/cms/sites/default/files/resources/2021-11/Cyber%20DFARS%20FAQs%20rev%203%20%207.30.2020%20%2B%20correction%2011.23.2021.pdf (last visited Feb. 22, 2023).

Establishing a system for compliance with reporting requirements should be a priority because DOD requires that contractors "rapidly report" cyber incidents, meaning "within 72 hours of discovery of any cyber incident."[49] The 72-hour reporting requirement is one of the most troubling parts of the regulation for contractors because it is much sooner than the disclosures required under FAR 52.203-13 (Contractor Code of Business Ethics and Compliance), which permit time to conduct an internal investigation, which could take weeks. FAR 52.203-13 requires timely disclosure of evidence of a violation of the civil False Claims Act or title 18 of the U.S. Code but does not require a specific time period, implying that a reasonable time to investigate is allowed.[50] Under the DFARS clause, by contrast, contractors are not only required to report "whatever information is available" within the 72-hour period, but also "should submit a follow-on report when additional information becomes available."[51] Although the initial time period for disclosure is starkly different from that of FAR 52.203-13, as we have discussed, both clauses contain a continuing obligation to disclose.

It is difficult for a contractor to meet the tight deadline without having a comprehensive understanding of which systems/information are covered under the clause and having a system already in place to quickly identify cyber incidents and respond in compliance with DFARS 252.204-7012. DOD takes the timely reporting of incidents very seriously. In its answers to comments, DOD stated that timely reporting is "a key element" in protecting DOD's information and "provides the clearest understanding" of what cyber information is targeted.[52]

To summarize, a contractor's cyber incident reporting system should have three components. First, it should establish a system for reviewing compromised CDI. Second, it should trigger reporting to DOD within 72 hours of an incident.[53] Third, it should ensure that all information is preserved and protected for 90 days following the incident.[54] DOD may

49. DFARS 252.204-7012(a) (codified at 81 Fed. Reg. 72,986).

50. FAR 52.2013-13(c)(ii)(F) (codified at 80 Fed. Reg. 38,293 (July 2, 2015)).

51. Frequently Asked Questions, *supra* note 48.

52. Cyber Incident Reporting and Cloud Computing, 53 Fed. Reg. 36,905 (July 30, 2019).

53. DFARS 252.204-7012.

54. *Id.*

require access to this information and, in some cases, may even require physical access to technical systems.[55]

(c) Step 3: Develop a System Security Plan and a Plan of Action

Next, the DFARS clauses require contractors to ensure that their technical systems are secure enough to withstand cyberattacks.[56] To accomplish this, contractors are required to develop a System Security Plan (SSP) and encouraged to develop Plans of Action (POAs) to help implement the SSP.[57] Until CMMC is required, SSPs and POAs are perhaps the most important evidence a contractor can produce in an investigation to prove that it has thoughtfully considered and taken steps to implement its safeguarding requirements. Their importance cannot be overstated, as mitigation efforts are essential in negotiating down potential suspensions and debarments and the severity of any penalty for a potential civil False Claims Act violation.

An SSP requires the contractor to develop and regularly update a plan that will describe its system, how it operates, its relationship with other systems, and its security controls.[58] The goal of an SSP is "to provide an overview of the security requirements of the system and describe the controls in place or planned for meeting those requirements."[59] Developing an accurate and detailed SSP is important because it will allow DOD to assess the overall risk of hosting CDI on your system.[60] DFARS clause 252.204-7012 requires contractors to implement NIST 800-171 standards into their system security plan and to comply with its guidelines.[61] Neither the DFARS clause nor NIST requires an SSP

---

55. 84 Fed. Reg. 36,905.

56. *See* DFARS 252.204-7012.

57. NIST SP 800-171 Rev. 1, *supra* note 8, ch. 3.

58. *Id.* ch. 3.21.4.

59. NIST SP 800-18 Rev. 1, *supra* note 14, ch. 1, at vii.

60. Memorandum from Office of Under Sec'y of Def., Implementation of DFARS Clause 252.204-7012, Safeguarding Covered Defense Information and Cyber Incident Reporting (Sept. 21, 2017), https://www.acq.osd.mil/dpap/policy/policyvault/USA002829-17-DPAP.pdf.

61. Office of Under Sec'y of Def., Guidance for Assessing Compliance and Enhancing Protections Required by DFARS Clause 252.204-7012, Safeguarding Covered Defense Information and Cyber Incident Reporting (2018).

to take on any particular format, but NIST provides a helpful template in NIST 800-18 Revision 1 Chapter 3.[62] The SSP must describe how the NIST security requirements are to be met.[63] DFARS clause 252.204-7012 makes it a requirement for contractors to comply with the guidelines in NIST 800-171. NIST 800-18 Revision 1 provides cybersecurity requirements that the federal government must follow.[64] Although contractors are not bound by NIST 800-18 Revision 1, it can be helpful in informing contractors on how to create an SSP.[65]

The question that plagues many contractors is how to implement over 100 pages of NIST SP 800-171's highly technical language into their SSP. Start with NIST 800-171 Chapter 3. Chapter 3 lays out the requirements of each part of the SSP. It contains eight pages of guidance and is easy to follow. Many contractors get bogged down with the highly technical language and mapping requirements set forth in Appendix D. However, Appendix D is intended to be a tool to help contractors navigate the requirements listed in Chapter 3. Therefore, contractors should focus first on Chapter 3 and then turn to Appendix D for clarification.

In June 2019, NIST published a draft of NIST 800-171 Revision 2. NIST has made it clear that "there are no changes to the basic and derived security requirements in Chapter Three."[66] NIST has also developed the NIST MEP (Manufacturing Extension Partnership) program to help small- and medium-size manufacturing businesses comply with cybersecurity requirements and has provided a guide for manufacturers to help them assess their SSP.[67]

Although not expressly required, NIST strongly recommends using a plan of action (POA) to enable ongoing real-time updates to the SSP

---

62. Memorandum from Office of Under Sec'y of Def., *supra* note 60.

63. NIST 800-171 Rev. 1, *supra* note 8, ch. 3.

64. *See* NIST 800-18 Rev. 1, *supra* note 14, at iii ("This guideline has been prepared for use by federal agencies. It may be used by nongovernmental organizations on a voluntary basis and is not subject to copyright.").

65. *See id.* ch. 3.

66. Nat'l Inst. of Standards & Tech., NIST 800-171 Rev. 2 DRAFT, Protecting Controlled Unclassified Information in Nonfederal Systems and Organizations (2019) [hereinafter NIST SP 800-171 Rev. 2 DRAFT].

67. *Cybersecurity Assessment Tool,* MEP Nat'l Network, https://www.nist.gov/mep/cybersecurity-services, (last visited Feb. 22, 2023).

and to help work towards implementing all NIST requirements.[68] NIST describes a POA as a "key document" to "describe how any unimplemented security requirements will be met."[69] A POA may be a separate document or may be combined with an SSP. A POA "identifies tasks needing to be accomplished" to reach certain milestones on your way to NIST compliance.[70] POAs also serve to "correct deficiencies and reduce or eliminate vulnerabilities" in a contractor's technical system.[71] Further, SSPs require periodic review and modification to ensure they are up to date.[72] Having a POA will help ensure the SSP is up to date. Keeping up with the SSP and POA is also good practice because those are the tools by which DOD will measure compliance, particularly if a cyber incident occurs. Outdated or vague documents could create problems.

4. Navigating DFARS 252.239-7020 (NIST SP 800-171 DoD Assessment Requirements)

Effective November 30, 2020, DFARS 252.239-7020 (NIST SP 800-171 DOD Assessment Requirements) together with its accompanying notice provision, DFARS 252.239-7019 (Notice of NIST SP 800-171 DOD Assessment Requirements), requires contractors subject to DFARS 252.204-7012 to complete a Basic Assessment in accordance with the NIST 800-171 DOD Assessment Methodology and post the score in the Supplier Risk Management System (SPRS) (pronounced like "spurs") prior to contract award.[73] Contractors may also send a copy, via encrypted email, of its summary level score to the Navy at webptsmh@navy.mil for posting to SPRS.[74] A Basic Assessment is simply a contractor's self-

68. NIST 800-171 Rev. 1, *supra* note 8, ch. 3.12.2.

69. *Id.* app. F, at 99.

70. *Id.* app. B, at 36.

71. Dep't of Def., *Cybersecurity Challenges: Protecting DoD's Unclassified Information: Implementing DFARS Clause 252.204-7012, Safeguarding Covered Defense Information and Cyber Incident Reporting* (2018), https://www.nist.gov/system/files/documents/2018/10/18/cui18oct2018-104501145-dod_dfars-michetti-thomas.pdf, (last visited Feb. 22, 2023).

72. NIST 800-18 Rev. 1, *supra* note 8, ch. 1, at vii.

73. 85 Fed. Reg. 61505 (Sept. 29, 2020) (interim rule that created DFARS 252.204-7019, -7020, & -7021); *see also* DFARS 252.204-7020(c), (d).

74. DFARS 252.204-7020(d)(1).

assessment of its implementation of the 110 security requirements in NIST SP 800-171.

This clause also allows the government to require the contractor to obtain a Medium or High Assessment, which will be completed by the government.[75] A Medium Assessment consists of the government's review and evaluation under NIST 800-171A (Assessing Security Requirements for Controlled Unclassified Information) of the contractor's Basic Assessment, a document review, and discussions with the contractor to obtain additional information as needed.[76] A High Assessment consists of the same, but also adds a requirement that government is to examine and verify the contractor's system security plan to validate that the NIST 800-171 security requirements have truly been implemented as described in the contractor's plan.[77]

5. DFARS 252.239-7021 (Cybersecurity Maturity Model Certification Requirements)

In September 2019, shortly after the DOD Inspector General issued a report finding inconsistent and poor contractor cybersecurity compliance, DOD's Office of the Under Secretary of Defense for Acquisition and Sustainment (OUSD (A&S)) released its first public, unclassified version of the CMMC.[78] According to the DOD, "[t]he CMMC is intended to serve as a verification mechanism to ensure appropriate levels of cybersecurity practices and processes are in place to ensure basic cyber hygiene as well as protect CUI that resides on the Department's industry partners' networks."[79] In essence, because the Office of the Inspector General (OIG) found that contractors were in compliance with NIST SP 800-171, DoD developed a means for contractors to prove

75. *Id.* at (c).

76. *Id.* at (a).

77. *Id.*

78. Carnegie Mellon Univ. & Johns Hopkins Univ. Applied Physics Lab LLC, Cybersecurity Maturity Model Certification (CMMC), Unclassified Draft Version 0.4 (Aug. 30, 2019).

79. *CMMC FAQ's*, Office of Under Sec'y of Def. for Acquisition & Sustainment, Cybersecurity Maturity Model Certification, https://dodcio.defense.gov/CMMC/ (last visited Feb. 20, 2023) (FAQ No. 5).

that they are compliant on the front end of a procurement, rather than through post-award compliance audits.

(a) What is CMMC?

CMMC is a mandatory third-party certification of DOD contractors and subcontractors' information systems intended to protect sensitive but unclassified data or CUI against cyber threats. The CMMC Accreditation Body (CMMC-AB) trains and certifies CMMC Third-Party Assessment Organizations (C3PAOs) to assess contractors' processes and practices. Based on those assessments, the CMMC-AB will award CMMC Level certifications. C3PAOs will explain certification process and provide training and gather information and report metrics on compliance. In 2020, 101 Provisional Assessors were selected by the CMMC-AB to test CMMC certification processes.[80]

On November 4, 2021, after contractors struggled to understand and ramp up to comply with CMMC 1.0 and the interim final rule, DOD announced its intent to suspend CMMC 1.0 and replace it with a simpler CMMC 2.0.[81] The changes reflected in the CMMC 2.0 framework will be implemented through the rulemaking process. DOD will pursue rulemaking in both title 32 of the C.F.R. and title 48, to establish CMMC 2.0 program content in 48 C.F.R.

CMMC 2.0 includes various modifications from CMMC 1.0. Notably, CMMC 1.0 had five ascending levels of cybersecurity practices (i.e., five levels of certification) that evaluated a contractor's cybersecurity maturity. They were Level 5 (Advanced/Progressive), Level 4 (Proactive), Level 3 (Good Cyber Hygiene), Level 2 (Intermediate Cyber Hygiene), and Level 1 (Basic Cyber Hygiene). Under CMMC 2.0, there will only be three maturity levels: Level 1 (Foundational), Level 2 (Advanced), and Level 3 (Expert). The CMMC 2.0 structure eliminates levels 2 and 4 from the model, which were intended to serve as steppingstones as contractors worked to achieve levels 3 and 5. The DOD has announced that Level 1 will remain the same as CMMC 1.0 Level 1.

80. https://cyberab.org/.

81. *Strategic Direction for Cybersecurity Maturity Model Certification (CMMC) Program,* https://www.defense.gov/News/Releases/Release/Article/2833006/strategic-direction-for-cybersecurity-maturity-model-certification-cmmc-program/.

CMMC 2.0 Level 2 aligns with the 110 security requirements in NIST SP 800-171, whereas CMMC 2.0 Level 3 is similar to CMMC 1.0 Level 5 and aligns with NIST 800-172 (Enhanced Security Requirements for Protecting Controlled Unclassified Information: A Supplement to NIST SP 800-171) (February 2021).

Another major change from CMMC 1.0 to 2.0 is that the government will allow companies, under certain limited circumstances, to make Plans of Action & Milestones (POAMs) to achieve certification.[82] This modification is a response to industry calls for flexibility in the event a contractor is close to achieving compliance.

(b) Unpacking CMMC Levels

CMMC Model 2.0 Level 1 includes 17 practices and an annual self-assessment. Level 2 includes 110 practices closely aligned with NIST SP 800-171. The assessment for Level 2 involves triennial third-party assessments for critical national security information but self-assessment for select programs. Finally, Level 3 includes 110+ practices based on NIST SP 800-172 and triennial government-led assessments. The emphasis on self-assessment for Level 1 and certain Level 2 contractors is intended to reduce assessment costs for lower-risk contractors.[83]

What this means in practice is that contractors at the "Advanced" level will have to meet scores of requirements and best practices across at least 14 Security Domains. For each ascending level of certification, the contractor must demonstrate its ability to satisfy a greater number of Best Practices. For example, to obtain a Level 1 certification under the domain "Access Control," a contractor must adhere to the following Best Practices:

1. Limit information system access to authorized users,
2. Limit access to the types of transactions and functions that authorized users are permitted to execute,
3. Verify and control/limit connections to and use of external information systems, and

82. CMMC Version 2.0, https://dodcio.defense.gov/CMMC/ (last visited Feb. 22, 2023).

83. *Id.*

4. Control information posted or processed on publicly accessible information systems.[84]

By contrast, to meet the higher Level 2 requirements, a contractor must follow such additional cybersecurity Best Practices as:

1. Separate the duties of individuals to reduce the risk of malevolent activity without collusion;
2. Prevent nonprivileged users from executing privileged functions and capture the execution of such functions to audit logs;
3. Terminate (automatically) user sessions after a defined condition;
4. Protect wireless access using authentication and encryption;
5. Encrypt CUI on mobile devices and mobile computing platforms.[85]

(c) CMMC Assessment Process

In July 2022, the government released a pre-decisional draft of the CMMC Assessment Process (CAP).[86] The CAP draft is nearly 80 percent complete,[87] and covers the overarching procedures and guidance for C3PAOs conducting official CMMC Assessments of organizations seeking CMMC certification for Level 2. The CAP is organized across four phases and describes the required activities to ensure that CMMC Assessments are conducted consistently. The four phases are:

1. Plan and Prepare the Assessment,
2. Conduct the Assessment,
3. Report Assessment Results,
4. Closeout POA&Ms and Assessment (if necessary).

The pre-decisional draft has received a lot of criticism from contractors for being simultaneously overly complicated while lacking important detail about important issues, such as whether contractors

84. *Id.* at A-3–A-6.

85. *Id.* at A-4–A-5.

86. https://cyberab.org/Portals/0/Documents/Process-Documents/CMMC-Assessment-Process-CAP-v1.0.pdf (last visited Feb. 22, 2023).

87. Daniel Wilson, *Assessment Draft for DOD Cyber Program Lacks Key Details*, Law360 (Aug. 5, 2022).

who receive conditional certification will be eligible for DOD contracts.[88] These issues will likely be resolved or clarified in the final version of the CAP.

6. *Navigating DFARS 252.204-7010 (Cloud Computing Services)*

DFARS 252.204-7010 (Cloud Computing Services) is, as its title suggests, "applicable when using cloud computing to provide information technology services in the performance of the contract."[89] This clause requires the contractor to (1) maintain all government data not located on DOD premises within the U.S. government unless permission is granted by the contracting officer; (2) implement administrative, technical, and physical safeguards and controls with the security level and services required in accordance with DOD's Cloud Computing Security Requirements Guide (SRG), which includes ensuring that the contractor's cloud service provider has gone through DOD's standardized assessment and authorization (certification) process; and (3) comply with a specific cyber incident reporting protocol and subsequent cyber incident damage assessment activities, discussed in detail later.[90]

DOD addresses cloud services separately in the Department of Defense Cloud Computing Security Requirements Guide (SRG), which is developed by the Defense Information Systems Agency, Department of Defense.[91] The SRG requires contractors to be certified under FedRAMP.[92] FedRAMP is a cloud services security certification program administered by GSA and applies to all federal contractors.

88. *Id.*

89. Carnegie Mellon Univ. & Johns Hopkins Univ. Applied Physics Lab. LLC, Cybersecurity Maturity Model Certification (CMMC) Version 1.0 (2020) [hereinafter CMMC Ver. 1.0] (citing Council of Econ, Advisors, The Cost of Malicious Cyber Activity to the U.S. Economy (2018), https://trumpwhitehouse.archives.gov/wp-content/uploads/2018/02/The-Cost-of-Malicious-Cyber-Activity-to-the-U.S.-Economy.pdf.; Ctr. for Strategic & Int'l Studies (CSIS) & McAfee, Economic Impact of Cybercrime-No Slowing Down (2018) (emphasis added)).

90. CMMC Ver. 0.7, *supra* note 41, at 1.

91. DFARS 252.239-7010(b)(2) (stating that contractors "shall implement and maintain . . . services required in accordance with the Cloud Computing Security Requirements Guide").

92. Def. Info. Sys. Agency for Dep't of Def., Department of Defense Cloud Computing Security Requirements Guide (2017).

Additionally, SRG points DOD contractors to DOD FedRAMP+, which imposes supplemental security requirements in addition to FedRAMP requirements.[93] DOD classifies information systems into four different levels based on the level of sensitive information they contain.[94] Contractors will have to comply with the appropriate FedRAMP and DOD FedRAMP+ level based on those requirements.[95]

Notably, under DFARS 252.204.7010 for Cloud Computing Services, Cloud Services Providers (CSPs) must:

- Provide adequate security to safeguard CDI that resides on or is transiting through a contractor's internal information system
- Report cyber incidents
- Submit malicious software
- Submit media to support damage assessment
- Flow down the clause in subcontracts for operationally critical support

The DOD has indicated that there will likely be some form of reciprocity between CMMC and FedRAMP.[96] Indeed, according to the CMMC 2.0 FAQ page "the Department is pursuing development of acceptance standards between CMMC and other cybersecurity standards and assessments, to include between CMMC Level 2 (Advanced) and the NIST SP 800-171 DoD Assessment Methodology for the high assessment confidence level, as well as CMMC Level 2 and the GSA Federal Risk and Authorization Management Program (FedRAMP) requirements for commercial cloud service offerings."[97]

93. *Id.*

94. *Id.*

95. *Id.*

96. J. Justin Doubleday, *Pentagon 'endorses' reciprocity for CMMC, FedRAMP requirements*, Federal News Network (July 6, 2022), https://federalnewsnetwork.com/defense-main/2022/07/pentagon-endorses-reciprocity-for-cmmc-fedramp-requirements/.

97. CMMC 2.0 FAQs, https://www.acq.osd.mil/asda/dpc/cp/cyber/safeguarding.html.

II. Who Pays for Certification?

Without question, the cost to obtain CMMC Level 2 or higher certification will be significant, and it is unclear whether or to what extent contractors will be able to seek reimbursement for those costs. According to the DOD Office of the Under Secretary of Defense for Acquisition & Sustainment's CMMC website, "[t]he cost of certification will be considered an allowable, reimbursable cost and will not be prohibitive."[98] Whether that refers to just the cost of the third-party certification or the work required to get to a Level 3 certification is unclear.

Further guidance may be found by looking further back. In 2013, when DFARS 252.204-7012 was first issued as a final rule, the FAR Councils stated in response to the question of whether "the cost associated with compliance to the DFARS changes is allowable under CAS" that "[t]here is nothing in FAR 31 or DFARS 231 that would make the costs of compliance unallowable if the costs are incurred in accordance with FAR 31.201-2 [Determining Allowability]."[99] The take-away is that, if compliance is allowable, allocable, and reasonable under FAR Part 31, it may be reimbursable. The FAR Councils further explained in response to another question that "[i]n many cases, this contract requirement will be spread across and benefiting multiple contracts—costs associated with implementation will be allowable and chargeable to indirect cost pools. The Government does not intend to directly pay for the operating costs associated with the rule."[100] In plain language, until there is a more clear answer from DOD, contractors will likely have to bear the full brunt of the cost of compliance and then build the cost into their proposals over time as overhead and hope that the increased price does not make their proposal uncompetitive.

98. CMMC FAQ's, *supra* note 79, Response to Question 19.

99. Safeguarding Unclassified Controlled Technical Information, 78 Fed. Reg. 69,273, 69,274 (Nov. 18, 2013).

100. *Id.* at 69,275.

III. Potential Consequences for Noncompliance

Failure to comply with these regulations can lead to serious consequences, including False Claims Act liability.[101] For example, in *United States ex rel. Markus v. Aerojet Rocketdyne Holdings, Inc.*,[102] the Eastern District of California refused to dismiss a qui tam case where an employee of Aerojet Rocketdyne Holdings claimed that his employer repeatedly made false cybersecurity certifications to the government.[103] It is likely courts will continue to find civil False Claims Act violations for noncompliance with cybersecurity requirements. Additionally, contractors face potential suspension and debarment for not complying with DFARS regulations.

IV. May 12, 2021, Executive Order Regarding Cybersecurity

On May 12, 2021, President Biden signed an Executive Order (May 12, 2021, EO) to improve the nation's cybersecurity and protect federal government networks. The May 12, 2021, EO was in response to recent cybersecurity incidents including, significantly, SolarWinds, Microsoft Exchange, and the Colonial Pipeline incident.[104] The Biden administration noted that each of these cybersecurity incidents "share commonalities, including insufficient cybersecurity defenses that leave public and private sector entities more vulnerable to incidents."[105]

The May 12, 2021, EO included several broad requirements and developments. Among those requirements, the May 12, 2021, EO included sections to:

- Remove barriers to threat information sharing between the Government and Private Sector.

101. *See* FAR 52.203-13.

102. 381 F. Supp. 3d 1240 (E.D. Cal. 2019).

103. *Id.*

104. https://www.whitehouse.gov/briefing-room/statements-releases/2021/05/12/fact-sheet-president-signs-executive-order-charting-new-course-to-improve-the-nations-cybersecurity-and-protect-federal-government-networks/.

105. *Id.*

    - The Executive Order requires IT Service Providers to share certain breach information with the Government by removing contractual barriers to sharing such information where it could impact Government networks.
- Modernize and implement stronger cybersecurity standards in the Federal Government.
    - The Executive Order works to secure cloud services and a zero-trust architecture, and mandates deployment of multi-factor authentication and encryption with a specific time.
- Improve Software Supply Chain Security.
    - The Executive Order establishes baseline security standards for development of software sold to the government, including requiring developers to maintain greater visibility into their software and making security data publicly available. It also creates a pilot program to create an "energy star" type of label so the government—and the public at large—can quickly determine whether software was developed securely.
- Establish a Cybersecurity Safety Review Board.
    - The Executive Order establishes a Cybersecurity Safety Review Board, co-chaired by government and private sector leads, that may convene following a significant cyber incident to analyze what happened and make concrete recommendations for improving cybersecurity.
- Create a Standard Playbook for Responding to Cyber Incidents.
    - The Executive Order directs the development of a standardized playbook and set of definitions for cyber incident response by federal departments and agencies. The playbook will ensure all Federal agencies meet a certain threshold and are prepared to take uniform steps to identify and mitigate a threat. The playbook will also provide the private sector with a template for its response efforts.
- Improve Detection of Cybersecurity Incidents on Federal Government Networks.
    - The Executive Order improves the ability to detect malicious cyber activity on federal networks by enabling a government-wide endpoint detection and response system and improved information sharing within the Federal government.

- Improve Investigative and Remediation Capabilities.
  - The Executive Order creates cybersecurity event log requirements for federal departments and agencies.[106]

A. Zero Trust Architecture

As indicated earlier, the May 12, 2021, EO announced that it would implement "Zero Trust Architecture" for cloud services. As defined in the EO:

> [T]he terms "Zero Trust Architecture" means a security model, a set of system design principles, and a coordinated cybersecurity and system management strategy based on an acknowledgement that threats exist both inside and outside traditional network boundaries. The Zero Trust security model eliminates implicit trust in any one element, node, or service and instead requires continuous verification of the operational picture via real-time information from multiple sources to determine access and other system responses. In essence, a Zero Trust Architecture allows users full access but only to the bare minimum they need to perform their jobs. If a device is compromised, zero trust can ensure that the damage is contained. The Zero Trust Architecture security model assumes that a breach is inevitable or has likely already occurred, so it constantly limits access to only what is needed and looks for anomalous or malicious activity. Zero Trust Architecture embeds comprehensive security monitoring; granular risk-based access controls; and system security automation in a coordinated manner throughout all aspects of the infrastructure in order to focus on protecting data in real-time within a dynamic threat environment. This data-centric security model allows the concept of least-privileged access to be applied for every access decision, where the answers to the questions of who, what, when, where, and how are critical for appropriately allowing or denying access to resources based on the combination of sever.

106. https://www.whitehouse.gov/briefing-room/statements-releases/2021/05/12/fact-sheet-president-signs-executive-order-charting-new-course-to-improve-the-nations-cybersecurity-and-protect-federal-government-networks/.

According to NIST, which published SP 800-207 on Zero Trust Architecture in August 2020, Zero Trust (ZT) is the term for an evolving set of cybersecurity paradigms that move defenses from static, network-based perimeters to focus on users, assets, and resources.[107] The May 12, 2021, EO signals that the government as a whole is moving toward ZT as a comprehensive cybersecurity solution—which could ultimately mean somewhat of a departure from NIST 800-171, which acknowledges the use of trusted users in many network topologies. It is difficult to predict how and to what extent this will impact the rollout of CMMC, but, at a minimum, the May 12, 2021, EO mandated a review of agency-specific cybersecurity requirements to recommend to the FAR Council standardized contract language across government agencies.

V. Private Sector Cybersecurity Risks and Solutions

Cybersecurity risks in the private sector can be significant—and are largely tied to the types of data a company manages and the legal and contractual frameworks that govern those types of data. Most of this chapter has focused on data that comes from the government, that is, in the case of CMMC, "controlled unclassified information." In the private sector, the types of data subject to the most rigorous statutory and contractual frameworks tend to fall (broadly) into the following categories: (1) personal identifiable information (PII) (i.e., social security numbers); (2) protected health information (i.e., medical records); and (3) protected consumer financial information (i.e., bank records). These types of data are protected by long-standing statutory frameworks such as the Health Insurance Portability and Accountability Act (HIPAA) for health information,[108] the Gramm-Leach-Bliley Act (GLBA)[109] for financial information held by financial institutions, and a vast array of both existing and emerging state and federal frameworks for PII, such

---

107. *Id.*

108. https://www.cdc.gov/phlp/publications/topic/hipaa.html (last accessed Feb. 20, 2023).

109. https://www.ftc.gov/business-guidance/privacy-security/gramm-leach-bliley-act (last accessed Feb. 20, 2023).

as the California Consumer Privacy Act (CCPA).[110] Moreover, all states have mandatory data breach notification laws that require certain private and public entities to report cybersecurity incidents within a period of time to state agencies and to individuals impacted by a breach.[111]

Standard-setting organizations, like the Payment Card Industry Security Standards Council,[112] also promulgate industry data security standards that are routinely incorporated into contracts between and among private entities. Notably, the Payment Card Industry Data Security Standard (PCI DSS) is a component of most contracts between credit card issuing banks and merchants that accept credit cards branded by the major credit card networks (i.e., Visa and Mastercard). Questions of compliance with the PCI DSS frequently arise in litigation regarding security breaches of credit card data.[113] The PCI DSS is often cited as the "standard of care" in lawsuits alleging that cyber incidents were the result of a company's negligence.

This section discusses, in broad terms, the fundamentals of conducting a risk assessment and best practices for cybersecurity in the private sector. There is, however, no "one size fits all" approach to private sector cybersecurity, particularly given the patchwork of regulations and standards that may govern an organization's data. Indeed, cybersecurity needs are best addressed through a comprehensive review of existing cybersecurity infrastructure, combined with an assessment of threats, vulnerabilities, and regulatory mandates. Ultimately, the decision of how best to protect the business assets and networks is a nuanced cost/benefit analysis based on the organization's needs, regulatory and contractual mandates, and what is, ultimately, affordable.

A. Risk Assessments

Risk assessments are essential to the development of cogent cybersecurity policies and practices. There are many standard-setting organizations

110. https://oag.ca.gov/privacy/ccpa (last accessed Feb. 20, 2023).

111. https://www.ncsl.org/research/telecommunications-and-information-technology/security-breach-notification-laws.aspx (last accessed Feb. 20, 2023).

112. https://www.pcisecuritystandards.org/pci_security/ (last accessed Feb. 20, 2023).

113. https://www.willkie.com/-/media/files/publications/2017/08/target_data_breach_ag_settlement.pdf (last accessed Feb. 20, 2023).

that provide cybersecurity frameworks that help organizations identify their risks, including, as discussed earlier, NIST and the PCI-DSS. Risk assessments can be conducted internally or with external partners, such as law firms specializing in cybersecurity and/or cybersecurity consulting firms. Best practices include engaging an external provider to provide an independent analysis at least every three years.

Put in basic terms, a cybersecurity risk is the likelihood of experiencing negative disruptions to sensitive data, finances, or business operations. Common security threats that may pose a risk to an organization include ransomware, phishing scams, insider threats, data leaks, and malware, among other threats. Companies often think about cybersecurity risks as those events associated with a potential breach of sensitive information (whether personal or commercial). Data breach risk is certainly paramount, but companies should also appreciate the operational risks—a ransomware attack, for example, can cripple operating systems and grind business to a halt.

Risk assessments focus on identifying vulnerabilities in addition to threats. A vulnerability is a control gap or weakness that may result in unauthorized access to a network. A vulnerability assessment will include a basic analysis of potential risks in terms of "low," "medium," or "high" risks. A risk assessment matrix may plot out the likelihood of the risk against the gravity of the risk to determine the importance of quickly (and fully) addressing the vulnerability. A network may have vulnerabilities in different domains of its information technology infrastructure, impacting different types of company assets. For instance, a network may have a vulnerability because it only requires users to log-in to their computers using single-factor authentication. This relatively weak authentication process may put certain assets (i.e., PII) at risk of an external threat (i.e., ransomware). However, while having only single factor authentication may carry a high risk that a third party could breach a user's computer, the overall risk may not be significant if that user does not have access to sensitive data.

Risk assessments overall identify, estimate, and prioritize risk to a business's operations, assets, individuals, and other organizations, resulting from the use of information systems. Prioritization is key—although certain cybersecurity protocols and practices may be required by contracts or state and federal law, much of the decision-making about how to identify and address cybersecurity risks and vulnerabilities is left to the discretion of business leaders within an organization. Many businesses (at their peril) fail to appreciate the potentially catastrophic impact a data breach may have on the company, which can and often does result in under-investment in cybersecurity. That said, the cost of a robust cybersecurity infrastructure can be significant and cost-prohibitive for many small and mid-sized companies. Thus, making strategic business decisions that prioritize higher-level risks over lower-level risks is essential for a company to protect itself while minimizing its costs of compliance.

B. Best Practices

As noted earlier, best practices in cybersecurity necessarily depend on the industry and type of data a company seeks to protect. However, the following is a nonexhaustive list of certain fundamentals that apply nearly universally:

- Keep software up-to-date
  - Companies provide software updates for a reason—many times this reason is to upgrade security and fix vulnerabilities.
- Keep hardware up-to-date
  - Outdated hardware may not support security upgrades. Thus, it is important to make sure your hardware can keep up with technological solutions to threats.
- Avoid opening suspicious content
  - Many data breaches begin with a single user opening a suspicious email. As noted later, companies should be mindful of these threats and train employees to identify and avoid suspicious content.
- Use secure file sharing
  - Using secure file sharing is key to both accessing and protecting sensitive data. Third-party secure file sharing services (or in-house services if company resources permit) allow a company to encrypt data while in transit and prevent unauthorized access. Depending on the type of data a company manages, such secure file sharing may be required by contract, state law, or federal law. Email should be avoided to transmit sensitive files.

- Use anti-virus and anti-malware protection software
  - Protection software can alert the company and/or user in the event of certain types of threats and allow the company to better contain or eliminate the threat. A company can achieve "defense in depth" with additional layers of protective technology (e.g., endpoint detection and response (EDR) solution; firewalls).
- Use a Virtual Private Network
  - A virtual private network (VPN) will encrypt a user's connection and protect private information, even from an internet service provider.
- Employ password protection
  - This is a basic level of protection. Training regarding strong passwords and policies that mandate passwords be changed periodically can greatly increase the efficacy of password protection.
- Enable multifactor authentication
  - Multifactor authentication moves away from reliance on a single (potentially vulnerable) password and requires at least one additional step to verify that the user is indeed the person attempting to log-in (e.g., a verification code sent to a cellular phone).
- Do not provide users with more access than necessary
  - This is also referred to as the "principle of least privilege" and is the concept that information is better protected if only those who need to access it can access it. Applying the principle of least privilege is particularly important for companies that maintain a large amount of sensitive data.
- Avoid public networks
  - When a user connects to a public network, she shares the network with other connected users. This can expose sensitive information to any third-party user on that network unless the company employee uses an otherwise secure connection (e.g., VPN).
- Back up important data
  - Discussions around cybersecurity often concentrate on protecting data from unauthorized access or attacks. Equally

important, however, is protecting data from deletion or corruption. It is essential that companies back up important data in the event of a physical disruption (e.g., destruction of servers) or other incident that may lead to the deletion of mission critical data (e.g., following a ransomware attack).

There are numerous other steps a company can take to protect its networks from a cyber threat. Some steps may be required by contract or applicable law. It is essential that a company undergo a full risk assessment and understand compliance obligations to ensure it has implemented the proper policies and practices.

C. Training

Training employees is critical to cybersecurity. When it comes to cybersecurity, a company is only as strong as its weakest link. All too often, that "weakest link" is a single employee who falls prey to a phishing scam or logs in to the company financials via a public network. Companies should have clearly defined user policies that are regularly updated and disseminated to employees. Further, employees should undergo cybersecurity training when they are onboarded and periodically over the course of their employment. Cybersecurity training should cover a range of topics, including:

- Identifying potential threats (e.g., suspicious emails, suspicious links, malware, phishing scams);
- Physical security (e.g., locking computers when away from one's desk, never leaving a laptop unattended in a public place, not allowing others to use a company computer);
- Log-in protocols (e.g., avoiding public networks, routinely changing passwords, employing dual-factor authentication);
- Secure file sharing (e.g., requiring employees to use secure file sharing that has been set up internally rather than other third-party services);
- Regulations governing data that employees access (e.g., employees must be trained to comply with applicable regulations that may apply to any data they can access and use).

A company's risk assessment can help guide what types of training are most necessary and beneficial. The more sensitive the data a company maintains, the more training is required to ensure adequate cybersecurity.

VI. Insurance for Cyber Risks

As noted earlier, the consequences for failure to comply with government cybersecurity regulations can be serious and may expose contractors to financial liability as well as result in exclusion from future government contracts. Beyond the government sanctions for failure to comply, companies maintaining data protected by any state or federal law (not limited to controlled unclassified information) may face significant financial liability from a data breach incident. The cost of a massive data breach can cripple a company—particularly a small or mid-sized company with limited financial resources to respond to the breach and subsequent litigation. As a result of the significant risk posed by data breaches, many companies purchase cybersecurity insurance to offset these risks.

There are multiple ways in which architects and engineers (A/E) or contractors may face exposure from a potential data security breach. Like most companies that manage any type of PII, A/Es and contractors may be subject to state laws requiring mandatory notification in the event of a data breach. Depending on the type of coverage, cyber security coverage may pay for a forensic investigator to determine the source and extent of a breach, attorneys to determine if notification is required and to draft notification letters, and breach response firms to provide notification services and credit monitoring for affected individuals.

Cyber insurance may also cover claims by clients or other third parties for the unauthorized disclosure of confidential information. Further, if A/Es or contractors accept credit cards, they may need insurance in the event they are noncompliant with PCI DSS. Indeed, some third-party contracts require contractors to carry cybersecurity coverage.

If a company is subjected to a ransomware attack, certain insurance may cover the cost (and negotiation) of the ransom. Companies should also explore coverage for fraudulent funds transfers (e.g., wire/ACH fraud) that may result from an email account takeover or social engineering scheme where someone within the company is tricked into directing funds to a cybercriminal posing as a trusted internal or third-party contact[114].

---

114. https://www.pindrop.com/blog/fbi-says-fake-ceo-email-scam-losses-hit-2-3-billion.

Cyber insurance may also cover losses in the event of data destruction or loss of profits associated with a network shutdown. It may also cover liabilities from a breach related to a vendor or subcontractor.[115] Finally, contractors may suffer reputational harm from a breach. Insurance may cover the costs of responding to negative press, among other things.

Insurance, however, comes with limitations and exclusions. Since cybersecurity insurance is an emerging industry, and cyberattacks have increased exponentially over the last several years, one should anticipate premiums will continue to rise and certain coverage may be limited in the event of a significant breach. In 2021, premiums increased by 74 percent, while available coverage has been shrinking.[116] Thus, there is no substitute for strong cybersecurity practices, policies, and protocols to protect a company against a cybersecurity threat.

VII. Conclusion

The rise in use of artificial intelligence (AI), wider use of the Internet of Things (IoT) through "smart" devices and sensors, increased data storage in clouds, and increased automation in design and construction projects create new vulnerabilities to cyber threats. As the design and construction industry embraces numerous new technologies,[117] owners, designers, contractors, subcontractors, and suppliers must recognize the need for constant vigilance to minimize the risk of cyberattacks and data breaches.

---

115. https://www.founderspro.com/2020/01/06/10-reasons-architects-engineers-need-to-buy-cyber-liability-insurance/.

116. National Association of Insurance Commissioners Memorandum, Report on the Cyber Insurance Market, October 18, 2022, https://content.naic.org/sites/default/files/cmte-c-cyber-supplement-report-2022-for-data-year-2021.pdf.

117. See Chapter 1 regarding new technologies being used in design and construction.

CHAPTER 4

Dealing with Construction Technology in Law Practice

Rebecca Sherman and Megan George, *Authors*
Chris Harnett and Sarah Glover, *Contributors*

I. Introducing Emerging Technology and Its Legal Concerns, Impacts on Existing Practices, and Vetting New Technology[1]

Construction sites are teeming with new technology. From collaboration software used when starting a project, to powered drones used to survey potential and ongoing job sites, to wearable devices providing data about workers' activity and health, the way the construction industry looks, feels, and operates has fundamentally changed in every step of the design, bid, and build process. Businesses recognize the critical need for advancements to increase productivity, particularly since many construction projects are not completed on time.[2] Contributing

1. This chapter focuses on issues that new design and construction technology raise for lawyers; it does not include discussion of various types of technology that affect lawyers generally, such as ChatGPT, digital signatures, block chain contracts, virtual hearings, and so on.

2. KPMG International, KPMG International Cooperative, Climbing the curve, 2015 global construction Project Owner's Survey (2015).

to project delays are fragmented and inefficient processes. One survey found that construction companies can lose upwards of 14 hours per week of optimal activity when workers face problem dealing with project data/information collection, conflict resolution in contract documents, and mistakes and reworks, which are all issues that technology could address and make more efficient.[3] While new and emerging technologies create enormous potential to increase productivity, reduce costs, and improve workplace safety, they also present novel and untested risks to the design and construction industry and its lawyers. With a wave of technological change sweeping the industry, new legal challenges have emerged.

A. Core Issues Regarding Construction Technology (BIM Technology)

Unlike newer on-site and integrated technology, design technology is well established in the industry. Building information modeling (BIM), design-based software that allows collaboration and virtual management of construction projects, is widely adopted for use on nearly all project sizes.[4] BIM use has risen over the last two decades, and the software has proven to increase productivity and efficiency between collaborators at all levels of the design process.[5] The United States and United Kingdom especially have emerged as pioneers in BIM adoption.[6] In fact, the United Kingdom mandated the use of BIM for all construction projects funded by the government starting in 2016.[7]

---

3. Eric Thomas et al., PlanGrid & FMI, 2018 Industry Report, Construction Disconnected (2018).

4. Salman Azhar, *Building Information Modelling (BIM): Trends, Benefits, Risks and Challenges for the AEC Industry*, 11 Leadership & mgmt. in Eng'g, 241–252 (2011).

5. F.H. Abanda, D. Mzyece, A.H. Oti, & M.B. Manjia, *A Study of the Potential of Cloud/Mobile BIM for the Management of Construction Projects*, 1 Applied Sys. Innovation (2018).

6. Andy K.D. Wong, Francis K.W. Wong & Abid Nadeem, *Attributes of Building Information Modelling Implementations in Various Countries*, 6 Architectural Eng'g & Design Mgmt. 288–302 (2010).

7. *BIM Activities Around the World 2020*, Vibim (2020), Vibim.com.

However, widespread adoption of BIM creates legal challenges and uncertainties. Use of BIM often leads to risk allocation issues, intellectual property protection issues, including potential infringement claims, and various other contractual issues.[8] Contractors, designers, and owners often have their own individual approaches in contracting out the use of BIM, which can lead to confusion and uncertainty.[9] Varying indemnification clauses often overshadow contractual agreements over use of BIM.[10] These indemnification clauses may touch and concern BIM at its creation, its transfer, or at receipt of electronic data comprising the BIM documents on any given project. Many industry-standard agreements include model language covering the use of BIM, but businesses and their attorneys must take care in modifying these terms to protect their unique interests and adequately allocate the risks associated with BIM use (an issue discussed further in this chapter).

B. The Rise of Drones and Wearable Technology

Newer technology, such as drones and various wearable devices, are likewise becoming commonplace on construction sites across the United States.[11] Drones have been rapidly adopted and are becoming increasingly popular. As of March 2020, nearly half a million drones were licensed for commercial use.[12] In construction, drones can assist in scouting potential construction sites, as well as providing data about established and ongoing projects. While the FAA currently oversees drone use,[13] privacy issues associated with drone use are largely unregulated. However, the American Law Institute and the Uniform Law Commission both attempted to address legal issues (such as trespass, nuisance, and some privacy concerns) related to drone use,[14] and the

---

8. Philip L. Bruner & Patrick J. O'Connor Jr., Bruner & O'Connor on Construction Law § 7.89: (Thomson West 2020).

9. *Id.*

10. *Id.*

11. See Chapter 1 for a discussion of drone use on construction projects.

12. Robinson & Cole Construction Group, Robinson & Cole LLP, *Balancing New Technology and Privacy When Using Drones in Land Use and Construction* Vol X The Nat.Law Rev. No 147 (May 26, 2020).

13. 14 C.F.R. §§ 107 *et seq.*

14. *Id.*

ABA House of Delegates recently sponsored Resolution 111 (adopted overwhelmingly by the 2020 ABA Midyear Meeting),[15] which urged legislators and regulators to enact laws and regulations addressing trespass and privacy concerns of drone usage.[16] More laws and regulations addressing drone use will likely soon be created, and will undoubtedly impact the way construction teams utilize drones in the future.

Wearable technology, which provides a worker's individual biometric data, is likewise on the brink of privacy-related regulation. "Wearables" expand far beyond smart watches. Among the many devices currently flooding the industry are "smart" work boots that give GPS coordinates and have motion sensors, sensor clips used to track falls and alert others when hazardous conditions arise, and smart glasses that contain mixed-reality technology to overlay 3D renderings in real time.[17] Wrist- and body-worn device production is expected to expand substantially in the coming years.[18] The data collected provides insight into specific medical and locational information about the wearers, which data is likewise subject to numerous medical and other privacy concerns. Because of these issues, the use of these devices, as well as the data they collect, will likely soon be addressed by statute or regulation.

In the meantime, employers should use due care in gathering this data on their employees. As an initial matter, employers should give their employees notice of data collected prior to wearable use,[19] and should recognize that jurisdictions have differing rules regarding the

---

15. Matt Reynolds, *ABA House of Delegates Passes Resolution on Drones; Delegate Calls It "a Hot Topic,"* ABA J. (Feb. 17, 2020, 6:45 PM), https://www.abajournal.com/news/article/resolution-111.

16. *Id.*

17. Asphalt Pro Staff, CPH Asphalt Pro, LLC, *Wearable Technology Makes Construction Safer, More Efficient*, https://theasphaltpro.com/articles/wearable-technology-makes-construction-safer-efficient/.

18. Allied Business Intelligence, Inc., *Enterprise Wearable Market to Soon See Shift from Wrist to Body-Worn Devices, ABI Research Forecasts Body-Worn Wearables Will Exceed 116 Million Shipments in 2021* (Jan. 7, 2017), https://www.abiresearch.com.

19. Allen Smith, J.D., *How to Limit Wearable Technology's Legal Risks*, Soc'y for Human Res. Mgmt. (May 29, 2018), https://www.shrm.org/ResourcesAndTools/legal-and-compliance/employment-law/Pages/wearable-technology-legal-risks.aspx.

collection of employee medical information. For instance, California recently enacted the California Consumer Privacy Act (CCPA), which became effective on January 1, 2020.[20] While this act directly addresses consumers, it *can* also apply to employers that meet certain criteria.[21] Employers that meet the statutory threshold must follow guidelines on the use of personal data collected, including numerous disclosure practices that must be followed in obtaining the data.[22]

Similarly, Illinois enacted legislation that addresses the collection of biometric data of individuals by private entities.[23] The Illinois Biometric Information Privacy Act (BIPA) requires employers to establish safe practices of storing and destroying biometric data it collects on employees.[24] The act imposes numerous disclosure practices on employers collecting biometric data and gives individuals standing to sue if an entity violates the act.[25] Washington state also recently enacted legislation imposing disclosure requirements and retention practices of biometric data.[26] A wave of new legislation addressing individual data is expected across the United States, as numerous states are evaluating or planning to enact legislation concerning biometric data.[27] In any case, employers should ensure that adequate precautions, protecting that data from theft or leak, are implemented any time data is collected and stored.[28] Employers should likewise implement written guidelines disclosing the collection of biometric data and establishing retention practices to

---

20. California Consumer Privacy Act of 2018, 1.81.5 CAL. CIV. CODE.

21. Mary Beth Downs, Risk Management, Sequoia Consulting Group, *Biometric Data Collection—State and Federal Legislation Recap*, SEQUOIA (Aug. 19, 2020), https://www.sequoia.com/2020/08/biometric-data-collection-state-and-federal-legislative-recap/.

22. CAL. CIV. CODE. § 1798.100(a).

23. 740 ILL. COMP. STAT. ANN. § 14/1.

24. *Id.* § 14/15.

25. *Id.* § 14/20.

26. WASH. REV. CODE ANN. § 40.26.020.

27. Downs, *supra* note 21.

28. Smith, *supra* note 19.

safely store and destroy this data.[29] Data breaches impacting employee personal information can expose businesses to legal, financial, and reputational risks, and may require companies to provide formal notification under the state data breach notification statutes.

As more and more companies mandate the use of wearables, counsel should consider the unique privacy risks associated with these devices and the data collected. For instance, wearables gathering information could reveal the existence of a disability, triggering ADA concerns for an employer.[30] Wearable technology could also trigger Fair Labor Standards Act liability issues because of additional control an employer exerts over employees through the use of wearable data.[31] Additionally, this data can trigger National Labor Relations Act protections if wearable devices are used to record or reveal unsafe working conditions.[32] As wearable data becomes more commonplace, counsel should expect more regulation of the use of both wearables and the data collected.

C. Technology's Impact on Insurance[33]

Privacy concerns surrounding the use of wearables are an obvious issue; their impact on insurance claims may be less direct but should not be overlooked. Wearable data will likely provide important claims evidence, particularly for workers' compensation. For example, unsafe work practices such as excessive speed may be able to be retrieved; if a significant fall occurs, wearables can track when and where it happened.[34] While wearable data could help to weed out fraudulent claims, the same data could also be used to corroborate employee injuries. As

---

29. Ana Tagvoryan, Brooke T. Iley & David J. Oberly, *Minimize Litigation Risks When Using Biometric Data*, SOC'Y FOR HUMAN RES. MGMT. (Apr. 1, 2019), https://www.shrm.org.

30. Smith, *supra* note 19.

31. *Id.*

32. *Id.*

33. See Chapter 3 for a discussion of cybersecurity insurance.

34. Mike Kroeber, Business Intelligence Associates, Inc., *Reduce Claims Payouts with Discoverable Data in Construction Wearables*, BIA BLOG (Oct. 1, 2020), https://www.biaprotect.com/blog/reduce-claims-payouts-with-discoverable-data-in-construction-wearables/.

the data from these devices establish a firmer presence in litigation, insurance companies will likely take notice.

Additionally, mandated wearable use may result in a reduction in insurance premiums for companies who provide the data to their insurers.[35] More efficient and quicker claim handling may occur with the assistance of wearable data. The presence of wearables could make employees more cognizant of their actions and result in an overall increase to workplace safety, thereby reducing workers' compensation claims (and potentially reducing premiums).

Despite technology's potential to reduce injuries, improve claims processing, and even lower premiums, wearables, drones, and other emerging technology may complicate insurance coverage planning. Coverage for drone accidents, for example, may be disallowed by a commercial general liability policy's "aircraft, auto and watercraft" exclusion.[36] Drone, or "unmanned aerial vehicle" (UAV) coverage, whether through endorsement to a general liability policy or standalone coverage, is quickly becoming mandatory on construction sites. Such coverage can be valuable, covering not just injury and property damage but also invasion of privacy claims.[37] Drone insurance products are available in both period and on-demand coverage, offering different coverage for regular and occasional users.[38] Yet, such policies have limitations and informational obligations insureds should fully understand before purchasing and relying on drone coverage. At a minimum, firms acquiring drone coverage should investigate whether an offered policy includes coverage for the damage to the craft itself, as well as any payload carried by the drone (cameras, sensors, etc.), what operator,

---

35. Procore Editorial Staff, Procore Technologies, Inc., *Reducing Insurance-Related Costs with Construction Technology* (May 6, 2018), https://www.procore.com/jobsite/reducing-insurance-related-costs-with-construction-technology/.

36. In the absence of a policy definition of "aircraft," courts interpreting the aircraft exclusion generally have found drones to be "aircrafts" as the term is commonly understood. *See, e.g.*, Philadelphia Indem. Ins. Co. v. Hollycal Prod., Inc., 2018 WL 6520412 (C.D. Cal. Dec. 7, 2018) (finding no coverage for a wedding guest's injury caused by the insured wedding photographer's drone due to the policy's "aircraft" exclusion).

37. RotorDroneMag.com, *Insurance Coverage 101* (Apr. 22, 2020), https://www.rotordronepro.com/drone_insurance/.

38. *Id.*

usage, and maintenance information the insured will need to supply the insurer, and any geographic or usage exclusions to coverage.

Collection and use of biometric data, as well as the ever-impending threat of a data breach, may also subject construction firms to private claims or regulatory concerns that reveal an insurance coverage gap. Directors and officers (D&O) coverage, employer liability coverage, and cyber liability coverage may offer a defense to certain claims, but alone, none of the foregoing coverages is adequate to afford an insured full protection.[39] D&O and employer liability policies may exclude coverage for invasion of privacy claims, while cyber liability policies are not intended to address shareholder litigation that might arise from a data breach.[40] Insurance carriers are also steadily adopting exclusions for regulatory violations and private actions concerning data privacy.[41] Firms should familiarize themselves with privacy laws applicable to their business and clients, and the scope and limitations of existing coverage to assess their risk and coverage needs now and in the coming years.

Firms should further consider the potential downsides of readily available data on insurance claim resolution. While expanded evidence relevant to an insurance claim may offer certain immediate benefits, an insurer's access to previously unavailable information may complicate claim processing, or even lead to limited or denied recovery. Photos, video, weather data, and even user biometric data may provide an insurer means to dispute the cause of an otherwise covered occurrence, the extent of an insured's loss, or even the insured status of the damaged party. In the long term, an insurer's access to unlimited biometric data on a macro scale may also drive data-driven decisions that ignore individual insured or claims information in favor of statistical stereotypes.

---

39. CRC Group, *Biometric Data Risks: Keep Eyes on Coverage Gaps*, https://www.crcgroup.com/Tools-Intel/post/biometric-data-risks-keep-eyes-on-coverage-gaps (last visited Dec. 30, 2021).

40. *Id.*; Kristine R. Argentine & Paul J. Yovanic, Jr., Seyfarth Shaw LLP, *The Growing Number of Biometric Privacy Laws and the Post-COVID Consumer Class Action Risks for Businesses* (June 5, 2020), https://www.consumerclassdefense.com/2020/06/the-growing-number-of-biometric-privacy-laws-and-the-post-covid-consumer-class-action-risks-for-businesses/.

41. *Id.*

This could create price spikes for companies or industries deemed high risk and drive complicated policy drafting that excludes critical losses to prioritize limiting carrier exposure. To the extent possible, inquiry into an insurer's data usage terms and conditions is a best practice when considering sharing data with an insurer.

D. Vetting New Technology

Recent surveys found that 40 percent of construction industry respondents implemented new technology in the last six months.[42] Technology development and implementation is not solely confined to the on-site worker or the inner mechanisms of the design, bid, build process of a construction project. As structures continue to be built, a cascade of ever-evolving modern technology is installed along with the building, ensuring that similarly constructed buildings can function in technologically dissimilar ways. This technology often allows safer maintenance and efficient repairs when buildings inadvertently present safety hazards, such as interior piping water flow monitors.[43] If an integral pipe fails and the sensors detect a failure, maintenance or security is immediately alerted and the water is automatically shut off, turning a potential nightmare into a routine repair.[44]

As new technology transforms how buildings are managed, such new technology does not always create benefits. Infamously, in 2015, a high-rise condominium tower located within Miami's financial district garnered media coverage when its robotic car retrieval garage malfunctioned. In response, condominium owners had to find alternative and costly arrangements to park their vehicles. A lawsuit was filed, and a jury verdict rendered in Miami-Dade Circuit Court found the developer, BrickellHouse Holding LLC, on the hook for over $40 million in

---

42. Grace Ellis, *The Legal Risks and Pitfalls When Using Construction Tech—and How to Avoid Them*, DIGITAL BUILDER BLOG, AUTODESK (Oct. 21, 2020), https://constructionblog.autodesk.com/.

43. Katie Dwyer, *5 Trends to Watch in Construction Technology*, RISK & INSURANCE (APR. 18, 2018), https://riskandinsurance.com/5-trends-in-construction-tech/.

44. The Hartford Staff, The Hartford Financial Services Group, Inc., *How Innovative Technology Is Changing Construction Risk Management* (May 9, 2021), https://www.thehartford.com/insights/construction/innovative-technology.

reparations to the condo association.[45] The developer was found to have breached statutory warranties it owed to owners of condo units and to the building's condo association.[46] While extreme, this example demonstrates the need for all project team members to carefully consider how emerging technology will be utilized.

Novel technology also can present unique challenges, since despite vetting efforts, defects are not always readily discoverable.[47] With billions of dollars rolling into new construction technology startups each year,[48] the market is likely to be flooded with shiny, yet unproven, technology at every corner of the design, bid, and build process. This funding is surging each year and sifting through this cascade of new technology being introduced into the market to find solutions either to address a contractor's problem or to create new efficiencies is a challenge.

Technology adoption can fail for a variety of reasons. Common barriers to successful implementation include the technology being a poor fit with current processes and procedures, poor integration with existing software and technology, and inadequate training.[49] Legacy systems that firms have used and relied on for years can present challenges when attempting to integrate into new technology, as a bad fit may not always be apparent at the outset of adoption. Nearly three-quarters of responding contractors in a recent survey expect to adopt new advanced tech

---

45. Scott Sowers, *The Law and Emerging Technology, Why Developers Should Be Careful about Using Untested Technology in Buildings*, Builder (Oct. 24, 2019), https://www.builderonline.com/technology/the-law-and-emerging-technology_o.

46. Rene Rodriguez, *The Robotic Garage at This Brickell Condo Broke. Now the Developer Must Pay $40.6 million*, Miami Herald (Sept. 4, 2019).

47. Lyndsey Christofer, *How Technology Is Revolutionizing Construction Risk Mitigation*, PropertyCasualty360 (Nov. 2, 2017), https://www.propertycasualty360.com/2017/11/02/how-technology-is-revolutionizing-construction-risk-mitigation/?slreturn=20220713185351.

48. Hamzah Shanbari, *Evaluating and Selecting Construction Technologies*, xplorexit, https://xplorexit.com/evaluating-selecting-construction-technologies/.

49. Eric Thomas et al., PlanGrid & FMI, 2018 Industry Report, Construction Disconnected (2018) (New Research from PlanGrid and FMI Identifies Factors Costing the Construction Industry More Than $177 Billion Annually).

within the next three years.[50] Proven manufacturers are the safest bet but could present higher costs not feasible for smaller construction projects or smaller firms.

Testing new technology that maintains compatibility with existing technology can ease the process of upgrading or implementing.[51] Construction sites generate a lot of data, and numerous options exist on how to input, collect, manage, and transfer this data, but not every new software or technology introduced will seamlessly coexist with other products. Implementing software tools that can coexist or seamlessly interact with each other or with existing systems can reduce confusion and streamline data utility. Construction industry leaders have developed creative means to implement new tools on a limited basis, including joint ventures or partnerships with tech sector companies aimed at exploring implementation and compatibility on a limited scale or on particular projects before attempting to integrate new technology across all projects. These partnerships are mutually beneficial, allowing construction firms to vet new technology without a major commitment or systems overhaul, while offering tech developers real-world insight into user-interface and efficiency optimization. With the right amount of planning and strategic approaches to tech integration, risks can be managed. Still, it is likely no amount of planning or vetting can provide as much safety as proper risk allocation.

In addition to operational vetting of new technology, valuable risk allocation and planning tools for construction firms include thorough investigation of clients, partners, subcontractors, and vendors supplying new technology, strategic relationship structuring, careful contract and warranty drafting, and broad insurance coverage. Take for example the Miami-Dade condominium case; if the tech company that supplied the malfunctioning car retrieval robotic was a startup, is the developer solely responsible for the $40.6 million settlement? Or, if the developer

50. Kathleen Brown, *74% of Contractors Expect to Adopt Advanced Tech in 3 Tears*, Construction Dive (Dec. 19, 2018), https://www.constructiondive.com/news/74-of-contractors-expect-to-adopt-advanced-tech-in-3-years/544757/.

51. Rose Hall, *Construction Industry's New Priority: Greater Tech Adoption*, Int'l Risk Mgmt. Inst., Inc. (IRMI) (Feb. 5, 2021), https://www.irmi.com/articles/expert-commentary/construction-industrys-new-priority-greater-tech-adoption.

lacks assets, how will damaged contractors or condominium owners be made whole? Which party's insurance, if any, will offer coverage for the robotic retrieval system's failure?

First, thorough vetting of relationships and strategic business relations is always a critical means to protect clients and companies. Firms must exercise due diligence before accepting risky engagements or forming business relationships involving new technology, ensuring all risks are known prior to project initiation. After assessing the risks and rewards of a proposed business arrangement, construction attorneys should advise clients on equitable risk allocation through contract terms. Risk should lie with the party best able to ameliorate the identified risk, and well-drafted contracts expressly identify the risks involved with a particular transaction and assign responsibility accordingly. Key terms for risk allocation in contracts involving emerging technology are discussed further in the next section, although the primary terms to be addressed are indemnification, warranties, data security, and responsibility for supply, use, and oversight of technology products contemplated for the project or the deal memorialized in the agreement.

Finally, ensuring all parties concerned carry appropriate and adequate insurance coverage is critical when using unfamiliar or complex technology in the construction arena. All project team members or parties to a contract should carry insurance covering the scope of risk posed by their respective roles on the project or in the business relationship, and those parties at risk of a loss covered by another's insurance should insist on contractual additional insured obligations. To protect the data generated and collected by technology involved in a transaction or a project, parties should consider cyber liability coverage or insurance products aimed at covering a loss caused by a data breach or a related privacy claim. Most importantly, the breadth of coverage afforded by, and exclusions to, carried coverages must be fully understood. Just as construction companies are steadily exploring new technology, insurance companies are adapting available coverage products to newly posed risks of that technology. Absent a complete understanding of the application of common exclusions to recent technological innovations and recently developed exclusions aimed at limiting insurer exposure to risks posed by tech integration, firms face considerable uninsured or underinsured loss exposure.

II. Contract Drafting, Risk Allocation, and Intellectual Property Concerns

The modern design, bid, build process involves a fluid and interactive exchange of information between multiple parties that has been revolutionized—particularly in the early to middle stages of the project—by technology. The owner, architect, contractor, and various subcontractors and vendors on any given project are more dynamically involved than ever before. Streamlined collaboration stemming from new technology has led to greater productivity, leading to more efficient design and build processes. Designing a building may contain over 100,000 objects to be placed into models.[52] Interoperability, while streamlined in many instances, may commonly comprise a large percentage of a project's budget. Additionally, this efficiency and reliance on new technology can manifest into unforeseen or unaccounted for potential legal pitfalls.

A. Allocation of Risk for Technology-Impacted Contracts

When drafting or negotiating a construction contract involving technology, an attorney's role involves two steps: (1) identify the risks created by the technology's involvement, and (2) allocate those risks to the party best able to mitigate or bear those risks through thorough and clear contract terms. The risks and liabilities associated with technology fall into three categories: (1) physical injury and property damage, (2) intellectual property concerns, and (3) cybersecurity and privacy threats. Although the general categories of threats remain constant, the parties best suited to bear those risks vary based on countless factors and circumstances, including but not limited to control or experience with the platform or product, investment in the technology's development or ownership rights, insurability, costs and power dynamics, and upside benefits offered by using the contemplated tools. Once due consideration has been given to risk identification and allocation, drafting or modifying existing indemnity, warranty, intellectual property ownership and freedom to operate, insurance, legal compliance, data security, and other terms and obligations of an agreement to clearly and plainly

52. Bruner and O'Connor, *supra* at § 7.68

highlight the risks and responsibility therefor places all parties in the best position to minimize risk and efficiently complete the desired venture.

B. Design and Construction Contract Templates

Frequently used construction contract form providers, including the American Institute of Architects (AIA®), the Engineers Joint Contract Documents Committee (EJCDC®), ConsensusDocs®, and the Design-Build Institute of America (DBIA®), strive to update their templates to accommodate changing technology in the industry. In recent years, these organizations have developed forms aimed at addressing legal risks posed by electronic communications, BIM considerations, green construction, and digital data licensing, all of which were previously unaddressed by readily available construction contract templates. When properly adapted to your client and your project's needs, or simply when used as a point of reference for developing a thorough and thoughtful manuscript agreement, these forms prove invaluable in accommodating the use of technology on a job site. However, "industry standard" forms are reactive to industry trends, and therefore inherently behind the curve in addressing adoption of emerging technology. Thus, while form templates may provide an excellent starting point for transactions or projects involving new technology, responsible counsel will adapt those forms to consider and allocate the risks associated with the products the parties plan to implement.

1. Adapting Contract Forms to Include BIM

Given the regular use of and integration of BIM into modern construction, almost all major contract template producers offer contract forms or addenda addressing the use of BIM on commercial projects. The AIA E-Series E203-2013 can be utilized and modified for projects of any size to establish the rights governing each party's use of BIM and associated data.[53] AIA also provides the G-Series G202-2013 form to

---

53. The American Institute of Architects (AIA), https://www.aia.org/resources/6150803-list-of-all-current-aia-contract-documents.

be used to establish BIM protocols. ConsensusDocs has a series of standard form contracts for formation of construction contracts utilizing BIM, last updated in 2017.[54] The ConsensusDocs 300 Series contains a BIM addendum in form 301 that addresses both legal and administration issues associated with use of BIM. While industry forms provide a good starting point for establishing BIM use, it is important that contracts be reviewed and tailored to adequately protect the parties involved and to incorporate project-specific considerations.

BIM is well established in the industry, but the contracts governing the use of this technology can lead to inequitable agreements, disputes over intellectual property ownership and license rights, and an overall lack of clarity on expectations concerning use of BIM. The AIA and the American Institute of Steel Construction (AISC®) have implemented best practices or standard codes of practice governing the use and collaboration through BIM software.[55] The AIA best practices contain guidance on inserting indemnification clauses into a BIM contract.[56] The AISC standard codes of practice provide guidance on streamlining the interoperability involved in the shared use of BIM. ConsensusDocs has also created a BIM addendum that serves as guidance on best practices and provides clarity of ownership rights when contributions are made to building design from various corners of the project team.[57] The individual responsibilities and ownership rights can be settled on at project outset with the use of such an addendum.[58] This addendum and the best practices just mentioned serve as tools that can be utilized to clarify the roles, responsibilities, and expectations of each party to a contract. These tools are a good starting point as reference for contract formation, but proper risk allocation and intellectual property protection often need to be individually tailored depending on the project. If

54. ConsensusDocs, https://www.consensusdocs.org/contract/301-2/.

55. Bruner and O'Connor *supra* at § 7:80.

56. *Id.*

57. Kevin F. Peartree, Theodore M.B. Baum & Timothy Boldt, ConsensusDocs Contract Documents Handbook § 10.01, 2031 Cum. Supp. (rev. ed. 2011).

58. *Id.*

all parties on a project have a clear understanding this can reduce tension and the likelihood of disputes.

A specified agreement concerning how and when BIM is to be utilized, and what each party's responsibility is in the use of BIM should be one of the first steps when forming a construction contract.[59] Intellectual property terms specifying ownership rights and the scope and duration of any licenses to those rights; for example, which party owns what model inserted into the BIM software can give a clearer understanding of who maintains ownership of designs. Minimal case law provides guidance on this issue, so a clear delineation of who maintains control and ownership rights at every level of the BIM model should be explicitly agreed to via contract.[60] Likewise, the allocation of risk associated with each level of the BIM model should be explicitly agreed to in conjunction with ownership. Providing a clear understanding of who retains ownership of design elements will help mitigate the blurred lines of liability that naturally accompany BIM usage.

In 2022, the AIA issued a suite of new documents focused on BIM and digital data.[61] The suite includes four BIM exhibits (E201-2022, E202-2022, E401-2022, and E402-2022), each specific to how the model is used and the parties with whom the model is shared. AIA also issued a template for a BIM Execution Plan (G203-2022).[62] Section 6.6 of the BIM Execution Plan has space for parties to outline their data security measures.

---

59. Justin L. Weisberg & Raymond M. Krauze, *Opening Communication Lines: Evolving Project Delivery Methods to Promote Collaboration*, 38 CONSTR. LAW. 14 (Spring 2018).

60. Jennifer M. Horn, *Bridging the Gap between Design and Construction*, 40 CONN. L. TRIB., CONSTR. & ENERGY L. S10 (Nov. 10, 2014).

61. The suite also includes G204-2022 (Model Element Table); G205-2022 (Abbreviated Model Element Table) and C106-2022 (Digital Data Licensing Agreement); *see* AIA Digital Documents Guide, https://zdassets.aiacontracts.org/ctrzdweb02/zdpdfs/digital-practice-docs_guide.pdf (last accessed on Feb. 20, 2023).

62. See Chapter 1 for discussion of BIM Execution Plans.

2. *Adapting Construction Contract Forms to Accommodate Emerging Technology*

While AIA, ConsensusDocs, and other industry organizations offer forms addressing sustainability objectives or BIM usage due to the ubiquity of BIM and green construction considerations in recent projects, fewer tailored templates exist to address the use of wearables, drones, virtual or augmented reality, or other emerging technology steadily being adopted on job sites. Construction attorneys drafting agreements for projects involving these products therefore must consider if and how to adapt existing terms to accommodate the risks and benefits involved. This first entails considering how technology will be used, what risks the anticipated (or unanticipated) use might create—including data security, to the extent relevant—and for whom, and finally, who should bear responsibility for those risks. Once those risks and their proper allocation are determined, a skilled attorney will tailor a contract's indemnity, warranty, and insurance terms accordingly.

The foregoing recommendations are best extrapolated by an example. Assume you represent a project owner engaging an architecture firm; while designing and overseeing construction of the project, the architect plans to use a drone to capture video footage of the project site, the project's progress, and the completed structure. You plan to modify AIA forms to tailor a contract suited to the client's needs. Under those circumstances, you might modify an AIA B101-2017's insurance terms to require the architect to carry appropriate drone coverage, the extent of which should be dictated by risks posed by neighboring properties or structures; the drone's characteristics (including the camera and payload attachments); the architect's experience using a drone; and state, federal, and local law applicable to drone operation and privacy rights. These factors should also be woven throughout the B101 modifications to ensure the architect is responsible for complying with both applicable law and licensure requirements, and the applicable standard of care for drone operation. Careful thought should be given to adding indemnity obligations to the B101-2017 to allocate the risk of drone accidents to the architect. Counsel should craft an indemnity clause that will be enforceable in the relevant jurisdiction.

Lawyers might also consider modifying an AIA G201-203, the Project Digital Data Protocol Form, or an AIA C106-2022, a Digital Data

Licensing Agreement, to address transmission and ownership of digital data created by the drone. While the C106-2022 is used for transmitting and licensing instruments of service or other digital design data, it can be tailored to suit any data stored in a digital format. Similarly, although the G201-2013 heavily references the E203-2013, it can be modified to address digital data protocols, ownership, and related rights and obligations for data beyond that traditionally included in BIM. The client and the architect must establish who owns the data collected by the drone and who has the right to use it; the drone's data may be useful to the client in soliciting prospective tenants, to the general contractor in constructing the project, or to any party filing an insurance claim.[63] To the extent the drone may capture proprietary information belonging to the owner client, the lawyer should address whether the architect or other parties should be permitted to use that information and, if so, to what extent. Modification of the C106-2022 may be appropriate to address these concerns; likewise, modifying an AIA E203-2013 BIM and Digital Data Protocol Exhibit may be useful if drone data will be incorporated into a BIM model for the project, particularly given the extensive coverage of transmission procedures, confidentiality, warranties, and indemnification for digital data included in the E203-2013.

When sensors in equipment or robots collect automated data, there may be an information log kept in a "black box" like that used in airplanes. The setup of the data logger is usually found in the user's manual. Contract language may be needed to allow this data and black box information to be obtained from the device suppliers. Sometime suppliers are reluctant to share this information so nondisclosure and confidentiality agreements may be required.[64]

Depending on the circumstances of the project and the parties and technology involved, additional modifications may be necessary beyond those discussed here. Regardless, the same process for contract drafting and negotiation remains: first, identify risks, then allocate those risks as appropriate to the parties' needs and ability to control or mitigate those risks.

---

63. Additional considerations regarding data and intellectual property ownership are addressed in the next section.

64. See discussion in Chapter 7, Section I.A.1 regarding "black boxes."

3. *Intellectual Property Issues*

Article 1, section 8 of the U.S. Constitution grants Congress the power, "To promote the progress of science and useful arts, by securing or limited times to authors and inventors the exclusive right to their respective writings and discoveries." Legal issues involving protection of intellectual property rights have long been of central importance to the construction industry. For example, the Supreme Court's 1877 decision in *City of Elizabeth v. Pavement Co.*[65] addressed issues of patent validity for the subject technology, "new and improved wooden pavement."

Intellectual property issues in the construction industry can arise in numerous ways. Trademarks, patents, copyrights, and trade secrets can pervade every step of the construction process. The mechanisms for protecting valuable intellectual property rights extend across all of these. Obtaining and enforcing those rights involves a complex statutory landscape; some rights are strictly federal in nature and others implicate a hybrid of federal and state law provisions. The specialized, sometimes arcane, nature of intellectual property law—coupled with the complexities of rapidly evolving technology—makes consultation with IP counsel at the outset of a significant construction project advisable.

Although the Supreme Court has stated that mathematical algorithms and use of a computer to implement an abstract mathematical concept are not eligible for patent protection,[66] intellectual property protection may be available under federal copyright law.[67] Aspects of such technological advancements can also be protected under the federal Defend Trade Secrets Act (DTSA)[68] and under the Uniform Trade Secrets Act, which has been adopted by 48 states. The DTSA protects "all forms and types of financial, business, scientific, technical economic or engineering information. . . ."[69]

Against the statutory backdrop of protecting intellectual property rights, the collaborative nature of construction projects raises numerous practical issues with respect to confidentiality, disclosure, and

65. City of Elizabeth v. Pavement Co., 97 U.S. 126 (1877).
66. Alice Corp. Prop. Ltd. v. CLS Bank Int'l, 573 U.S. 208 (2014).
67. 17 U.S.C. § 101-122.
68. 18 U.S.C. § 1836.
69. *Id.* § 1836(3).

ownership of the proprietary technology to be implemented. As with most contractually defined issues, an ounce of prevention is worth a ton of cure and express delineation of rights and obligations concerning ownership and use of proprietary technology should, wherever possible, be addressed at the outset of a project. Doing so will enhance the prospects for owners, contractors, and design professionals operating seamlessly in completing the project. For example, establishing the parameters for ownership of jointly developed inventions or technological improvements should be memorialized contractually as early as possible. The licensed use of such jointly developed technology in future projects is one issue that should be addressed in advance.[70]

The ability for owners, contractors, and architects to collaborate seamlessly on projects using collaborative software and technology may create uncertain boundaries of when ownership of certain materials is established or retained. The easiest way to protect intellectual property rights is via contract, but misguided attempts to protect one's interest can result in a slew of indemnification clauses or other provisions that can muck up the negotiation process. Without clear contract terms at the outset, the fluid nature of BIM especially can present heightened risk of dispute over intellectual property. Protecting the more traditional two-dimensional drawings prepared for a project allows a more straightforward means to protect one's interests, but when every facet of a building is created through a three-dimensional medium such as BIM, properly protecting an individual's interests is both more important and more nuanced than ever.

Unambiguous agreements regarding ownership rights for project contributions should be one of the first steps in ensuring a clear understanding each party's rights and interests. The contract should make clear that a contributor owns the rights to their contributions, and indemnity obligations should be established and agreed to with others who may use these contributions.[71] Once ownership is established, any

---

70. Robert F. Cushman & Michael C. Loulakis, Design-Build Contracting Handbook § 14.05, at 61 (Jesse B. Grove III, Richard P. Dyer eds., 2d ed. 2021).

71. Steve Crow, *Building Information Modeling and Intellectual Property*, Clarion Solicitors Ltd.: Our insights (Nov. 9, 2020), https://www.clarionsolicitors.com/articles/building-information-modelling-and-intellectual-property.

conditions or limitations that may be placed on ownership should be specified. Moreover, numerous trade secrets may be present in these three-dimensional models. Implementing provisions for identifying confidential data, and then contractually protecting this data with non-disclosure or confidentiality clauses no matter who retains ownership of the final model can help ensure adequate protections are in place. Confidential data found in a BIM commonly includes both technical and commercial data, such as drawings or designs, distribution processes, or supplier information.[72]

Once design ownership is unambiguously established and agreed to, careful consideration must also be made regarding licenses for future use of designs or models. Parties should provide specific provisions designating whether the project owner, architect, or contractors can use plans entered into a BIM model on future projects as well as for future use on the ongoing project itself.[73] Typically, what results from these use agreements are considered nonexclusive licenses—a licensee may only use the protected work solely in connection with the current project.[74] However, alternate arrangements may be appropriate based on a project, or a project team member's particular needs.

Owners often seek to retain all intellectual property rights for the Instruments of Service and other proprietary content and data associated with a project, without any discussion of how the use of BIM on a project complicates those rights. Although project owners have valid reasons for seeking ownership of designs for a building or other structure they will be responsible for operating and maintaining, those needs do not extend to designers' and contractors' sensitive information often included in BIM models, which go well beyond project plans and specifications. Designers and other entities actively engaged in BIM usage should be vigilant in identifying these broad ownership terms. Modifications may be necessary to protect trade secrets and other proprietary information included in BIM data, and such modifications need not impact ultimate ownership or usage rights for the final project design model.

---

72. *Trade Secrets*, World Intellectual Prop. Org. (last visited Aug. 17, 2022, 1:44 PM) https://www.wipo.int/tradesecrets/en/.

73. Cushman & Loulakis, *supra* note 71.

74. *Id.*

Issuing narrow guidance for intellectual property concerns over the use of BIM is difficult. Standard contractual ideology will chiefly govern any contract formation. Depending on the needs and the type of client, as well as the nature of the project itself, no two separate and distinct contract considerations will be the same. Establishing a clear understanding for each of the parties concerning ownership, licenses, and BIM use is the most critical component to successful contract formation and mitigation of intellectual property disputes. Caution should be exhibited in using boilerplate language, as the provisions may be tilted toward granting one party more ownership or license rights than intended or desired.

Where proprietary information used in a construction project constitutes a trade secret, preserving the confidentiality of the trade secret information is a prerequisite to legal protection.[75] The DTSA provides protection for trade secret material only if "the owner thereof has taken reasonable measures to keep such information secret" and "the information derives independent economic value, actual or potential, from not being generally known to, and not being readily ascertainable . . . by another person who can obtain economic value from the disclosure or use of the information."[76] Accordingly, execution of broad confidentiality agreements before disclosing any potential trade secrets is essential. Negotiation of such agreements should involve discussion of how broadly the trade secret should be disclosed and, possibly, identify the specific individuals who are qualified to receive the subject information.

Similarly, to the extent that any proprietary software or underlying source code must be shared with a collaborator during a construction project, well-defined software license agreements delineating the terms, scope, and duration of use should be executed before disclosure.

In today's tech-heavy competitive environment, it is good practice to consider intellectual property rights beyond those owned or licensed by the parties involved in the construction project. Third-party rights can also present injunction roadblocks and potential damages claims for infringement. Seeking freedom to operate evaluations by experienced

---

75. *See* Chapter 6, Section V. for discussion of protecting trade secrets and confidential information in discovery.

76. 18 U.S.C. § 1836(c)(A) and (B).

intellectual property counsel can help identify potential proprietary landmines and can permit licensing and design-around efforts before the project begins.

C. Addressing Data Security in Contracts

For any business relationship where sensitive or confidential information will be exchanged, or where access to such information will otherwise be afforded by one party to another, the governing contract should address data security. Standard provisions that should incorporate allocation and mitigation of data security risk include those dealing with indemnification, warranties, insurance, use of subcontractors, limitation of liability, and dedicated provisions for data security safeguards. State and federal privacy and security laws, where applicable, will often require at least high-level treatment of data security in contracts.[77] For example, Alabama's Data Breach Notification Act requires covered entities maintaining sensitive personally identifiable information of Alabama residents to adopt reasonable security measures such as retaining service providers that are contractually required to maintain appropriate safeguards to protect such information if they have access to it.[78] At a minimum, contracts should meet such legal requirements. When it comes to negotiating contracts with third-party service providers, construction firms should make sure that any contractual requirements in their agreements with government entities, clients, and/or business partners are also met (e.g., contractually requiring service providers with potential access to data maintained by the construction firm on behalf of these other third parties to protect such data in certain ways).

Allocation of data security risk in indemnification and limitation of liability provisions should be dealt with as any other liability risk in the contract—if the other party will have access to sensitive data, then the construction company should ensure that the contract holds the other party liable for data breaches to help offset the risk of allowing access to such data. Beware of boilerplate limitation of liability clauses that limit the other party's liability for a data breach to a nominal or low amount of fees (e.g., fees paid to a service provider), as such amounts may not

77. See Chapter 3 for further discussion of cybersecurity laws and regulations.

78. Ala. Code § 8-38-3 (1975).

offset the data breach risk inherent in the relationship adequately. Cyber liability insurance of an appropriate amount should also be required if sensitive data will change hands. Finally, the other party should be contractually required to protect sensitive data from unauthorized access or disclosure. At a minimum, reasonable and appropriate security measures should be required, but also consider enumerating specific safeguards that align with industry standards, compliance requirements, and best practices (e.g., data encryption, multifactor authentication).

III. Ransomware, Law Firm Considerations, and Cybersecurity Best Practices[79]

With the increased use of and reliance on technology in the construction industry comes an increase in cybersecurity risk for construction companies as well as the law firms that support them. Cybersecurity is a hot topic in nearly every major industry—cyberattacks continue to plague businesses in the United States. The Federal Bureau of Investigation's Internet Crime Complaint Center received a record number of complaints in 2020: 791,790, with reported losses exceeding $4.1 billion.[80] In particular, ransomware (through which hackers encrypt [render inaccessible] a company's files or operating systems until a payment is made) has become a significant threat to businesses of all sizes and types. The FBI alone saw nearly 2,500 ransomware attacks reported in 2020, with a total victim loss of $29 million.[81] These attacks have quickly evolved from nuisance threats to the biggest cyber risk facing companies today. The effects of ransomware attacks are wide-ranging—regardless of whether a ransom is paid. The ransoms demanded by cybercriminals are just one piece of the risk puzzle, as companies suffering ransomware attacks can forfeit significant revenue by losing the ability to operate for days or weeks at a time, and liability risks (e.g., costs associated with

---

79. For a discussion of cybersecurity concerns and best practices in government contracts, refer to Chapter 3.

80. Federal Bureau of Investigation Internet Crime Complaint Center, Internet Crime Report 2020, at 5, https://www.ic3.gov/Media/PDF/AnnualReport/2020_IC3Report.pdf.

81. *Id.* at 14.

forensic investigation, data mining, notification costs, credit monitoring, regulatory fines and penalties, and litigation) emerge when protected data is compromised. As technology improves and pervades the market more and more, secured electronic data management becomes a costly but necessary component to how design and construction firms, big and small, operate. Otherwise, the construction industry is likely to see a rise in cybersecurity breaches and costs due to increasing volume and sophistication of attacks coupled with inadequate preparation or security controls to help businesses prevent, detect, and respond to these targeted attacks.

A. Ransomware Attacks in Construction Businesses and Law Firms

In a survey conducted in 2020, over 13 percent of construction companies reported experiencing a ransomware attack in the last year.[82] Small- to mid-size firms are often at increased vulnerability, as firms this size commonly report not having any response plan in place or the resources to combat cyberattacks such as ransomware.[83] These cyberattacks, which cumulatively costs businesses billions of dollars each year, are expected to continue to rise in frequency.[84]

It is natural that cybercriminals target construction companies. A typical construction company is likely to have thousands of files hosted by various sources and applications. Sensitive information such as trade secrets, other confidential business information, or even classified information used by government contractors[85] can commonly be present throughout the company's file systems. Additionally, these companies often operate on thin margins—with no room to experience downtime.

---

82. R. Dallon Adams, *Infographic: Ransomware Attacks by Industry, Continent, and More*, TECHREPUBLIC: SECURITY (Oct. 12, 2020, 11:00 AM), https://www.techrepublic.com/article/infographic-ransomware-attacks-by-industry-continent-and-more/.

83. Infrascale Press Release, *Infrascale Survey Reveals Close to Half of SMBS Have Been Ransomware Attack Targets*, INFRASCALE, INC.: PRESS RELEASES (Apr. 21, 2020), https://www.infrascale.com/press-release/infrascale-survey-reveals-close-to-half-of-smbs-have-been-ransomware-attack-targets/.

84. Adams, *supra* note 82.

85. For additional information on cybersecurity requirements for government contractors, refer to Chapter 3.

Because the downtime of a company experiencing a ransomware attack can easily last weeks, hackers specifically target construction companies assuming there is an increased incentive to pay the ransom and restore operations.[86]

For similar reasons, law firms are also frequent targets of cyberattacks. The ABA has recognized, "[d]ata breaches and cyber threats involving or targeting lawyers and law firms are a major professional responsibility and liability threat facing the legal profession."[87] Data breaches can expose legal professionals not only to ethical complaints and bar sanctions but also to criminal penalties and civil damages. Law firms large and small are exposed to and have suffered cyberattacks such as ransomware and business email compromise and other phishing incidents in recent years, exposing not only the firms themselves but also their clients to significant risks.[88] There have been several high-profile data breaches at prominent international law firms in recent years.[89]

Law firms host their clients' most sensitive data,[90] and the breadth and variety of information hosted presents a treasure trove of valuable information for cybercriminals, who also understand the pressure the

---

86. *Ransomware in the Construction Industry*, EGNYTE, INC. 1, HTTPS://WWW.EGNYTE.COM/SITES/DEFAULT/FILES/2021-02/INFOGRAPHIC-RANSOMWAREINTHECONSTRUCTIONINDUSTRY.PDF (last visited Aug. 17, 2022).

87. Standing Committee on Ethics and Professional Responsibility, *Lawyers' Obligations After an Electronic Data Breach or Cyberattack*, 2018 A.B.A., Formal Opinion 483, at 1, https://www.americanbar.org/content/dam/aba/images/news/formal_op_483.pdf.

88. Gerry Grealish, *Law Firms Increasingly Targeted by Cybercriminals*, SECURITY BOULEVARD: SECURITY BLOGGERS NETWORK (December 15, 2021), https://securityboulevard.com/2021/12/law-firms-increasingly-targeted-by-cybercriminals/.

89. *Id.*

90. Ipro Tech, *Law Firms and Cyber Attacks: InfoGov Isn't Just for Corporate Legal Teams Anymore*, JDSUPRA: TOPICS: LAW PRACTICE MANAGEMENT (Aug. 31, 2021), https://www.jdsupra.com/legalnews/law-firms-and-cyber-attacks-infogov-isn-5734706/. (In February 2021, a major law firm suffered a ransomware attack, exposing sensitive client information, including "certain individuals' names, dates of birth, driver's license numbers / state identification numbers, financial account information, Social Security numbers, passport numbers, payment card information, medical information, health insurance information, biometric data, and/or online account credentials (i.e., usernames and passwords)[.]".

law firms would face if confidential client data was compromised.[91] Law firms also often have access to substantial sums of client money, which can make them optimal targets for business email compromise schemes involving fraudulent funds transfers.[92] "Law firms are often behind other industries (including their clients) in implementing adequate information security measures, and these deficiencies can make law firms attractive targets for cybercriminals, as well as making them more susceptible to cyberattacks."[93]

Moreover, attorneys' ethical obligations to secure client information not only increase law firms' exposure to the potential fallout from a data breach, also serve as heightened incentives for firms to pay a ransom demand if they get hit with ransomware.[94] Rule 6.1(c) of the ABA Model Rule of Ethics requires a lawyer to "make reasonable efforts to prevent the inadvertent or unauthorized disclosure of, or unauthorized access to, information relating to the representation of a client." The ABA issued Formal Opinion 483, "Lawyers' Obligations After an Electronic Data Breach or Cyberattack" (October 17, 2018), which discusses lawyers' ethical obligations to detect, prevent, mitigate, and investigate data breaches, and also establishes the connection between the obligation to prevent a data breach of client data under Model Rule 6.1(c) and other Model Rules, such as Model Rule 1.1 (Duty of Competence) (which extends to keeping abreast of changes in technology), Model Rule 1.15 (Safekeeping Property) (which extends to electronic client data), and Mode Rule 5.3 (Responsibilities Regarding Nonlawyer Assistance) (which extends to supervising third party service providers who have access to electronic client data).[95] Law firms may have a

91. Adams, *supra* note 82.

92. *Id.*

93. *Id.*; *see also* Julie Sobowale, *Law Firms Must Manage Cybersecurity Risks*, ABA J. Online (Mar. 1, 2017), https://www.abajournal.com/magazine/article/managing_cybersecurity_risk.

94. Adams, *supra* note 82.

95. Standing Committee on Ethics and Professional Responsibility, *supra* note 87, at 15–16. ("Even lawyers who, (i) under Model Rule 1.6(c), make 'reasonable efforts to prevent the unauthorized disclosure of, or unauthorized access to, information relating to the representation of a client,' (ii) under Model Rule 1.1, stay abreast of changes in technology, and (iii) under Model Rules 5.1 and 5.3, properly supervise other lawyers

duty to notify their clients of data breaches pursuant to state and federal breach notification statutes as well as governing agreements and guidelines from their clients. Law firms should take the foregoing ethical and legal requirements into account when managing information security risk but also when responding to ransomware attacks. All businesses should implement and maintain written incident response plans that incorporate all response requirements they may face.

B. Best Practices for Mitigating Cybersecurity Risks[96]

Although cybersecurity insurance is becoming a more commonplace method to mitigate the damage of cybersecurity breaches, no business should rely on insurance alone to protect itself from cyber risks.[97] Implementing a few standard security practices designed to prevent or mitigate the effects of cyberattacks can go a long way to minimizing the threats and costs associated with security breaches. Limited budgets and internal technical expertise are often cited as reasons for failing to maintain standard security measures and lack of information security investment;[98] but some security measures offer a great deal of bang for your buck in terms the level of security they offer in exchange for often minimal cost and effort. Such measures include implementing multi-factor authentication for remote access to applications where sensitive data is stored, providing regular cybersecurity awareness training to employees, maintaining adequate backups of data, and properly vetting and monitoring third parties with access to data. Each of these measures are all cost-effective ways of increasing a firm's resiliency against cyberattacks. Hiring internal information technology personnel with experience managing security risk also will help an organization

---

and third-party electronic-information storage vendors, may suffer a data breach. When they do, they have a duty to notify clients of the data breach under Model Rule 1.4 in sufficient detail to keep clients 'reasonably informed' and with an explanation 'to the extent necessary to permit the client to make informed decisions regarding the representation.'") (https://www.americanbar.org/content/dam/aba/administrative/professional_responsibility/aba_formal_op_483.pdf).

96. Best practices for mitigating cybersecurity risks in government contracts are discussed in more detail in Chapter 3.

97. Bruner and O'Connor *supra* § 7:93.

98. Sobowale, *supra* note 93.

to shore up its cybersecurity program; however, adequate support can be outsourced to third-party service providers. Finally, it is important for both construction companies and outside counsel to keep abreast of legal requirements regarding data security and privacy, as well as the ever-evolving cybersecurity threat landscape. Understanding the risks facing an organization's information systems is critical to maintaining the safeguards needed to protect its sensitive data.

For example, one of the easiest ways for hackers to gain access to a firm's information systems is through phishing. Phishing is a type of social engineering meant to trick employees into inadvertently giving hackers access or means of disrupting a firm's data and operating systems.[99] Educating employees on how to spot and report phishing attacks is critical to reducing the risk this common threat poses. Phishing often manifests itself in emails meant to mimic internal emails from other employees asking the recipient to click on a link, offer personal information and passwords, or give specific financial information. Key small details to look for that indicate an email may be or is part of a phishing scam can become apparent to the trained eye. These details include mismatched URLs in the email body, poor spelling and grammar, and misspelled names or email addresses.[100] These emails will often ask for financial information. More sophisticated emails will attempt to impersonate real coworkers in a firm and could address an individual by name in a specifically targeted attack termed spearfishing.[101]

Consistently integrating software updates, utilizing multistep employee authentication, and backing up data are all cost-effective tactics to mitigate outside threats. Computers, software, and any tech utilized by a firm should be updated consistently when updates are released. When large software companies push updates, these are often issued to improve security or shore up gaps that can be exposed and utilized by cybercriminals to gain access. Two-factor authentication is a simple

---

99. Reece Guida, *How Law Firms Can Prevent Phishing and Malware*, X(35) NAT'L L. REV. (Feb. 4, 2020), https://www.natlawreview.com/article/how-law-firms-can-prevent-phishing-and-malware#:~:text=Establish%20a%20secure%20login%20process,anti%2Dmalware%2C%20and%20MFA.

100. Kriyansh Roy, *How to Identify a Phishing Attack*, LINKEDIN (July 12, 2021), https://www.linkedin.com/pulse/how-identify-phishing-attack-kriyansh-roy.

101. *Id.*

yet effective security measure that can be easily implemented.[102] This requires employees to open an app on their phone or other device before access to emails or other systems within the organization is allowed. This provides a robust level of security standing between a hacker and direct access to an organization's files—even where a hacker may have learned a correct password or achieved another level of access.

Consistently backing up data allows a company to take the potential sting out of a ransomware attack—which can render impacted files inaccessible—or other types of data loss. No business should underestimate the operational impact that cyberattacks can have on an organization. The inability to use critical applications or files can grind business to a halt and cause significant financial and reputational damage to a business. Maintaining adequate backups can minimize these risks.

Companies should also anticipate an increase in state and federal legislation governing hackers and data protection. The Stop Hacks and Improve Electronic Data Security (SHIELD) Act enacted by New York in 2019, and the California Consumer Privacy Act (CCPA) enacted by California in 2020 are just two examples of recent legislation addressing issues in this area.[103] The SHIELD Act requires any businesses or persons that own or license computerized data which includes private information of residents within the state to implement and maintain reasonable safeguards to protect this information from unauthorized access.[104] Discussed in more detail earlier in this chapter, the CCPA imposes a number of disclosure practices on entities collecting individual's personal information,[105] as well as data retention practices governing how an entity is to store personal information or release it upon

102. Bruner & O'Connor *supra* § 7:93.

103. John G. Loughnane, *2020 Cybersecurity*, AM. BAR ASS'N (Oct. 18, 2020), https://www.americanbar.org/groups/law_practice/publications/techreport/2020/cybersecurity/.

104. N.Y. GEN. BUS. LAW § 899-bb(2) (Consol. 2020), https://www.nysenate.gov/legislation/laws/GBS/899-BB.

105. California Consumer Privacy Act of 2018, *supra* note 20, at § 1798.100. Colorado, Connecticut, Utah, Virginia and Indiana have also enacted consumer data privacy laws.

request.[106] It is likely these two pieces of legislation are only the tip of the iceberg of legislation to come guiding the practice of collecting, maintaining, and releasing personal data.

In-house counsel and law firms can work in tandem to ensure their companies or clients' data is secure and invulnerable to attacks. In keeping with an attorney's ethical obligation to maintain client confidences and protect client data, attorneys can, and should, recommend and implement the products, training, and best practices discussed in this chapter and elsewhere in this book. In-house counsel should work to implement these measures internally, and carefully vet vendors and business partners. Cybersecurity products and services are ubiquitous, but not all cybersecurity programs or vendors are created equal. Ask questions to ensure complete understanding of your company's existing and prospective systems, and carefully review terms and conditions of newly acquired products. When selecting outside counsel, in addition to evaluating available expertise and experience, companies should pay meaningful attention to external counsel's security capabilities and competence. A firm with appropriate expertise means little if the firm exposes your company's information to cyber risk.

Separately, law firms should fully disclose to clients the security measures in place to protect client information, and clearly delineate client security and communication expectations. If clients require specific information security measures, attorneys must learn and understand those requirements and reach agreement on how those needs will be met. Likewise, attorneys should communicate to clients how security expectations are enforced with third-party vendors, such as experts, document hosting vendors, and others. When engaging consultants, experts, vendors, or others with access to sensitive data, consider including cybersecurity requirements in engagement agreements. Requisite security measures might include requiring two-factor authentication for systems access, email encryption, cyber insurance, and competent policies and procedures for safeguarding sensitive information and guarding against threats.

106. California Consumer Privacy Act of 2018, *supra* note 20, at § 1798.105.

An engagement letter or agreement, whether between a client and attorney or attorney and a third-party vendor, is the ideal means to record expectations. Sample clauses addressing cybersecurity and confidentiality concerns between attorney and client, and attorney and expert, are included in the following appendix to this chapter. These clauses are provided only as reference materials; as with any engagement letter or contract, the terms used in practice should be tailored to suit the context of the relationship, the services and/or products contemplated, and the needs of both parties to the engagement, as well as adjusted to meet any applicable state or jurisdiction-specific cybersecurity concerns.

APPENDIX TO CHAPTER 4

Sample Cybersecurity Clauses

Sample Attorney/Client Cybersecurity Clause

During our representation, we may communicate with you or others by email, and send and store electronic data over the internet or with computer software applications hosted in cloud-based applications. Electronic data that is confidential may be transmitted or stored using these methods. In using these data communication and storage tools, our firm makes reasonable efforts to keep such communications and data access secure in accordance with applicable law and professional ethics. This includes requiring third-party vendors, experts, consultants, and others who may be entrusted with your data to implement and adhere to reasonable cybersecurity and confidentiality policies and procedures. However, if you require specific or particular security measures, those must be communicated to us in writing.

By signing below, you acknowledge [SELECT ONE: "our firm will use unencrypted email communications to communicate with you and others" or "we will use encryption when communicating electronically with you concerning the following matters: [LIST MATTERS SUBJECT TO ENCRYPTION]."] Furthermore, your cooperation is critical to maintaining confidentiality and promoting cybersecurity. You acknowledge and agree that despite any security methods that we might implement, our firm has limited control over unauthorized interception or breach of communications or data, particularly after it has been disclosed to a third party or has been subject to unauthorized access. Our firm assumes no responsibility for cybersecurity losses arising from vulnerabilities in your systems or technological security practices.

Sample Attorney/Expert Cybersecurity Clause

During your engagement, we expect that you will communicate with us via email, and possibly receive, send, and store electronic data over the internet or with computer software applications hosted in cloud-based applications. While electronic data that is confidential may be transmitted or stored using these methods, you agree to use best efforts to keep such communications and data access secure in accordance with applicable law and professional obligations. This includes, but is not limited to, implementing, and adhering to cybersecurity policies and procedures that requiring third party vendors, experts, consultants, and others who may be entrusted with client data shared with you to implement and adhere to cybersecurity and confidentiality policies and procedures at least as rigorous as those required herein.

By signing below, you agree to use encrypted emails for communications concerning the engagement and your services and to disclose, upon request, the identity and terms and conditions shared with any third-party vendors that may have access to the client's data by virtue of this engagement. You further acknowledge and agree to immediately notify us of any actual or reasonably suspected breach of any safeguards, or any actual or reasonably suspected unauthorized access to, or loss, destruction, compromise, or disclosure of the data shared with you pursuant to this engagement. You shall indemnify, defend, and hold harmless our firm and the client against any claims, liabilities, damages, or judgments, including reasonable attorney's fees and costs, arising from your failure to meet the cybersecurity obligations under this engagement agreement. This indemnification obligation includes, but is not limited to, costs for notification to clients, governmental entities, and other interested parties in the event of a data breach.

CHAPTER 5

Overview of Electronic Discovery in Construction Law Cases

Brett Lamb and Elisabeth Malsch, PhD, PE, *Authors*
Leslie King O'Neal, *Contributor*

I. Introduction

A. E-Discovery in Construction Litigation

Electronic discovery, or "eDiscovery," has been part of civil law practice in the United States for decades. "E-discovery is simply the discovery of information and data that is stored electronically, including email, instant messages, social networking content and any other information that may be stored on desktops, laptops, file servers, mainframes or on a variety of other platforms."[1] A complete discussion of all aspects of eDiscovery in construction litigation is beyond the scope of this chapter. For more thorough discussion of eDiscovery generally, see some of the

1. Shira A. Scheindlin, The Sedona Conference®, Electronic Discovery and Digital Evidence in a nutshell (2d Ed.) (West Academic Publishing 2016), at 11.

comprehensive books on the subject.[2] This chapter focuses on eDiscovery issues raised by the new types of construction technology currently being used, and offers some practical suggestions and resources for practitioners.

B. Electronically Stored Information on Construction Projects

In today's world, almost all business and personal information is exchanged electronically. As discussed in Chapter 1, the design and construction industries, while initially slow to adopt technology, are now doing so at an ever-increasing pace. Use of BIM[3] continues to expand, while collaboration software[4] platforms allow project participants to share, modify, and view project data and integrate data from different sources and software. Electronic design drawings, shop drawings and submittals, schedules, pay applications, photos and videos, wearable technology data, GPS mapping data, and data from sensors and robots as well as emails, texts, chats, videoconferences, and social media postings are commonly used in modern construction projects, regardless of size.

---

2. *E.g.* MICHAEL D. BERMAN, COURTNEY I. BARTON & PAUL W. GRIMM, MANAGING E-DISCOVERY AND ESI FROM PRE-LITIGATION THROUGH TRIAL (ABA Publishing 2012); ELECTRONIC DISCOVERY IN A NUTSHELL, *supra* note 1; Bruce Olsen & Tom O'Connor,ELECTRONIC DISCOVERY FOR SMALL CASES: MANAGING DIGITAL EVIDENCE AND ESI (ABA Press 2013).

3. "BIM" is the acronym for Building Information Modeling. See Chapter 1 for additional discussion of the use of BIM in design and construction projects. *See also* Howard A. Ashcraft, "Building Information Modeling: A Framework for Collaboration," THE CONST. LAW., Vol. 28, No. 3; Trevor Arnold, et. al., "BIM—Useful Tools and Key Legal Considerations," 2022 Florida Bar RPTL Section, Construction Law Institute, March 11–12, 2022, Orlando, FL.

4. "Collaboration software is a set of tools that enable group members to execute tasks that are characteristic to team work, such as collaboration, idea sharing, co-operation, and networking. This is done with a set of computers that allow working with the same documents and projects, either close by or remotely from each other." Sakari Ikäläinen, "Collaboration Software Adoption: Factors Affecting Adoption of Collaboration Software in Organizations," Aalto University School of Business (https://core.ac.uk/download/pdf/80709111.pdf) (last accessed 3-14-23).

"Electronically stored information," or "ESI,"[5] provides a wealth of potential evidence for construction cases. ESI includes not only the basic data in the emails, spread sheets, or other documents but also includes "metadata" which is data about the data. "Metadata is an electronic 'fingerprint' that automatically adds identifying characteristics' to electronically stored information, 'such as the creator or author if the file, the name of individuals who have accessed or edited the file, the location from which the file was accessed, and the amount of time spent editing the file.'"[6] Reviewing ESI metadata to determine if information produced is incomplete or has been altered may require forensic expert assistance.

Attorneys have an ethical obligation to stay abreast of changes in technology that affect their clients as well as changes that affect law practice generally.[7] In addition to fulfilling this ethical duty, however, lawyers able to locate, gather, and organize the large quantities of ESI data produced from design and construction projects have an edge in presenting their clients' cases to a mediator, arbitrator, judge, or jury. Marshaling this information allows counsel to understand the relevant facts and present them more effectively on the clients' behalf. The vast number of different sources of data and information create opportunities for construction lawyers knowledgeable about eDiscovery to locate an array of information that can be used as evidence.

In addition to understanding the technology that clients and other parties use in designing and constructing a project, the construction lawyer must advise clients about the duty to preserve information once there is a reasonable probability of litigation. Also, counsel should know

---

5. The Federal Rules of Civil Procedure and many state rules use the term "ESI." Although the federal rules do not define the term "ESI," the Comments state that it is, "intended to be broad enough to cover all current types of computer-based information and flexible enough to encompass future changes and developments." Rule 34, Committee Notes on Rules—2006 Amendment.

6. Melissa B. Withy, Patrick R. Kingsley & Peter Bogdasarian, "E-Discovery—Managing the Risks to Get the Reward: Best Practices for Construction Lawyers and Their Clients" THE CONST. LAW. Vol. 41, No. 3, at 24, citing, "What is Metadata? HARV. L. SCH. INFO. TECH. SERV., HTTPS://HLS.HARVARD.EDU/DEPT/ITS/WHAT-IS-METADATA/.

7. ABA MODEL RULE 1.1 cmt. 8; see Chapter 2 for further discussion of the attorney's ethical duty of technological competence.

how to use the applicable discovery rules in the jurisdiction to coordinate discovery with opposing counsel to make the eDiscovery process economical and efficient.

C. Data Retention Policies and Preservation

It is important for design and construction companies and their counsel to develop data retention policies considering potential litigation. The plan must comply with the company's legal, statutory, and contractual retention duties. Government contracts are subject to more stringent and comprehensive data retention requirements than other types of contracts.[8] In the private sector, contracts may include data and document retention requirements as well as confidentiality requirements. Preservation duties can arise under statutes or contracts before litigation is reasonably anticipated. The jurisdiction's applicable statute of repose may require certain contract documents (plans, specifications, as-builts) to be retained. Best practice is to retain documents as long as a party to a construction project has potential legal liability. Internal email correspondence or voicemails may not be subject to a statutory retention period unless there are contract provisions stating otherwise.[9] The company and its legal counsel must determine retention requirements and create a retention schedule that complies with legal and contractual requirements but also protects the company from unnecessary and potentially counterproductive data retention.

Preservation for litigation is a primary consideration in selecting backup methods for data being retained. Courts have stated that the risk of litigation should be considered when selecting backup methods.[10] The *Sedona Principles* provide:

---

8. See Chapter 3 regarding government contractor data security requirements.

9. Construction document retention requirements may be related to an entity's contractual documents or jurisdictional statutes of limitations or repose, which vary from there being no statute of repose up to 15 years from a specified time. Public work projects may have their own statutory retention requirements. Documents relevant to accidents or workers' compensation claims may have significantly longer retention requirements. Admiralty laws may apply for those in construction of seagoing vessels and equipment or involved in projects related to navigable waters.

10. *See* United States ex rel. Guardiola v. Renown Health, 2015 U.S. Dist. LEXIS 112511, 2015 WL 5056726 (D. Nev. 2015); Starbucks Corp. v. ADT Sec. Servs., Inc.,

> Organizations that use backup tapes for archival purposes should be aware that this practice is likely to cause substantially higher costs for evidence preservation and production in connection with litigation. Organizations seeking to preserve data for business purposes or litigation should, if possible, consider employing means other than traditional disaster recovery backup tapes. They should not be used for record keeping.[11]

Companies should think about the costs and benefits of technology selected considering their needs, litigation risks, and potential discovery obligations.[12]

Discovery of legacy data created on outdated software that is no longer supported by the software creator can be difficult. Retaining a copy of the latest version of software to provide accessibility to data necessary for a future case is advisable.

Safeguards for private and privileged data as well as custody and control of data stored on noncompany servers or cloud-based sites must be included in any retention plan. And, of course, any retention plan must be workable and must be complied with at all organizational levels.

II. Locating ESI in Construction Projects

ESI in design and construction projects is created in a multitude of ways and from a multitude of sources, both corporate and personal. The forms of ESI frequently found on construction projects include (1) design and management software, including BIM, project management software, scheduling software, computer aided-design (CAD); (2) proprietary software; (3) email and other forms of messaging; (4) texts and IM; (5) social media postings; (6) BIM model and digital twin data;

No. 08-CV-900-JCC, 2009 U.S. Dist. LEXIS 120941, 2009 WL 4730798, at *6 (W.D. Wash. Apr. 30, 2009).

11. Comment 5h, The Sedona Conference, The Sedona Principles: Best Practices Recommendations & Principles for Addressing Electronic Document Production, at 35 (2d ed. 2007).

12. United States ex rel. Guardiola, 2015 U.S. Dist. LEXIS 112511*13 (to the extent that restoration costs in this case owe to Renown's failure to earlier implement a sensible email retention policy and its choice to use an archival/backup solution that did not maintain ESI in an indexed or otherwise searchable manner, Renown must bear some responsibility within the consideration of whether the restoration cost is undue).

(7) contracts, leases, and purchase orders; (8) plans and specifications; (9) shop drawings and submittals; (10) photos and videos; (11) drone data; (12) robot data; (13) wearable technology data; (14) vehicle or equipment technology data; (15) sensor data; (16) security cameras; (17) device and cloud-based backup systems; (18) data generated by project information management software; (19) daily reports; (20) safety reports; (21) punch lists; (22) inspection and progress reports; (23) business and financial data; (24) meeting minutes; (25) insurance and surety data.

Some companies use project information management systems, such as ProCore or Autodesk Construction Cloud, which integrate with tools such as BIM, Primavera, Egnyte, Docusign, Drone Deploy, HoloBuilder, or other applications. These collaboration programs allow owners, general contractors, design professionals, subcontractors, and suppliers to share, view, and modify project data in real time. The project information management programs can integrate the data from different sources and may also provide data analytics to create reports or to assist users in decision-making. The data from these sources is kept in the cloud or in data lakes.

"A data lake is a massive collection of datasets that: (1) may be hosted in different storage systems; (2) may vary in their formats; (3) may not be accompanied by any useful metadata or may use different formats to describe their metadata; and (4) may change autonomously over time."[13] "Data lakes make it easy to collect disparate data sets in one place, which is why they are so popular."[14] Counsel should ask clients what type of data storage they use so client data can be properly preserved and collected. This information is also important in drafting specific discovery requests for other parties. Data within a data lake may not be organized or structured. Because of this, "companies

13. Fatemeh Naregsian, Erkang Zhu, Ren'ee J. Miller, Ken Q. Pu, Patricia C. Arocena. Data Lake Management: Challenges and Opportunities, Proceedings of the VLDB EndowmentVolume 12 Issue 12, at 1986–1989, https://doi.org/10.14778/3352063.3352116.

14. Olga V. Mack, "Data Lakes and Data Warehouses: What Lawyers Need to Know," ABOVE THE LAW, Jan. 23, 2023, file:///C:/Users/loneal/Downloads/Data%20Lakes%20And%20Data%20Warehouses_%20What%20Lawyers%20Need%20To%20Know%C2%A0%20-%20Above%20the%20LawAbove%20the%20Law.html (last accessed 3-14-23).

may opt to 'structure' data in data warehouses to make it easier to find and work with more exact data points, just as workers organize actual warehouses to make it easy to locate specific items."[15] Structuring data can be costly, however.

Collaboration software platforms use Application Program Interfaces (APIs) to link (integrate) two or more systems.[16] APIs used in collaboration software can complicate data collection, verification, and authentication because APIs lack perfect synchronicity with the original (authentic) content. Also, there may be limits on the amount of data collected through an API.[17] Collecting, sorting, and authenticating API-impacted data from collaboration applications such as Zoom, Jive, Confluence, and Microsoft Teams safely and accurately may require forensic expert assistance.[18] While many construction companies today provide employees with mobile phones and tablets, some companies prefer the BYOD ("bring your own device") approach, meaning that the employees own the devices. This can complicate collecting data from these devices. Counsel should be aware that individuals may store work information on their private devices despite company policy prohibiting this. Also, neighbors, inspectors, visitors, or others may have relevant data on their personal devices. However, obtaining data from personal devices raises privacy issues that must be resolved.[19] In addition, forensic assistance may be necessary to retrieve the data from these devices.

As design and construction projects become more global and as virtual platforms allow parties in other countries to collaborate, issues of

15. Olga V. Mack, "Data Lakes and Data Warehouses: What Lawyers Need to Know," Above the Law, Jan. 23, 2023.

16. Brian Cooksey, An Introduction to APIs 7 (Zapier, Inc., 2014), https://cdn.zapier.com/storage/learn_ebooks/e06a35cfcf092ec6dd22670383d9fd12.pdf (last accessed 3-14-23).

17. The Sedona Conference, *Commentary on ESI Evidence & Admissibility, Second Edition*, 22 SEDONA CONF. J. 83, 139-40 (2021), https://thesedonaconference.org/publication/Commentary_on_ESI_Evidence_and_Admissibility.

18. Collecting these types of data is discussed more fully in Chapter 6.

19. "A Court must be mindful of the potential intrusiveness of ordering forensic imaging, however. Before compelling such imaging the court must weigh inherent privacy concerns against its utility." Wynmoor Community Council v. QBE Ins. Co., 280 F.R.D. 681 (S.D. Fla. 2012) (citations omitted).

cross-border discovery become more common.[20] Cross-border discovery creates additional privacy concerns because the European Union's General Data Protection Regulation (GDPR) applies to any organization, no matter its location, if it collects data related to EU residents. The GDPR imposes harsh penalties, including fines, for violations of the act.[21]

Security cameras or websites under a third party's control are another potential source of evidence. This type of data may be subject to routine destruction, so preserving it is crucial. To prevent an opposing party or a nonparty from deleting known ESI under its control, counsel should send a request for preservation of the specific information as soon as possible. For example, if a website controlled by a third party or opponent has existing content that is relevant, counsel should send a written preservation request to the controlling party asking it to preserve the current website content.[22]

For maximum efficiency in eDiscovery, counsel must learn about how clients and others involved in the project create, use, share, and store information. Early data assessment helps avoid potential discovery issues and challenges. After discussing types and locations of relevant data with the client, counsel should consider targeted preliminary discovery from parties holding relevant information. Because ESI can be ephemeral, counsel and the client should discuss early in the case what ESI parties and nonparties have, where it is located, how to preserve it, and how much it will cost to obtain it. While the Federal Rules of Civil Procedure and several state rules have "meet and confer" requirements

---

20. Discovery and data protection laws vary widely worldwide and may conflict. European countries have higher standards for protection of private digital information than those in the U.S. Information discoverable under U.S. rules may not be discoverable if located in the United Kingdom or Germany. *See* The Sedona Conference Practical In-House Approaches for Cross-Border Discovery & Data Protection, 17 SEDONA CONFERENCE J. 397 (2016).

21. *See* General Data Protection Regulation, Art. 1 (European Union, May 25, 2018).

22. A good resource for a preservation letter is CRAIG BALL, THE PERFECT PRESERVATION LETTER, https://craigball.net/2020/09/10/the-perfect-preservation-letter-a-new-guide/ (last accessed 3-18-23). Note this is a template for a preservation letter that should be tailored to the specific case.

regarding discovery, there is no reason to wait for discovery to begin before discussing preservation and other issues.[23] This holds true in arbitration as well as in litigation. Rule 17(a), JAMS Comprehensive Arbitration Rules provides:

> The Parties shall cooperate in good faith in the voluntary and informal exchange of all non-privileged documents and other information (including electronically stored information ("ESI")) relevant to the dispute or claim immediately after commencement of the Arbitration. They shall complete an initial exchange of all relevant, non-privileged documents, including, without limitation, copies of all documents in their possession or control on which they rely in support of their positions, and names of individuals whom they may call as witnesses at the Arbitration Hearing, within twenty-one (21) calendar days after all pleadings or notice of claims have been received.

Because eDiscovery and technology are evolving constantly, checklists are essential tools to identify data sources. The Sedona Conference "Jumpstart Outline," which has been carefully drafted and vetted, is an excellent resource for preparing for the initial client meeting and for the "meet and confer" with opposing counsel.[24] While generic checklists are helpful, the legal team, the client, and any eDiscovery consultant involved should develop a case-specific checklist for discovery, which should be revised as the case progresses.

Lead counsel's supervision and involvement are necessary to ensure discovery is targeted to the key issues in the case. The 2015 amendment to Rule 26(b)(1) changed the language regarding discovery from allowing

---

23. https://www.cand.uscourts.gov/filelibrary/1117/ESI_Guidelines-12-1-2015.pdf; *see, e.g.*, Fed. R. Civ. P. 26; r. 26(f); Ala. R. Civ. Proc. 16 ARS, Rules of Civ. Proc., r. 16 (https://govt.westlaw.com/azrules/Document/N39ECE0013B2411ED96AAFC15E831ABE3?viewType=FullText&originationContext=documenttoc&transitionType=CategoryPageItem&contextData=(sc.Default); r. 25, Rules of the Sup. Ct. State of NH (https://www.courts.nh.gov/rules-superior-court-state-new-hampshire).

24. Ariana J. Tadler, Kevin F. Brady & Karin Scholz Jenson, The Sedona Conference "Jumpstart Outline": Questions to Ask Your Client & Your Adversary to Prepare for Preservation, Rule 26 Obligations, Court Conferences & Requests for Production (March 2016), https://thesedonaconference.org/download-publication?fid=562.

what is "reasonably calculated to lead to the discovery of admissible evidence" to what is "proportional to the needs of the case."[25] Because of this requirement and because of the enormous amount of data created on many construction projects sending expansive and over-broad discovery requests is no longer appropriate.[26] eDiscovery practice—like all discovery under the current Federal Rules of Civil Procedure and most state rules—must be proportional to the needs of the case.[27]

A. Discovery Planning

Some aspects of e-Discovery planning depend on the tribunal's rules and procedures and the governing law in the jurisdiction. In addition, the judge's or arbitrator's experience with eDiscovery also plays a role.[28] While basic discovery rules and principles apply to eDiscovery, the plan for each case must consider the applicable case law, statutes, local rules, guidelines, and the judge's or the arbitrator's requirements or preferences.[29]

---

25. *Id.*

26. Russell v. Kiewit Corp., Case No: 1802144-KHV (order denying plaintiff's motion to compel production entered 6/14/19). Court denied plaintiff's request to produce his entire email file, including nine previous versions, as not proportional, rejecting plaintiff's argument that request "would lead to discovery of admissible evidence." https://cases.justia.com/federal/district-courts/kansas/ksdce/2:2018cv02144/120917/49/0.pdf (last accessed 3-16-23).

27. Rule 26(b)(1), Fed. R. Civ. P. provides: "DISCOVERY SCOPE AND LIMITS. (1) Scope in General. Unless otherwise limited by court order, the scope of discovery is as follows: Parties may obtain discovery regarding any nonprivileged matter that is relevant to any party's claim or defense and proportional to the needs of the case, considering the importance of the issues at stake in the action, the amount in controversy, the parties' relative access to relevant information, the parties' resources, the importance of the discovery in resolving the issues, and whether the burden or expense of the proposed discovery outweighs its likely benefit."

28. In many instances federal district and magistrate judges have more eDiscovery experience than state court judges. When selecting arbitrators in a case involving voluminous or complicated eDiscovery, consider the candidates' eDiscovery experience. Also, AAA and JAMS offer special masters to assist parties in eDiscovery, in litigation as well as in arbitration. Federal District Courts may appoint special masters under Fed. R. Civ. P. 53(a)(1)(B)(i).

29. It is good practice to check whether the judge has issued standing orders regarding discovery. Arbitrators' discovery preferences should be discussed at the preliminary hearing.

I. Client Meetings

Effective discovery planning begins with the client meeting. Here, counsel can discuss many important topics with client representatives, such as: preservation obligations; spoliation; the litigation hold; eDiscovery costs and budget; data custodians and their locations; how ESI relates to case issues and strategies, and the benefits of a cooperative approach to discovery with other parties.

At the beginning of the matter, outside counsel should meet with the client representatives—in-house counsel, if any, as well as project management and IT representatives—to determine where relevant data may be located. This discussion should take place early to ensure the proper legal hold or preservation requests are sent. Counsel should instruct client IT representatives to disable any automatic deletion or destruction features for project emails, text messages, or other data.

Some aspects of the meeting will vary depending on the client's needs and sophistication. Some types of clients have reputational concerns about a lawsuit or claim; others may be concerned about maintaining confidentiality of trade secret information. Government contractors may have ESI subject to government security regulations.[30] The litigation may affect the client's business relationships, insurance coverage or surety line of credit, or standing on bid lists. By discussing these issues during this meeting and follow-up meetings, counsel can gain a better understanding of the client's business and its attitudes toward litigation and discovery.

The following topics should be discussed at or before the meeting:[31]

- Have preservation obligations been triggered? Has automatic destruction or deletion been disabled?
- Has a legal hold been sent? Who should receive the legal hold? What should it encompass?
- Should preservation letters be sent to the opponent or to third parties?

---

30. See Chapter 3 regarding government security requirements for data.

31. *See* Twigger, K., *Issue Spotting in eDiscovery: How and When to Start* found at Issue Spotting in eDiscovery Part I: How and When to Start - eDiscovery Assistant found at: https://www.ediscoveryassistant.com/issue-spotting-in-ediscovery-part-i-how-and-when-to-start/.

- What is the jurisdiction or tribunal for the matter? Federal or state court? Or arbitration? What rules apply?
- Who is the judge or arbitrator (or arbitrators)?
- Who are the key players and witnesses on both sides?
- What types of data are in the client's possession or control? What is the scope of data?
- What data is in the opponent's possession or control? Or that of third parties?
- What is the date range for the issues in the case?
- What experience and knowledge do the client, client's IT personnel, witnesses, and employees have about technology related to the issues and facts of the case?
- Does the client know of any immediate data issues?

2. *Phased Discovery*

The best method to obtain adequate discovery within a reasonable budget is through phased or staged discovery. To do this counsel must understand the relevant, discoverable ESI under the client's control. The "meet and confer" with opposing counsel provides an opportunity to discuss phased discovery as an economical approach, which can benefit both parties. This approach can reduce the cost of privilege and trade secret review as well as limiting the chances of mistakenly producing privileged, protected, or irrelevant information.

The "data dump" (producing all possible data) is the opposite of phased discovery. Using the data dump approach can be costly since counsel must ensure the production does not include privileged or confidential material in the voluminous records. To do this, counsel must create a defensible search term and statistical sampling analysis or conduct an eyes-on review of every document. Judges may not be sympathetic to lawyers or parties when data dumps go awry.[32] Even with a claw back

---

32. In Blythe v. Bell, 11 CVS 933, 2012 NCBC 42 (Sup. Ct. N.C. 2012), the trial court denied a Motion to Return Privileged Documents that were produced by defendants in data dump fashion (also found at https://www.ncbusinesslitigationreport.com/wp-content/uploads/sites/71/uploads/file/2012NCBC042.pdf). Voluminous discovery is also contrary to the hallmark principles of economy and efficiency in arbitration.

agreement or 502 order in place, no lawyer or client wants inadvertent disclosure of privileged information to occur.[33]

3. *The eDiscovery Team*

Some large and complex construction cases require a team composed of trial counsel and staff, the client and client's staff, and consultants or experts to manage the legal and technical aspects of ESI and eDiscovery.

Consultants, vendors, experts, and eDiscovery counsel can assist counsel in drafting discovery requests, motions to compel or motions for protective order, discovery responses, and ESI planning and budgeting. They may use Artificial Intelligence (AI) to assist with tasks such as search and privilege review, including active machine learning of large volumes of data, commonly referred to as Technology Assisted Review (TAR). Expert assistance may also be needed for (1) forensically sound collection and storage and testimony about authenticity of evidence;[34] (2) planning and handling technical access to challenging software or media,[35] backup systems, cloud or internet sources, or other ESI location; and (3) creating and providing a foundation for ESI-based trial exhibits. Consultants can also assist counsel in analyzing the opposing party's exhibits, summaries, and other things for cross-examination or challenge.[36]

In addition, consultants or knowledgeable client IT staff can assist in drafting focused requests to other parties or third parties. It is nonproductive and often counterproductive to request information outside

---

33. Fed. R. Evid. 502(d). *See* discussion in Chapter 6, Section V.C of 502 orders and protecting privileged information.

34. See Chaper 6, Section I.A for discussion of the pros and cons of collection by staff or by consultants.

35. Slack and other collaboration applications such as Jive, Confluence, Microsoft Teams, are challenging and potential costly forms of evidence to obtain, usually requiring expert forensic assistance. *See* The Sedona Conference, *Commentary on ESI Evidence & Admissibility, Second Edition*, 22 Sedona Conf. J. 83, 139–40 (2021), also found at https://thesedonaconference.org/publication/Commentary_on_ESI_Evidence_and_Admissibility. Forensic experts can assist in minimizing such issues and authenticating the collaboration application ESI generated in discovery.

36. See Chapter 7 for more discussion on the expert's role in creating and presenting exhibits.

the scope of relevant ESI that would be admissible in the case. Other technical issues that may require special expertise are forensic review of devices or data, determination of the cost or scope of a given discovery request for burdensomeness or proportionality assessment, and ESI planning and budgeting. Experts may be needed for (1) forensically sound collection and storage followed by testimony on authenticity of evidence; (2) planning and handling technical access to challenging software or media;[37] backup systems, cloud or internet sources, or other places ESI may reside; and (3) creation and introduction of trial exhibits.[38] Consultants can also assist in analyzing and replicating opposing party summaries, recreations, demonstrative aids, and the like for critical cross-examination.

An important, but sometimes overlooked, task where consultants or knowledgeable client IT staff can play a key role is in drafting focused discovery requests to the opposing party. Focused discovery is not only important for managing cases efficiently and economically, but also for maintaining credibility with the tribunal and opposing counsel.

4. Lead Counsel's Role

Lead trial counsel plays a critical role in leading the eDiscovery team. Lead counsel must supervise other lawyers and team members; understand the discovery plan and oversee its execution; manage and execute discovery filings with the tribunal and with opposing counsel; meet and confer with opposing counsel to reach agreement on various issues and inform the client about case progress and compliance with the discovery

---

37. Slack or other collaboration applications like Jive, Confluence, or Microsoft Teams may require forensic assistance to collect. Collaboration apps may use API's to access and share information. Collection from apps that use API's can be complicated because API collection lacks perfect synchronicity with the original (authentic) content, and there may be limits on the amount of data that may be collected through an API. *See* The Sedona Conference, *Commentary on ESI Evidence & Admissibility, Second Edition*, 22 SEDONA CONF. J. 83, 139–40 (2021), also found at https://thesedonaconference.org/publication/Commentary_on_ESI_Evidence_and_Admissibility. Forensic experts can assist in minimizing such issues and authenticating the collaboration application ESI generated in discovery.

38. See Chapter 7 for further discussion of an expert's role in developing trial exhibits or demonstrative aids.

budget. In addition, lead counsel must ensure that the client understands and will comply with preservation obligations and the discovery plan and that the legal team understands client concerns regarding ESI, such as privacy, trade secrets, equipment or data security, and other issues.

One of lead trial counsel's key responsibilities is conferring and negotiating with opposing counsel about eDiscovery issues. ESI by its nature requires early and persistent attention to efficient, economical, and proportional discovery.[39] Accordingly, the federal civil rules and almost all state civil rules require collaboration and cooperation to obtain just, speedy, and inexpensive determination of every action and proceeding.[40] Similarly, arbitration rules recognize the need for discussing ESI protocols and maintaining ESI for discovery in an economical fashion.[41]

In some cases, lead trial counsel may need assistance from another attorney knowledgeable in eDiscovery and possibly a technical expert who can bridge the gap between the client's IT staff and the outside counsel trial team. They can review the client's IT systems to gain a deeper understanding of how the data is created, shared, and stored and to inform the client's IT personnel about the duties for preservation, search, collection, and data production in light of the case issues.[42]

Experienced construction lawyers understand the need for open communication and cooperation with opposing counsel. Cooperating with opposing counsel in discovery does not mean counsel ceases being a zealous advocate. It means counsel advocates for the client's best interest in resolving the case fairly and cost effectively. As stated by U.S. District Court Judge Paul Grimm, "cooperation is not capitulation."

---

39. William Matthewman, *Towards a New Paradigm for E-Discovery in Civil Litigation: A Judicial Perspective,* 71 Fla. L. Rev. 1261 (2019) also found at https://scholarship.law.ufl.edu/flr/vol71/iss5/4.

40. Rules 1, 26f, Federal Rules of Civil Procedure.

41. *See* American Arbitration Association Discovery Best Practices for Construction Arbitration https://www.go.adr.org; and JAMS Arbitration Discovery Protocols www.jamsadr.com.

42. https://thedailyrecord.com/2016/09/23/federal-rules-amendments-practice/.

B. eDiscovery Budget

For almost all construction cases, all the relevant ESI cannot—and should not—be collected, processed, reviewed, and produced. For many cases, the costs for gathering, reviewing, and producing all available relevant ESI may exceed the value of the case. Such discovery is neither proportional nor reasonable. One of the topics for the initial client meeting is developing an eDiscovery budget. As the case develops the eDiscovery budget should be revised, allowing the client to make informed decisions about discovery options.

One topic for the meet and confer or for informal discussions with opposing counsel should be agreement about allocating costs for ESI production among the parties.[43] This is another area where expert assistance is helpful. If the type, scope, and volume of ESI data are known, experts can calculate the costs of ESI preservation, collection, search, organization, and review, including privilege review.

C. eDiscovery Protocols[44]

The approach to management of discovery issues varies among state and federal courts (and arbitration panels).[45] Federal Rule of Civil Procedure 26(f) requires parties to meet early in a case to develop an ESI discovery plan, which is an excellent time to develop an ESI protocol. There are numerous examples of model protocols, but any model protocol is merely a starting point for discussion.[46] The most effective

---

43. Ralph Artigliere & William Hamilton, Florida Ediscovery and Evidence § 6.02 (Matthew Bender LexisNexis 2020).

44. A comprehensive multipart series by Kelly Twigger on how to draft and leverage an ESI protocol is found at https://www.ediscoveryassistant.com/esi-protocols-part-i-planning-for-ediscovery-when-how-and-why/.

45. Despite the limitations on discovery in arbitration, both AAA and JAMS have discovery protocols regarding eDiscovery. *See* AAA discovery best practices for construction arbitration https://go.adr.org/rs/294-SFS-516/images/AAA341_AAA_Discovery_Best_Practices_Construction_Arbitration.pdf (last accessed Feb. 20, 2023); JAMS Discovery Protocols, https://www.jamsadr.com/arbitration-discovery-protocols/.

46. *See, e.g.*, United States District Court Western District of Washington Model Protocol for Discovery of Electronically Stored Information

protocols are case specific. Protocols may address issues such as data preservation, scope of discovery, data collection, search and filtering of data, TAR usage, form, and timing of production, confidentiality agreements, how the information will be secured and handled, FRE 502(d) orders, cost of production, and case-specific considerations.

Because construction cases often involve multiple parties, ESI protocols are sometimes difficult to obtain. However, even a partial protocol may be worthwhile if parties can agree on significant elements for ESI discovery. One method for successful protocol negotiation is for each party to designate an eDiscovery liaison who is knowledgeable about and responsible for discussing ESI issues.[47] The liaisons should be familiar with the technical aspects of eDiscovery in the case and they must have authority to bind the party to the eDiscovery protocol.

While the amount of data produced on a construction project can seem overwhelming, the solution is not simply to exclude large swaths of data from potential discovery. However, last year a federal judge entered an order with an agreed discovery protocol declaring whole categories of collaboration data not to be "reasonably accessible" (and thus not discoverable).[48] The order stated: "Absent a showing of good cause, voicemails, text messages, PDAs, mobile phones, and other forms of non-e-mail business communications such as Google Hangouts, Microsoft Teams, Skype, WhatsApp, and Slack are deemed not reasonably accessible and need not be collected and preserved."[49] Agreeing to such

---

in Civil Litigation, found at https://www.wawd.uscourts.gov/sites/wawd/files/61412ModeleDiscoveryProtocol.pdf; United States District Court for the District of Maryland Suggested Protocol for Discovery of Electronically Stored Information, found at https://www.mdd.uscourts.gov/sites/mdd/files/ESIProtocol.pdf.

47. E-Discovery liaisons may be lawyers, special masters, or consultants. Both AAA and JAMS have lists of eDiscovery special masters. Federal courts may appoint special masters in some cases. *See* Rule 53, Federal Rules of Civil Procedure.

48. Evrythng Ltd. v. Avery Dennison Retail Info. Servs., Civil Action 1:21-cv-04411-LJL (S.D.N.Y. Mar. 22, 2022).

49. *Id.* While there may be a case-specific reason known to the parties and the court that such data should be excluded from discovery, the *Avery* case case should not be cited for the proposition that such information is not reasonably accessible.

exclusionary language may seem an easy solution, but it may eliminate the ability to obtain important information.

The next chapter will discuss methods for requesting various types of ESI commonly used on construction projects.

Excluding whole categories of collaboration software documents from preservation should have a sound basis, lest valuable evidence be destroyed.

APPENDIX A TO CHAPTER 5

Litigation Early Stages: Data Collection Checklist

1. Litigation Hold: Ask your client if a litigation hold notice has gone out to all project personnel and if not, offer to send law firm's litigation hold notice. The litigation hold should be broad and include all data sources that are potentially responsive to the matter (i.e., email, IM, text messages, and documents saved to a hard drive or network share). **Note, send instructions to suspend auto delete text messages in cell phones.
2. Interview: Arrange interviews with the lead project manager, document specialist, and employee who interfaced the most with the entity with whom we are in a dispute.
    a. Meet with the project team and identify likely document custodians and potential search terms.
    b. During the interview, identify the locations of where the user-stored data was stored. This includes databases and cloud-based applications.
3. IT Personnel: Have the senior client contact coordinate a meeting between an in-house eDiscovery resource or technical consultant and client's IT personnel to discuss sources of data and best process for collection.
4. Email Type: I What type of email platform is being used (this will affect data collection)? Ascertain if the client uses Outlook at the workstation level or if it is only reserved for corporate.
5. Project Files: Are they using a shared Windows file server, SharePoint, Home Shares, or Dropbox?
6. Third Party Applications: Were there any construction-specific databases used on the project (ProCore, Newforma, Aconex, etc.) or file-sharing applications (box.com, dropbox, etc.)?
7. Mobile Devices: Does the client provide company phones or do employees use their own (BYOD)? Were the project personnel "heavy texters"? Did the project team exchange texts with opposing party?

8. Pause Auto-Deletion: Confirm with your client's IT that they have disabled any auto-delete functionality with the relevant systems and preserved the hard drives of employees who have left the company. Confirm the names of the employees that are no longer employed, and preserve their data. If using Office365, implement Litigation Hold within Office 365.

9. Collection Best Practices:
   a. Email: Client's IT should only apply a date cut to email inboxes and collect by individual custodian. Search terms should be run in eDiscovery processing/searching tools in the event search terms change throughout the course of early eDiscovery stages. IT systems don't consistently run keyword searches the same way, which could cause problems with productions down the line.
   b. Project Records: Client's IT should collect the entire project server vs. select folders. Folders can later be withheld due to nonrelevance or logged on the privilege log.
   c. Collection Log: IT can create an excel spreadsheet that lists each custodian/data source and the size of the email export. This will be cross-referenced when the data is received to confirm complete mailboxes were collected and transferred. eDiscovery consultant can provide a collection workbook if needed.

Data Collection: Potential Scenarios

1. Client does not want to do broad collection because their costs have been too high in the past.
   a. A broad collection on the front end avoids needing to do a recollection down the line.
   b. A broad collection also ensures preservation—if a custodian is requested much later in the case and their data wasn't preserved or collected, that could present problems with production.
   c. Make sure your vendor is not charging you to store data, and charges only apply once data is processed and promoted into the review platform.

2. Client wants to "cherry-pick" folders for collection from the project server.

   a. While the client may send select documents at the onset of a claim for law firm to review, or potentially to share with experts, it is critical the entire project server is collected once the eDiscovery process begins.
   b. This will ensure no gaps in the production to opposing parties.
   c. Anything withheld will be logged (which the courts and arbitration panels like) versus withheld on the basis it was never collected due to client preference.

3. Special handling for senior executives.

   a. Special search terms can be used for senior executives, but must be agreed upon by both parties.
   b. Exclusion terms can be used, which will weed out communications related to other projects.

4. Client wants to collect email by running search terms over global email environment (typically when responding to a subpoena). This approach is NOT recommended. You will end up with an unwieldy data set with hundreds of custodians and no way to piece the data sets back together.

5. Exclusion terms, near dupe + sampling.

   a. Exclusion terms, when written correctly, can be valuable to weeding out irrelevant documents and reducing your data set.
   b. Near dupe, while not perfect, can reduce your data set. We also recommend applying threading and reviewing the most inclusive thread, meaning the last thread that contains all replies.
   c. Excluded doesn't mean carved out and forgotten; you can review a statistical sample of the documents excluded to confirm they are in fact all irrelevant.

Transparency Is Key

1. The ESI protocol is your opportunity for transparency so the opposing party cannot argue later regarding your productions.

2. Disclosing the use of search terms, junk terms, privilege terms, and exclusion terms, as well as the use of threading, TAR, and near-dupe technologies.

Broad Collection Advantages

A thorough and broad collection is one of the greatest opportunities to create efficiencies and save the client time and money down the line because:

1. Broad collection avoids the need to recollect.
2. Broad collection enables outside counsel to respond quickly to a change in scope or introduction of a new search term or custodian.

APPENDIX B TO CHAPTER 5

Sample Litigation Hold and Data Preservation Notice

[Insert Name]

What You Must Do

The purpose of this legal hold notice is to notify you that you are required to preserve documents related to [INSERT PROJECT NAME]. You have been identified as a company representative who we believe may have records related to potential issues noted in [Insert Matter Name. Attach relevant document if needed and reference. "For your reference, a copy of the (Order, Subpoena, Petition, Demand Letter, etc.) is attached to this legal hold notice."].

This legal hold notice applies to any and all documents that relate to [INSERT PROJECT NAME].

Instructions

Please take all reasonable steps to retain and preserve, and not delete or otherwise destroy, any such documents that are in your possession, custody, or control. In this regard, "documents" includes both (1) hard copy and paper records, and (2) electronic records. The first category (hard copy and paper records) includes, but is not limited to, the following:

- Handwritten notes, work papers, calendar entries, diaries, daily logs, reports, written phone messages, checks and other records of payment, receipts, invoices, ledgers and other financial and accounting records, records of shipment, memos, letters, computer spreadsheets, computer models, meeting minutes, drawings, design documents, and maps.

The second category (electronic records) includes, but is not limited to, the following:

- Emails, electronically stored materials (such as correspondence, calendars, spreadsheets, and other materials stored on a computer, server, PDA, or other electronic device), backup tapes, archives and copies of electronically stored materials (such as DVDs, CDs, zip disks, and external hard drives), voicemail messages stored electronically, and any audio and video recordings.

Please note that, in order to retain and preserve emails, you must ensure that you have placed them into a retention email folder, instead of keeping them elsewhere (*e.g.*, in your "inbox," "sent items," or "deleted items"). If you have any questions regarding retention of electronic records, contact [Insert designated contact within client IT department] for assistance.

The above lists are not intended to be exhaustive. If you have an item that you believe may be relevant in any way, please err on the side of caution and comply with this legal hold notice.

If there are any other company representatives who you believe should receive this notice, please notify [Insert legal point person].

Questions

If you have questions or concerns regarding this notice, you should contact:

- NAME, EMAIL ADDRESS, PHONE NUMBER

Thank you for your prompt and careful attention to this matter.

Please respond to [Insert legal point person] with your acknowledgment and ability to comply with this request.

CHAPTER 6

Gathering ESI from Construction Projects

Brett Lamb and Elisabeth Malsch, PhD, PE, *Authors*
Leslie King O'Neal, *Contributor*

This chapter provides practical suggestions regarding how counsel can gather the ESI frequently generated on construction projects and data for use in a construction dispute. It also discusses methods for protecting confidential or sensitive data during discovery and afterward.

I. ESI Collection and Review

A. Who Should Perform Data Collection?

Trial counsel and the client should select the person or entity to be responsible for data collection and organization. Factors to consider in making this selection are:

- Technical competence of the collector;
- Possible/perceived self-interest or bias on the part of the collector;
- The collector's desirability as a witness; and
- The collector's competence to testify on authenticity, hearsay, or other foundation issues.

Because most in-house IT professionals serve their company's business needs but have little or no experience or training in retrieving and collecting data for litigation, in many cases they should not perform the data collection. If the ESI collection will be technically complex or difficult, consultant or expert assistance may be necessary.

As mentioned earlier, having the client perform data collection raises issues of competency as well as issues of potential bias. Also, counsel must consider whether the client personnel performing collection may be required to testify on other substantive matters in the case. If so, it may be wise not to put the witness in the position of being cross-examined on collection issues where his or her credibility could be undermined. It may be preferable to have a qualified consultant testify about how the data collection was performed and other foundational issues.

I. Scope of Discovery

Because of the large amounts of data that construction projects generate, and the numerous entities and personnel involved in most projects, producing every document and all data files that a project generates is impractical and cost prohibitive. The shotgun approach to discovery requests is no longer appropriate. Wise lawyers attempt to limit discovery scope, while still retrieving relevant information through cooperation with other parties. Court or arbitrator intervention may be needed if cooperation fails.

Whether through order or by agreement, the following categories serve to limit scope or conduct phased discovery with focused requests:

- **Time:** Limiting requests by time is the simplest and most effective way to limit data production. This requires determining the earliest date data regarding the issues could exist, as well as last possible date for creating relevant data. This is a separate analysis from a preservation request or litigation hold; the dates for data preservation should be broader than the date range for productions.
- **Custodian:** Identify the persons who have the most knowledge of the case issues, the "key custodians." Identifying key custodians within the client organization will also reveal key non-party custodians, who will appear more frequently in the key

custodians' communications. Having information about key ESI custodians can assist counsel in negotiating to limit data sets produced while still capturing needed data.

- **Enterprise ESI:** Another method for segregating is ESI enterprise sources (server/cloud location or software type). Counsel and client representatives can analyze enterprise sources, which may show that only a specific server has relevant data or even that relevant data is limited to certain folders within that server. Counsel or the eDiscovery liaison should know the different software types that the client uses regularly; having a map of servers and folder structure is also helpful.
- **Excluding Data Sources:** Excluding certain data sources is another clear limitation but should be done with the understanding that such exclusion does not mean the data will be destroyed. Excluding certain sources allows limiting the data set to critical data and limiting the review required. Some data sources that may be excluded in early production are:
    - Deleted, fragmented, or other data only accessible by forensics;
    - Random access memory (RAM), temporary files, or other ephemeral data;
    - Personal digital assistants, pagers, and mobile telephones;
    - Instant messages, text messages, and voicemails; and
    - Obsolete or legacy systems.

Discussion with the client may identify additional exclusion techniques that can increase savings.

2. Proportionality

Determining proportionality requires counsel and the judge or arbitrator to consider whether relevant information is discoverable considering case needs. Not all relevant information is proportional to case needs case or issues. Federal courts use the nonexclusive list of factors in Rule 26(b)(1) to determine proportionality:

> Unless otherwise limited by court order, the scope of discovery is as follows: Parties may obtain discovery regarding any

> nonprivileged matter that is relevant to any party's claim or defense and proportional to the needs of the case, considering the importance of the issues at stake in the action, the amount in controversy, the parties' relative access to relevant information, the parties' resources, the importance of the discovery in resolving the issues, and whether the burden or expense of the proposed discovery outweighs its likely benefit. Information within this scope of discovery need not be admissible in evidence to be discoverable.

Other states have adopted similar proportionality rules governing discovery.[1] Meeting proportionality requirements means the client must understand and agree on the scope of discovery and its limitations, and counsel must manage discovery keeping proportionality in mind. However, achieving proportionality in practice can be difficult. There is inherent tension between the role of the judge and that of the attorneys in managing discovery in a case.[2]

3. Requesting ESI

(a) Required Disclosures

Federal Rule of Civil Procedure 26(a)(1)(A)(ii) requires disclosure of nonprivileged, proportional, relevant, and responsive ESI and Federal Rule of Civil Procedure 34 requires this ESI to be produced. Counsel who engage in "gamesmanship" in responding to production requests may find that this strategy backfires and puts them and their clients in a difficult position with the tribunal. Opposing counsel are not permitted

---

1. *See* ALA. R. CIV. P. 26(b)(1); ARIZ. R. CIV. P. 26(b)(1); COLO. R. CIV. P. 26(b)(1); DEL. CH. CT. R. 26(b)(1); DEL. SUPER. CT. R. CIV. P. 26(b)(1); D.C. SUPER. CT. R. CIV. P. 26(b)(1); IND. COMMERCIAL CT. R. 6(A); KAN. STAT. § 60-226(b)(1); MICH. CT. R. 2.302(B)(1); MINN. R. CIV. P. 26.02(b); 2019 MO. S.B. 224 (amending MO. SUP. CT. R. 56.01); NEV. R. CIV. P. 26(b)(1); OHIO R. CIV. P. 26(B)(1); OKLA. STA. tit. 12 § 3226(B)(1); VT. R. CIV. P. 26(b)(1); WIS. CODE § 804.01(2)(a); WYO. R. CIV. P. 26(b)(1).

2. *See* Michael Thomas Murphy, *Occam's Phaser: Making Proportional Discovery (Finally) Work in Litigation by Requiring Phased Discovery*, 4 STAN. J. COMPLEX LITIG. 89 (Spring 2016) (advocating mandatory phased discovery in federal civil cases).

to determine disclosures and productions based on what he or she thinks is important in the case.[3]

(b) Preserving Metadata and Production Form

Requests or agreements for production form or metadata must be specific to minimize postproduction arguments about a party's compliance. Request for production of file types and metadata to be produced should be specific and should be tailored to the specific case and project. Some topics to consider regarding wording document requests are:

- **Document Format:** Requests, agreements, or orders should specify document format. Such recommendations might include a requirement to provide documents as searchable, multi-page PDF images named by Bates numbers on the first page of the document. The producing party should affix a legible Bates number electronically branded into the PDF image so as not to interfere with any source document information.
- **Native Format:** A party should request certain files in native format. Due to the data size of certain file when imaged as well as embedded information, certain files serve reviewers better in native format. These files include, but are not limited to, presentation applications (e.g., PowerPoint), spreadsheet applications (e.g. Excel), multimedia audio/visual files such as voice and video recordings (e.g., .avi, .mpeg), and engineering or plan files (e.g., CAD). The requesting party should also specify PDF image placeholders be added between native files indicating that such file was produced in native format and providing a corresponding Bates number location.
- **Text Files:** The request, agreement, or order should specify that the producing party shall provide document level extracted text files corresponding to each document produced. If the produced document has no corresponding text file, the document should be run through an optical character recognition (OCR) program so it is fully searchable.

---

3. DR Distributors, LLC, v. 21 Century Smoking, Inc, & Brent Duke, 513 F. Supp. 3d 839, 940, n.46, 2021 U.S. Dist. LEXIS 9513, 2021 WL 185082 (N.D. Ill. Jan. 19, 2021).

- **Metadata:** Document specificity, particularly with metadata, helps to secure proper production compliance. A litigant, therefore, must come prepared with pointed metadata items to request. Some examples follow:
  - Beginning Bates Number
  - End Bates Number
  - First Bates Number of Family Range
  - Last Bates Number of Family Range
  - Name of Person from Whose Files the Document Produced
  - Author of the Document or Attachment
  - Sender of Communication
  - Recipient of Communication
  - Additional Recipients of Communication
  - Blind Recipients of Communication
  - Size of File
  - Number of Pages in Document
  - Date Communication Received
  - Time Communication Received
  - Date Sent
  - Time Sent
  - Date Created
  - Date(s) Edited

4. Review Platforms

The large amount of data everyday construction projects create requires an adequate review platform to locate pertinent data efficiently. This requires the platform to (1) locate relevant data and (2) organize data gathered at a high level. Because the amount of data generated even in a small construction project can be beyond the limits for human review, robust review platforms are critical. A platform allowing targeted searches to locate key pieces of evidence and allowing culling of privileged or confidential documents is the minimum necessary. Platform features, such as artificial intelligence, become more important with larger data sets. Platforms with machine learning capabilities can search through millions of documents, constantly reordering them by relevance. Some courts accept and have upheld review methodologies based on artificial intelligence.[4]

5. Deduplication and Avoiding Duplication

It is common for identical, or near identical data to be found in different places and forms across platforms, in different media, and on multiple devices. To address this issue, software platforms have been developed to identify and cull duplicates. Such data may be excluded from the data set if it lacks relevant information or metadata. If such reduction is challenged, the producing party must be able to justify the reason for the exclusion and the methodology used.

In the deduplication process, software compares the unique hash values of two or more electronic records to eliminate additional identical copies. Even though a production set may contain multiple (sometimes numerous) copies of the exact same document, after deduplication only one copy of a particular file will exist. Deduplication can be tailored to the case and issues at hand. For example, it may be important to know if a particular custodian had a copy of a particular file. Platforms can apply deduplication by custodian, enterprise source, or production set.

Near deduplication is closely related to deduplication. Near deduplication can be a powerful search efficiency enhancement allowing reviewers to search more documents more quickly. The most sophisticated platforms direct reviewers to specific text differing from document to document in near deduplication groupings helping them locate exact changes to key documents.

(a) Key Word Searches and Other Search Methods

The accuracy of electronic searches depends on the knowledge and care used to create and perform them.[5] Choosing a search method requires a party and its counsel to consider the nature and volume of the data

4. Da Silva Moore v. Publicis Group, 28 F.R.D. 182 (SDNY 2012); *see also* Hon. Craig B. Shaffer, *"Defensible" by What Standard?* 13 Sedona Conf. J. 217 (2012).

5. Bankdirect Capital Fin., LLC v. Capital Premium Fin., Inc., 2018 U.S. Dist. LEXIS 224705, *11–12 (N.D. Ill. Nov. 8, 2018).

to be searched and proportionality requirements.[6] Because key word searches are familiar to many attorneys and their paralegals, they are often the only means used to find relevant documents. Key word search is a fast, economical, universally available, and useful manner to identify potentially relevant data. However, key word searching has some limitations, such as the amount of knowledge the person selecting key words has about how the information was created. Determining possible synonyms, versions, or abbreviations for key terms requires understanding the industry terminology. Use of acronyms, slang, misspelling, or codes can also limit the effectiveness of a key word search.

Courts are reluctant to deal with key word search disputes. In *United States v. O'Keefe*,[7] the court noted:

> Whether search terms or "keywords" will yield the information sought is a complicated question involving the interplay, at least, of the sciences of computer technology, statistics, and linguistics. . . . Indeed, a special project team of the Working Group on Electronic Discovery of the Sedona Conference is studying that subject and their work indicates how difficult this question is. . . . Given this complexity, for lawyers and judges to dare opine that a certain search term or terms would be more likely to produce information than the terms that were used is truly to go where angels fear to tread. This topic is clearly beyond the ken of a layman and requires that any such conclusion be based on evidence that, for example, meets the criteria of Rule 702 of the Federal Rules of Evidence. [*citations omitted*]

Some strategies for using key word searches include:

- Recognize key word search limitations;
- Study the linguistic and business culture where the data set was produced to improve key word selection;

---

6. *See* The Sedona Conference, The Sedona Conference Best Practices Commentary on the Use of Search & Information Retrieval Methods in E-Discovery, 15 SEDONA CONF. J. 217, 224 (2014), found at https://thesedonaconference.org/publication/Commentary_on_Search_and_Retrieval_Methods.

7. 537 F. Supp. 2d 14, 2008 U.S. Dist. LEXIS 12220, 69 Fed. R. Serv. 3d (Callaghan) 1598 (D.D.C. Feb. 18, 2008).

- Do not rely on narrow terms; use alternatives to obtain broader document selection for testing before doing a full search;
- Obtain opposing counsel's cooperation to select search terms acceptable to both sides;
- Where required, take disputes to the court or arbitrator, but remember that evidence meeting the criteria of the applicable rules must be provided to support the client's position; and
- Phasing discovery—start with limited custodians and obtain samples before broadening the search.

6. *Machine Learning, Artificial Intelligence (AI), Technology Assisted Review (TAR)*

AI use in eDiscovery is widely accepted because it increases efficiency and economy. Technology assisted review (TAR), which uses machine learning to review data and documents is decreasing in cost as its use becomes more accepted. Creating a TAR search program involves machine learning, in which the software learns from human reviewers while refining and applying observed standards to data sets.

Despite increasing use of AI and TAR in eDiscovery document review, there are few court cases discussing proper use of these tools. Further, "[T]here are no standards for the conduct of AI product testing and many tools that are in use today would not pass muster if they were subjected to the scientific method."[8] Consequently, determining reliability of an AI tool is done on a case-by-case basis. Currently, challenges under the *Daubert* standards under Federal Rule of Evidence 702 and its state court equivalents are the only mechanism for testing expert opinions about reliability of such tools. This is an expensive and time-consuming process, which may result in inconsistent results as judges and arbitrators (who may have little experience in these types

8. Paul W. Grimm, Maura R. Grossman & Gordon V. Cormack, *Artificial Intelligence as Evidence*, 19(1) Nw. J Tech. & Intell. Prop. 48 (2021), https://scholarlycommons.law.northwestern.edu/njtip/vol19/iss1/2. ("In an ideal world, the accuracy and reliability of AI tools should be established by independent testing. Even so, it is necessary to consider carefully whether the results from such testing really transfer to the problem at hand. In practice, progress in AI has occurred so quickly that often such independent testing has not yet occurred." *Id.* at 83.

of technical issues) make decisions on complex and obscure technical issues.[9] Parties may resist providing information about their proprietary systems to allow opponents to develop a challenge.

Selecting a reliable vendor and confirming that its AI tools have undergone rigorous testing is the best method for successful AI use. If possible, ask the vendor to explain the nature of the testing done, the protocols, and the results. Determine whether the vendor can provide factual support for their AI product before the tribunal—has it done so successfully before this or similar tribunals? Unfortunately, until more rigorous disclosure is required, "unvetted AI technologies will continue to be deployed, and it will be necessary to estimate their effectiveness and reliability on an ad-hoc basis. It would be unwise to consider such ad-hoc determinations as judicial notice, absent rigorous independent testing."[10]

7. Self-help Discovery

Self-help discovery can be appropriate, but it must be done ethically, effectively, and legally. Investigating publicly available social media or websites of opposing parties or witnesses early in a dispute can lead to important information, which may be difficult or impossible to obtain later. While clients may want to obtain information through self-help to save costs, there are risks of inadequate or improper collection. "Friending" a target on Facebook to obtain information not available to public view has been deemed unethical.[11] The best person to collect the

---

9. Some potential issues that may give rise to challenge are bias, function creep, lack of robust testing for validity and reliability, failure to account for data privacy and data protection, lack of transparency and explainability, lack of accountability, and/or lack of resilience. *Id.* at 34–75.

10. *Id.* at 80.

11. Is it permissible for the attorney's staff to "friend" a witness on Facebook® to gain access to restricted information on the witness's Facebook® page for use in an upcoming deposition? The lack of candor in a request to "friend" a witness simply to obtain information about them is proscribed by Pennsylvania Rules of Professional Conduct against engaging in dishonesty or deceit or knowingly or assisting others to do so. *See* The Philadelphia Bar Assoc. Professional Guidance Committee, Op. 2009-2 (Mar. 2009). *See* FLA. R. OF PROF. COND. 4-4.1 (Truthfulness in Statements to Others) and 4-4.4 (Respect for Rights of Third Persons). Other jurisdictions may have similar rules.

electronic evidence may be an unbiased, qualified expert who can also testify regarding the collected information if needed.

II. Discovery and Production of Different Types of ESI Used in Construction Projects

A. Construction Design and Management Software

Computer-aided design software (CAD), such as AutoCAD by Autodesk, has been used for many years by architects, engineers, interior designers, contractors, and property owners. However, this software varies in format and technical capabilities depending on the version and the manufacturer. CAD software may include authentication for the ESI it creates. Building design and building information modeling (BIM) software often contains CAD products tailored to the architectural design and construction industries.[12] There are specialized BIM tools for civil engineering and for process piping used in manufacturing, wastewater treatment plants, and oil refineries.[13] BIM tools allow project participants to collaborate and to share information and to perform advanced analysis.

When requesting ESI, remember that prior versions of work on BIM and CAD software may not appear in the available ESI, but may exist in printed or analog form. Some CAD software can print two-dimensional drawings or three-dimensional models on a 3D printer. This can be helpful in preparing trial exhibits. It may also create discoverable analog versions of two- and three-dimensional work relevant to the case. Such versions may show markups or design or operation changes during design.

Metadata from BIM and CAD software may disclose who created or modified designs, when it was done, and other substantive and authenticating data. BIM and CAD files can be shared with other devices,

---

12. See Chapter 1, Section I.B for further discussion of use of BIM in design and construction.

13. Autodesk has BIM versions for architects, for civil engineers, and for manufacturing, wastewater treatment plants and oil refineries using specialized process piping. *See* https://www.autodesk.com/campaigns/aec-collaboration.

allowing other parties to alter or manipulate the files, so such metadata can be critical in determining responsibility for design changes. It is important to request CAD software in native format and with metadata preserved (rather than in PDF format) so the data can be searched and relevant information can be extracted. To replicate information in its richest form, requesting parties must ask for the proper version of CAD software. Where certain applications integrate with ProCore or Autodesk, the better practice is to request the data from the native application rather than through ProCore or Autodesk so the critical metadata is kept intact.

Proprietary software such as BIM and CAD creates challenges for requesting parties. Finding out the specific software the target entity or person uses, how it is used, and how to request the ESI in useful form and how to access it are important questions for the meet and confer with opposing counsel and possibly for deposition or interrogatories. The final versions of design or workflow software generates, or printouts of such data, may not provide the complete story. This is often the case when obtaining a spreadsheet-type database. The receiving party will not be able to see the internal calculations and commands unless the database is provided in native form. Forensic expert assistance may be needed to draft requests and to analyze the ESI for complicated proprietary software, such as BIM, CAD, and workflow software.

Counsel or the eDiscovery vendor should do a privilege and confidential document sweep before producing any collaboration software data. Project teams sometimes save email communications or documents shared with the legal team on collaboration software without noting they are privileged.

Some important questions to ask when considering discovery from collaboration software platforms are (1) who is in control of the system? (2) who had access to it? and (3) was the data in question shared with other parties? If the requesting party had access to the data, it may not be necessary to produce it again, thus saving time and cost for all parties.

B. Email

Almost all businesses and individuals now use email communication. Different types of email software are used; some have common features and some have distinctions. Because email has been part of eDiscovery for many years, there are established methods for reviewing, collecting, preserving, and producing it.

Because email is so common, the volume of emails in a case may be substantial. Also, relevant emails may exist on employee's personal devices as well as company-provided devices. The sheer volume of emails in a matter can make screening for privilege very challenging. Most eDiscovery platforms can load, organize, and search email accounts from most common email software available. E-Discovery vendors can perform collection, deduplication, and email threading, which reduces and logically groups emails to improve evaluation and analysis. Successfully handling email discovery requires coordination between trial counsel, client IT personnel, and the vendor, so that it is done efficiently and economically.

C. Photos, Video, Drone Data

Construction litigators have long used photos and videos to illustrate job site conditions, design or construction defects, and other issues. Now project photos and video may be taken using many devices, including handheld cameras, drones, digital phones or pads, robots, security cameras, IoT devices (discussed later), vehicle or equipment cameras. Daily 360-degree photos or videos of the interior and exterior of a project can be taken and shared through use of ProCore, Autodesk Construction Cloud, or other project information management platforms.[14] Workers may take personal photos on their own devices. Drafting requests to produce interrogatory and deposition questions to identify the information needed to secure all relevant and proportional project photos and video requires considerable thought and effort. As mentioned earlier, having a data map of the client's data sources and locations is helpful in this effort.

---

14. See Chapter 1, Section II.D for further discussion of use of 360° photography. For example, apps such as Holobuilder 360° Photo Site Documentation and Drone Deploy can be embedded in ProCore. *See, e.g.*, https://support.procore.com/integrations/holobuilder-360-photo-site-documentation-embedded (last accessed 3-19-23) and https://help.dronedeploy.com/hc/en-us/articles/1500004861001-Procore (last accessed 3-19-23). Oculo integrates with Autodesk Construction Cloud; *see* https://www.oculo.ai/blog/oculo-announces-integration-with-autodesk-construction-cloud (last accessed 3-19-23).

In addition, all manner of persons or entities, including neighbors, bystanders, spectators, and government officials, may have camera, phone, drone, surveillance, or security camera images relevant to a case. As noted earlier, securing security or surveillance camera footage must be done early in the case or else the data may be automatically deleted before it can be secured. Counsel must tell the client about preservation duties for security footage in its possession to avoid possible deletion and spoliation claims. If other parties, entities, or individuals are known or suspected to have such data, counsel should send a preservation request to trigger a duty to preserve this information.[15]

D. IoT Sensors

Internet of Things (IoT) sensors are a broad category of data sensing and collecting devices.[16] Sensors may set, control, and maintain climate within a building or may be used to sense jobsite or building activity. Passive sensors may monitor temperature, humidity, gas pressure, and air particulates for worker safety or to provide data on efficiency and cost. Active sensors for motion detection or proximity can detect presence of persons or equipment and cause an immediate reaction or notification. These include motion-sensitive lighting, camera, or alarm devices; proximity sensors indicating or measuring room occupancy; detection sensors triggered when an employee sits in a chair or on a piece of equipment or when equipment is activated and turned off; and optical or infrared sensors. The data from various sensors, active and passive, may be sent to an integrated workplace management system (such as ProCore or AutoDesk Collaboration Cloud) that interprets the information and can be used for workflow or for determining macro efficiencies and costs. In addition, the data may be relevant to construction litigation issues. If so, it can be requested once the specific type and location of the data is learned.

---

15. In *Shamrock-Shamrock, Inc. v. Tracey Remark*, 271 So.3d 1200 (Fla. 5th DCA 2019), a Florida appellate court held that a nonparty does not have a duty to preserve evidence as a matter of law.

16. See Chapter 1, Section II.F for further discussion of use of IoT sensors.

E. Wearable Technology and Robots

Construction workers may use camera or activity detection wearable devices for safety, workflow, or to measure activity or work progress.[17] Data may provide information on an individual's location as well as activity; this information may supplement other jobsite data and provide relevant evidence. Robot technology often uses built-in wearable technology; such data may include operator or programming input as well as the data generated in accomplishing jobsite activities. For example, many construction companies are now testing robots for use in project layout. Robots may also provide photos, video, and IoT sensing of conditions and activity on a jobsite.[18]

To request this data, counsel must ask the client representatives what types of wearable technology or robots were used on the job, what types of data were collected from them, and where this data is located.

F. Enterprise Video Meeting Recordings[19]

The COVID-19 pandemic widely expanded commercial and personal use of Zoom, Microsoft Teams, and similar applications, which allowed project teams to meet from remote locations and to record the proceedings. Video and voice content, chat, Q and A, and screen-sharing data can be retained on these apps, sometimes without the participants' knowledge. Some platforms automatically generate transcripts; however, machine-created transcripts may not be accurate, depending on the machine's ability to identify voices and language. Such transcripts are becoming more common, although the users may not be aware they exist. Specific request should be made for all portions of the video meeting recording, including chat, Q and A, screen-sharing data, and any transcript.

G. Texts and IM, and Other Collaboration Applications

Text messages and instant messaging within various applications, including through social media platforms and some software or software

---

17. See Chapter 4, Section I.B regarding privacy issues related to use of wearable technology.

18. See Chapter 1, Section II.E for discussion of use of robotics on projects.

19. *E.g.*, Zoom, Microsoft Teams, GoogleMeet.

suites, are well known and often used in construction litigation. Text messages provide nearly instant, but sometimes truncated, communication between two or more devices. Some difficulties in using text messages as evidence are loss of context or abbreviated wording and the use of abbreviations and emoji[20] that are sometimes difficult to understand.

Teams within a business or project teams of people from different organizations often communicate using Slack or other collaboration applications like Jive, Confluence, or Microsoft Teams in lieu of email or texting. The ESI generated by messaging on these apps may be on company servers or in the cloud. As discussed earlier in Section II, collaboration apps may use APIs (application programming interface technology) to access and share information, which may complicate discovery of their data. Forensic experts' assistance may be needed to manage and authenticate ESI generated by collaboration platforms.[21]

Also, although BIM and other applications integrate with project collaboration platforms such as ProCore and Autodesk, in some instances it is advisable to request the data from the native application rather than through the collaboration platform. This keeps the critical metadata intact.[22]

H. Social Media

Parties' social media postings or sites and social media parties accessed or used during times relevant to the dispute can provide relevant evidence in construction disputes. Social media of employees, workers,

---

20. Emoji are frequently used in text messages and chat applications and may mean different things to different people, especially where differences in culture or age are involved. Emoji may vary from one type of software to another, further complicating the true meaning of a communication. Also, emoji can be difficult to collect, as the collection may appear as a blank box or different image than the original. *See* The Sedona Conference, Commentary on ESI Evidence & Admissibility, Second Edition, 22 SEDONA CONF. J. 83, 142–47 (2021), also found at https://thesedonaconference.org/publication/Commentary_on_ESI_Evidence_and_Admissibility.

21. For additional resources regarding discovery of collaboration software, *see* Ralph Artigliere and Leslie O'Neal, "Winning Strategies for Discovery of Collaboration Program Evidence—Collaboration Platform Data," Paper presented at The Florida Bar Real Property Probate & Trust Law Section Construction Law Institute (March 17–18, 2023), Orlando, FL.

22. See Section I.A.3.b regarding metadata.

independent contractors, suppliers, bystanders, and eyewitnesses can also provide information or relevant evidence. Two complications in social media discovery are (1) privacy issues and (2) the evidence must be produced by the owner of the social media account rather than the host organization. Certain social media content is subject to discovery.[23] Social media content, especially content shared in public, is neither privileged nor protected by an absolute right of privacy. However, the requesting party must make a threshold showing of relevance and proportionality for social media discovery. Parties do not "have a generalized right to rummage at will through information that Plaintiff has limited from public view" and are not allowed to engage in the proverbial fishing expedition, "in the hope that there *might* be something of relevance in Plaintiff's Facebook account.[24]

I. Proprietary Software and Databases[25]

Because proprietary software creates, manipulates, and stores information in many different ways and there are a variety of such sources, it is challenging to discover this information. Frequently, the owner is reluctant to allow access to proprietary software. Access to or search of databases can be complex, especially if there are multiple data sources and information about how the proprietary software creates and manipulates data is not available. If the software exports data only in reports or static format, the data exported may not resemble how the data was entered or manipulated. This is especially true of collaborative software if the objective is to determine who entered or manipulated data and when it was done. When data was edited, who entered or edited the information, and what the original data or information looked like may be relevant to a construction case. Owners or creators of software may resist giving permission to access data through use of the proprietary software. Expert assistance may be needed to answer these types of questions.

---

23. *See* Tompkins v. Detroit Metro. Airport, 278 F.R.D. 387 (E.D. Mich. 2012).

24. *Id.*

25. Proprietary software is software which is owned by an individual or company and only the owner has control over its development. Examples of proprietary software include Microsoft Windows, Adobe Flash Player, PS3 OS, Orbis OS, iTunes, Adobe Photoshop, and Google Earth.

As for traditional databases, such as Excel, requests for these should include not only what is on the face of the database but also the underlying formulas, calculations, and instructions leading to the information shown in a particular cell.

J. Contract Documents, Plans, Specifications, and Shop Drawings

With the advent of CAD and BIM, contract documents, design drawings, embedment drawings, erection bracing drawings, erection drawings, shop drawings, site plans, as-builts, and other drawings and papers now exist in both digital and paper form. In some cases, both paper and digital formats may be relevant because metadata in the digital format may disclose differences from paper documents as well as details on how the final document was created and when and how modifications were made to the original.

Most construction litigation will require discovery of the project plans, specifications, and shop drawings. Now that drawings are created and modified in digital media with collaboration software, it can be difficult to determine when data was edited, who entered or edited the information, and what the data or information looked like as of a given date and time using standard or proprietary software. This is not that different from distinguishing variations between the plans and the actual work or determining who made analog entries to plans on a jobsite and why they were made. Digital media may include a useful search functionality which provides a reliable trail to answers with help from the software or with forensic assistance from an expert.

Specifications for construction are valuable in construction litigation because they provide instructions on project intent, performance, and construction. Also, the specifications reference the applicable quality and standards. Digitally created, modified, and stored specifications include a search functioning tool and metadata that can show how, who, and when changes were made. Where a case involves issues about changes to or compliance with specifications, counsel should send a document request seeking preservation of metadata to collect all aspects of the data on specifications.

K. Device and Cloud Backup Systems

Backup data may provide important evidence and impeachment data. However, obtaining backup data and legacy data creates issues of reasonable accessibility and proportionality.[26] Whether this data is subject to discovery will depend on where the data is backed up and whether the original software is still available.

III. Inspecting Opposing Party Devices

Obtaining direct access to the computers and computer devices of opposing parties or their employees or an opposing party's complete database is a frequent ESI discovery issue. Justification for inspection of opposing party computers or databases includes evidence of misconduct by the opposing party in discovery,[27] inexplicable anomalies in data received, potential alteration or spoliation, missing data or documents, or variations in data produced from that which was promised or that the court ordered. Having a qualified expert inspect the device directly may eliminate questions about whether the data was fully and properly collected, copied, and produced. In some cases, the inability to replicate outcomes or calculations from a produced data set may require limited access to the opposing party's device. Direct inspection may be warranted if information is generated by unique and proprietary software or devices, and the output produced is not in a data set of all discoverable information in understandable form.

Federal Rule of Civil Procedure 34(a)(1) authorizes access to devices; however, inspecting a party's devices should not be a routine

---

26. The determination of whether data is retained in a reasonably accessible fashion and who should bear the cost of recovery of the data is a case-dependent issue. *See* United States ex rel. Guardiola v. Renown Health, 2015 U S. Dist. LEXIS 112511, 2015 WL 5056726 (D. Nev. 2015); Starbucks Corp. v. ADT Sec. Servs., Inc., No. 08-CV-900-JCC, 2009 U.S. Dist. LEXIS 120941, 2009 WL 4730798, at *6 (W.D. Wash. Apr. 30, 2009).

27. *In re* Ford Motor Co., 345 F.3d 1315 (11th Cir. 2003) (Plaintiff not entitled to unlimited access to Defendant's databases without factual showing and court-imposed limitations).

method for ESI discovery because such access to digital devices could result in overbroad access, including access to irrelevant, confidential, or private information.[28] There is a substantial body of federal[29] and state[30] case law about access to devices because direct inspection of the opposition's computer devices requires a showing of good cause before such an inspection is allowed. Access to personal devices is disfavored because traditional discovery of documents and things required the producing party to produce the documents or things, not the files where they were stored. The factors considered regarding forensic examination of an opponent's devices are (1) the privacy interests of the party whose devices are to be examined, (2) whether the party withheld requested discovery or would not search for requested discovery, and (3) the extent

---

28. *See I id.* (while some kind of direct access might be permissible in certain cases, in this case the requesting party is not entitled to this kind of discovery without a factual finding of some non-compliance with discovery rules by the producing party). The 2006 Committee Notes to Rule 34(a)(1) state: "Inspection or testing of certain types of electronically stored information or of a responding party's electronic information system may raise issues of confidentiality or privacy. The addition of testing and sampling to Rule 34(a) with regard to documents and electronically stored information is not meant to create a routine right of direct access to a party's electronic information system, although such access might be justified in some circumstances. Courts should guard against undue intrusiveness resulting from inspecting or testing such systems."

29. *See* Peskoff v. Faber, 251 F.R.D. 59 (D.D.C. 2008); Bro-Tech Corp. v. Thermax, Inc., No. 05-CV-2330, 2008 WL 724627 (E.D. Pa. Mar. 17, 2008); Sterle v. Elizabeth Arden, Inc., No. 3:06 CV 01584 (DJS), 2008 WL 961216 (D. Conn. Apr. 9, 2008); Xpel Tech. Corp. v. Am. Filter Film Distribs; No. SA-08-CV-0175 XR, 2008 WL 744837 (W.D. Tex. Mar. 17, 2008); Henry v. Quicken Loans, Inc., No. 04-40346, 2008 WL 474127 (E.D. Mich. Feb. 15, 2008); *In re* Honza, 242 S.W.3d 578 (Tex. App. 2008); Coburn v. PN II, Inc., No. 2:07-cv-00662, 2008 WL 879746 (D. Nev. Mar. 28, 2008); Ferron v. Search Cactus, LLC, No. 2:06-CV-327, 2008 WL 1902499 (S.D. Ohio Apr. 28, 2008); Johnson v. Wells Fargo Home Mortg., Inc., No. 3:05-CV-0321-RAM, 2008 WL 2142219 (D. Nev. May 16, 2008); Anadarko Petroleum Corp. v. Davis, No. H-06-2849, 2006 WL 3837518 (S.D. Tex. Dec. 28, 2006); Hedenburg v. Aramark Am. Food Servs., 476 F. Supp. 2d 1199 (W.D. Wash. 2007); *In re* Ford Motor Co., 345 F.3d 1315, 1316 (11th Cir. 2003); Ameriwood Indus. v. Liberman, No. 4:06CV524-DJS, 2006 WL 3825291 (E.D. Mo. Dec. 27, 2006).

30. *See, e.g.*, Antico v. Sindt Trucking, Inc., 148 So. 3d 163 (Fla. 1st DCA 2014); Menke v. Broward Cnty. Sch. Bd., 916 So. 2d 8 (Fla. 4th DCA 2005).

to which the party complied with past discovery requests.[31] Mere speculation that electronic data must exist is not sufficient to permit forensic examination of a party's personal computer or cell phone.[32]

Allowing access to devices not only raises privacy and confidentiality concerns but also prevents the owner from using the device during inspection, which could create a hardship as well as possible harm to the owner's data, hardware, and software. In allowing such searches, tribunals must weigh the need for access against infringing on the owner's rights.

Direct inspection by the requesting party should be conditioned on having a qualified expert conduct the inspection with a specific inspection protocol and method for protecting private, privileged, or trade secret information. The inspecting expert should disclose any relevant document located in the search to the producing party to allow it to inspect and designate any privileged or confidential documents subject to protection. The non-objected to relevant documents and a privilege log are provided to the requesting party, who may contest the items withheld. The tribunal can resolve issues regarding privilege for withheld documents.

IV. Cost Shifting

The Federal Rules of Civil Procedure allow cost shifting[33] for providing discovery of information if the producing party establishes that production imposes an undue burden[34] or to enforce proportionality limits.[35] The federal rules and many state court rules presume that the respond-

31. *See* Classic Soft Trim, Inc. v. Albert, no: 6:18-cv-1237-Orl-78GJK, 2020 U.S. Dist. LEXIS 218317, at *21 (M.D. Fla. June 15, 2020); Garrett v. Univ. of S. Fla. Bd. of Trs., No. 8:17-cv-2874, 2018 U.S. Dist. LEXIS 156996, at *3–4 (M.D. Fla. Sept. 14, 2018).

32. Garrett v. Univ. of S. Fla. Bd. of Trs., at *4; Klayman v. City Pages, No. 5:13-cv-143, 2014 U.S. Dist. LEXIS 150253, at *13–14 (M.D. Fla. Oct. 22, 2014).

33. *See generally* Fed. R. Civ. P. 26(b)(2)(B) ("The court may specify conditions for the discovery.").

34. *See* Kabelis v. NCL (Bahamas) Ltd., 2021 U.S. Dist. LEXIS 38481, at *11; 2021 WL 790067 (S.D. Fla. Mar. 2, 2021).

35. FDIC v. Brudnicki, 291 F.R.D. 669, 676 (N.D. Fla. 2013).

ing party bears the expense of complying with discovery requests.[36] However, Rule 26(c) of Federal Rules of Civil Procedure permits a court to "condition discovery on the requesting party's payment of the costs of discovery."[37] Shifting all or part of the costs of production to the requesting party is within the court's discretion.[38] In a motion for cost shifting, the responding party has the burden of proof to show that the production constitutes an undue burden or expense.[39] Since extensive (and expensive) ESI discovery has become more common, parties are more likely to seek cost shifting, which is helpful where there is an imbalance of resources between parties.

Cost shifting is appropriate only when electronic discovery imposes an "undue burden or expense on the responding party."[40] This requires a case-by-case analysis turning on whether the requested ESI is in a reasonably accessible format or not. The expense of producing requested data determines its accessibility. "Accessible data" is stored in a readily usable format that "does not need to be restored or otherwise manipulated to be usable,"[41] while data that is "not reasonably accessible" must be restored to an accessible state to be usable. Backup tapes may be considered not reasonably accessible, so shifting costs to produce data from them is possible.[42]

Zubulake v. UBS Warburg (Zubulake I)[43] sets forth a seven-factor analysis to determine whether cost shifting is appropriate:

1. The extent to which the request is specifically tailored to discover relevant information;

---

36. *See, e.g.*, Oppenheimer Fund, Inc. v. Sanders, 437 U.S. 340, 358, 98 S. Ct. 2380, 57 L. Ed. 2d 253 (1978).

37. *Id. See also* Zubulake v. UBS Warburg LLC, 216 F.R.D. 280, 283 (S.D.N.Y. 2003) ("Zubulake III").

38. *See* Peskoff v. Faber, 251 F.R.D. 59, 61 (D.D.C. 2008).

39. *Id.* at 358. *See also* Wiginton v. CB Richard Ellis, Inc., 229 F.R.D. 568, 573 (N.D. Ill. 2004).

40. 217 F.R.D. 309 (S.D.N.Y. 2003) at 318. This is the first in a series of opinions written by Judge Shira Scheindlin regarding eDiscovery and is referred to as "Zubulake I."

41. *Id.* at 320.

42. *Id.*

43. *Id.* at 322–23.

2. The availability of such information from other sources;
3. The total costs of production, compared to the amount in controversy;
4. The total costs of production, compared to the resources available to each party;
5. The relative ability of each party to control costs and its incentive to do so;
6. The importance of the issues at stake in the litigation; and
7. The relative benefits to the parties of obtaining the information.

The court in *Zubulake I* weighed the factors in descending order, the first factor being the most important and the seventh factor the least.[44]

V. Protecting Client Confidences

A. Duty of Confidentiality

Maintaining confidentiality of client data is one of counsel's most important duties. Client information should be disclosed only to the extent required by law or reasonably necessary to serve the client's interest.[45] Lawyers must take reasonable efforts to prevent inadvertent or unauthorized disclosure of, or unauthorized access to, client information.[46] The fact that ESI is created, stored, and disseminated so easily creates difficulties in maintaining confidentiality. Privilege review and searches for other protected materials can be one of the most expensive and time-consuming aspects of the discovery process. If the discovery process is not secure, important confidential information, including privileged communications, work product, trade secrets, and private employee data, can be leaked.

One of the first discussions counsel should have with the client is about areas of data protection the client deems critical. Special attention must be paid to privileged and work product information to avoid waiver of privilege or divulging information legally protected from discovery.

---

44. *Id.* at 323; Quinby v. WestLB AG, 245 F.R.D. 94, 102 (S.D.N.Y. 2006) (explaining Zubulake I).

45. Rule 1.6, ABA Model Rules of Professional Conduct.

46. Rule 1.6(c), ABA Model Rules of Professional Conduct.

Fortunately, AI and other technology can search ESI and identify privileged information. Nevertheless, clawback agreements should be drafted to remedy inadvertent disclosure of privileged or secret information. The preliminary meet and confer with opposing counsel is an excellent opportunity to discuss the potential need for protective orders, Rule 502(d) orders, and the methodology for privilege logs.[47]

B. Protective Orders

Protective orders can be extremely important in ESI discovery in construction cases. Construction cases may involve individuals' personal identifiable information (e.g., employment or personnel records) or information subject to contractual or statutory confidentiality requirements.[48] Relevant information in construction matters may be in documents or data sets including private, trade secret, research data, or other protected information, or may be found in proprietary databases needing protection. Under Rule 26(c)[49] and state court equivalents,[50] courts can issue protective orders preventing dissemination of such information.

47. Discussion of the topic in the Rule 26(f) meet and confer is often included in court ESI guidelines, local rules, or orders. *See, e.g.*, U.S. District Court for the District of Maryland, Principles for the Discovery of Electronically Stored Information in Civil Cases, found at https://www.mdd.uscourts.gov/sites/mdd/files/ESI-Principles.pdf; Guideline 2.02(f), U.S. District Court ND of California, Guidelines for the Discovery of Electronically Stored Information, found at https://www.cand.uscourts.gov/filelibrary/1117/ESI_Guidelines-12-1-2015.pdf; and Item VIII, U.S. District Court ND of California, Checklist for Rule 26(F) Meet and Confer Regarding Electronically Stored Information, found at https://cand.uscourts.gov/forms/e-discovery-esi-guidelines/.

48. See Chapter 3 for discussion of confidentiality requirements for government contractors.

49. Fed. R. Civ. P. 26(c) (a party or any person from whom discovery is sought may move for a protective order in the court where the action is pending; the motion must include a certification that the movant has in good faith conferred or attempted to confer with other affected parties in an effort to resolve the dispute without court action; and the court may, for good cause, issue an order to protect a party or person from annoyance, embarrassment, oppression, or undue burden or expense).

50. *E.g.*, Fla. R. Civ. P. 1.280(c); Tex. R. Civ. P. 192.6(a) and (b).

Early adoption of an agreed tailored protective order assists in designating information subject to protection.

It is important to note that a protective order is not the same thing as an order sealing information disclosed or filed in court. Counsel should be aware of the differences between protecting information in discovery and protecting ESI used in court.[51] Confidential information used as evidence in a case may require both types of protection.

C. Privilege Logs and Clawback Agreements or Orders

The concept of privilege logging began in 1993 (before the major growth in ESI) when Rule 26(b)(5) was amended to require notice if a party was withholding material otherwise subject to disclosure on privilege grounds.[52] Rule 26(b)(5) does not describe the information required in a privilege log, but the Advisory Committee Notes provide some guidance.[53] The large volume of ESI now common in the litigation process has overwhelmed parties' ability to identify and catalogue privileged information without costly effort. Unfortunately, neither court rules nor case law has provided a uniform and universally accepted method of preparing a privilege log. Despite these problems, privilege logging is required, and failure to provide a privilege log for withheld material may result in waiver of privilege or other sanctions.[54]

Proportionality standards apply to privilege logs, as well as other types of discovery.[55] Some emerging approaches to reduce the burden of privilege logging include metadata logs, categorical logs, and logs of

---

51. Sealing court records is discussed in Section E.

52. The Sedona Conference, Commentary on Protection of Privileged ESI, 17 Sedona Conf. J. 95 at 154–55 (2016).

53. *Id.*

54. *Id.* at 154. The Advisory Committee Note to Fed. R. Civ. P. 26(b)(5) stated that the failure to notify the other party could result in either sanctions under Rule 37(b)(2) or waiver of the privilege.

55. U.S. Bank Nat'l Ass'n v. Triaxx Asset Mgmt. LLC, No. 18-CV-4044 (BCM), 2021 U.S. Dist. LEXIS 205644, 2021 WL 4973611 (S.D.N.Y. Oct. 25, 2021) (proportionality is an issue in evaluating privilege logs, just as it is with other aspects of discovery).

samples of privileged documents.[56] Courts routinely approve categorical logs, which can be a less costly alternative to privilege logging on a document-by-document basis.[57]

Federal Rule of Evidence 502[58] can provide a way to reduce some costs and burdens of privilege review and logging. A Rule 502(d) order is a clawback agreement requiring return of and protection for privileged information inadvertently produced in discovery. Rule 502(d) orders provide protection that extends to cases in other federal and state courts. Not all state courts have similar rules, but parties may draft a Rule 502-type stipulation and seek a court enforcement of it where there is no specific state rule.

D. Protecting Trade Secrets

Trade secret protection can be extremely important to the client; thus, counsel must determine whether client data contains trade secrets or government-regulated confidential information[59] that must be protected. This type of protection should be considered early in the case since it may be possible to obtain protection by stipulation or an agreed protective order, which is far easier than having to litigate the issue before the judge. The stipulation may describe who has access to trade secret or other confidential information, how access will be managed during the litigation, and limitations on the information's use or disclosure after the case.

---

56. P. Favro, What Litigants Should Know About New Court Decisions on Categorical Privilege Logs (Dec. 2, 2021), found at https://www.driven-inc.com/blog-what-litigants-should-know-about-new-court-decisions-on-categorical-privilege-logs/.

57. *Id.*, Maxus Liquidating Trust v. YPF, S.A. (*In re* Maxus Energy Corp.), 2021 Bankr. LEXIS 2215, 2021 WL 3619900 (D. Del. Aug. 16, 2021) (using categorical privilege logs is a common practice in litigation involving the review of an extremely large number of documents and is an efficient and appropriate accommodation to allow production of meaningful privilege logs without undertaking the huge expense and significant delay arising from the production of a document-by-document log).

58. Rule 502(d), Fed. R. Evid. permits a federal court to enter an order stating that production of documents protected by the attorney-client privilege or work product doctrine does not waive those protections in the specific litigation or any other federal or state proceeding.

59. Confidentiality and cybersecurity of government data are discussed more fully in Chapter 3.

It is also important to protect trade secrets from public access; this may involve redaction of information filed in the case, sealing the court record,[60] sealing the courtroom when trade secrets may be disclosed at a hearing or trial, and an admonition to jurors concerning nondisclosure of trade secret information.[61] In arbitration, counsel should consider requiring all parties, counsel, and witnesses to sign a confidentiality and nondisclosure agreement regarding trade secrets involved in or discussed in the proceedings. Although arbitration proceedings are private, they are not necessarily confidential, so having such an agreement is advisable.[62] Technology assisted review (TAR) can be helpful in searching voluminous data for trade secrets. Trade secrets may be in many forms, such as formulae, work processes, inventions, source codes, and pricing or bidding data. Identifying and labeling confidential and trade secret information when it first appears in a document facilitates locating such information for purposes of discovery and protective orders.

E. Managing What Goes in the Court File and Sealing Court Records

Counsel should assume that all documents and data filed in the record or admitted as evidence in civil cases may be publicly accessible; therefore, sensitive client and third-party information must be protected. Depositions and deposition exhibits, pleadings and motions with attachments, and exhibits submitted to the court, whether introduced into evidence or not, are all subject to search and download by almost anyone, regardless of motive.

60. *See* Section IV.E. regarding sealing the court file

61. For extensive treatment on how attorneys and courts should deal with trade secret information, *see* The Sedona Conference Commentary on Protecting Trade Secrets in Litigation About Them (Public Comment Version March 2022) (https://thesedonaconference.org/sites/default/files/2022-March-Handout-Protecting-Trade-Secrets-in-Litigation-About-Them.pdf).(last accessed 5-15-23)

62. *See* Richard C. Reuben, *Confidentiality in Arbitration: Beyond the Myth*, 54 U. Kan. L. Rev. 1255 (2006). https://scholarship.law.missouri.edu/cgi/viewcontent.cgi?referer=&httpsredir=1&article=1323&context=facpubs (last accessed 3-30-23).

A request to seal court records must overcome a "strong presumption in favor of access." [63] The standard for overcoming the presumption of public access to court records depends on why the records are filed with the court. A party asking to seal court records relating to motions that are "more than tangentially related to the underlying cause of action" must demonstrate "compelling reasons" that support secrecy.[64] For records attached to motions that are "not related, or only tangentially related, to the merits of the case," the lower "good cause" standard of Rule 26(c) applies.[65] Sealing the court records also requires compliance with the procedures established by applicable local rules.[66]

Federal Rule of Civil Procedure 5.2 provides rules for sealing personal information, including social security, tax-ID, and financial account numbers, but provides no further guidance on sealing records of other confidential information. Sealing records for other types of confidential information is subject to local rules, which not only vary from district to district but also differ between districts within the same state.

Given the problems with local procedure, the best approach is to obtain an unopposed motion to seal. State court rules for sealing records and protecting confidential information vary from jurisdiction to jurisdiction. In some cases, states require certain confidential information to be located and redacted from court filings.[67] Counsel must know what is going into the record and determine and employ the correct process for dealing with these important issues.

---

63. Kamakana v. City and County of Honolulu, 447 F.3d 1172 ,1178 (9th Cir. 2006), (quoting Foltz v. State Farm. Mut. Auto. Ins. Co., 331 F.3d 1122, 1135).

64. Calhoun, 2022 U.S. Dist. LEXIS 69297, at *6 (quoting Ctr. for Auto Safety v. Chrysler Grp., 809 F.3d 1092, 1099 (9th Cir. 2016)).

65. Ctr. for Auto Safety, 809 F.3d at 1099 (9th Cir. 2016); Kamakana, 447 F.3d at 1179.

66. Calhoun, 2022 U.S. Dist. LEXIS 69297, at *6.

67. Under Florida Rules of General Practice and Judicial Administration 2.420, attorneys filing in civil court cases are solely responsible for ensuring some 22 types of confidential information designated by rule contained in filings is appropriately redacted or identified for redaction, whether the information is that of the client, the opponent, or a third party.

VI. Conclusion

Requesting, gathering, and protecting ESI data in construction cases requires construction lawyers to understand their clients' data for the specific project and to work with the client, the legal team, and possibly with experts to develop a practical, cost-effective strategy for eDiscovery to obtain the relevant information for the case while ensuring confidentiality where needed.

APPENDIX TO CHAPTER 6

Sample ESI Protocol for Construction Matters #1

NOTE: Any model protocol, and there are many of them, is merely a starting point for discussion. Components may need to be removed, added, or amended considering the nature of the case, the amount in controversy, agreements of the parties, the relative ability of the parties to conduct ESI discovery, and other factors relevant under the circumstances.

Stipulation Establishing Discovery Protocol

The parties hereby provide the Panel/Court with the following stipulated proposal governing the discovery of electronically stored information (ESI) and paper documents in the above-captioned matter.

I. Scope

A. **Date.** Discovery will be limited to ESI and hard copy documents in the parties' custody, possession, or control created on or after ____________________through ____________.

B. **Data Sources**

1. **Custodian ESI.** With respect to non-enterprise, custodial ESI (email and other electronic files), the parties agree to produce responsive ESI for the following limited list of custodians:

Plaintiff	1. Name 2. Name 3. Name
Defendant	1. Name 2. Name 3. Name

2. **Enterprise ESI.** The parties agree to produce responsive ESI from the following limited list of enterprise (non-custodian specific) sources:

Plaintiff	1. [Examples: project server, files from project management software etc.] 2. 3.
Defendant	1. 2. 3.

3. **Excluded Data Sources.** The parties agree the following data sources will not be subject to discovery absent a particularized need as established by the facts and legal issues of the case:

a. Deleted, slack, fragmented, or other data only accessible by forensics
b. Random access memory (RAM), temporary files, or other ephemeral data
c. Online access data (temporary internet files, history, cache, cookies, and the like)
d. Backup and archival files
e. Personal digital assistants, pagers, and mobile telephones
f. Instant messages, text messages, and voicemails
g. Obsolete or "legacy" systems

4. **Structured Data.** To the extent a response to discovery requires production of discoverable electronic information contained in a database, in lieu of producing the database, the parties agree to meet and confer to, with an understanding of which fields are relevant, agree upon a set of queries to be made for discoverable information and generate a report in a reasonably usable and exportable electronic file (e.g., Excel or CSV format) for review by the requesting party or counsel.

C. **Search Terms**

1. **Initial Search Methodology.** With the objective of limiting the scope of review and production, and thereby reducing discovery burdens, the parties shall meet and confer regarding search terms by [date].

2. **Exclusion Terms.** Each party reserves the right to exclude documents from production with certain domains or terms based on their non-relevance, privilege, PII, or proprietary nature. The receiving party may request disclosure of any domains or terms used to identify documents for exclusion.

D. **Predictive Coding.** Before any party begins using predictive coding through technology assisted review (TAR) as a means of identifying responsive and/or relevant documents for production, such party shall advise the other parties of its intention, whereupon the parties will meet and confer regarding the use of predictive coding. Nothing in this provision shall require any party to disclose its use of predictive coding solely for its own internal prioritization or review of ESI materials.

II. Production

ESI PRODUCTION SPECIFICATIONS

Standard Load File Specifications ESI format when producing documents to [Insert Name]	
Scanned Paper Documents	**Electronic Documents**
Single-Page TIF for B&W or color	Single-Page TIF for B&W or color (if image exists)
Document Level OCR/Text	Document Level OCR/Text
Date and Time in separate fields (if an option)	Date and Time in separate fields (if an option)
Date format: MM/DD/YYYY	Date format: MM/DD/YYYY
Concordance DAT delimited file for fielded data: • BEGBATES (required) • ENDBATES (required) • BEGBATESATTACH (required if applicable)	Concordance DAT delimited file for fielded data (if available): • BEGBATES (required) • ENDBATES (required) • BEGBATESATTACH (required if applicable)

Scanned Paper Documents	Electronic Documents
• ENDBATESATTACH (required if applicable) • PAGECOUNT (required) • OCR_PATH (required) • BOX (if applicable) • FOLDER (if applicable) • CUSTODIAN (if applicable) • VOLUME (if possible) OPT image load file Folder Structure: • Data (for load files) • Images (for image folders) • Image name must match BEGDOC • 1,000 images per subfolder if possible • OCR/TEXT (for OCR/text files) • Text file name must match BEGDOC • 1,000 text files per subfolder if possible	• ENDBATESATTACH (required if applicable) • PAGECOUNT (required if applicable) • CUSTODIAN (if applicable) • VOLUME (if possible) • EMAILFROM • EMAILTO • EMAILCC • EMAILBCC • EMAILSUBJECT • EMAILSENTDATE • EMAILSENTTIME • EMAILRECEIVEDDATE • EMAILRECEIVEDTIME • EMAILATTACHMENT (attachment names) • EMAILATTACHNUMBER • MD5HASH • NATIVE (link to Native) • NATIVEAUTHOR • NATIVECREATEDDATE • NATIVECREATEDTIME • NATIVEFILEEXTENSION • NATIVEFILENAME • NATIVEFILETITLE • NATIVEFILETYPEDESC (Adobe, MS Word, MS Excel, etc.) • NATIVEFOLDERPATH • (include entire file path) • NATIVEFOLDERNAME • (base level subfolder name) • NATIVEMEDIATYPE (eMail, eAttach, eDoc) • NATIVEMODIFIEDDATE • NATIVEMODIFIEDTIME • EXTRACTED_TEXT_PATH (required) • PLACEHOLDER (if document produced in native format, indicate with "Y")

Scanned Paper Documents	Electronic Documents
	OPT image load file Folder Structure: • Data (for load files) • Images (for image folders) 1. Image name must match BEGDOC 2. 1,000 images per subfolder if possible • OCR/TEXT (for OCR/text files) 1. Text file name must match BEGDOC 2. 1,000 text files per subfolder if possible • Native (for Native files if applicable) 1. Native file name must match BEGDOC 2. 1,000 native files per subfolder if applicable

III. Conidentiality Designations and Privilege Clawback

A. If a document qualifies for confidential treatment pursuant to the terms of Joint Stipulated Confidentiality and Protective Order in this case, the designation shall be shown on the face of PDFs pertaining to such documents and in the appropriate data field in the load file.

B. The parties will collectively consider the entry of a court order preventing waiver for privileged documents produced in the proceeding in the form of a Rule 502(d) non-waiver order [Federal Court] or its reasonable equivalent [state court or arbitration].

See The Sedona Conference, Commentary on the Effective Use of Federal Rule of Evidence 502(d) Orders, 23 Sedona Conf. J. 1 (2022). Also found at https://thesedonaconference.org/sites/default/files/publications/Rule%20502%28d%29%20Orders%20August%202021_0.pdf.

Sample ESI Protocol #2

I. General Principles:

A. An attorney's zealous representation of a client is not compromised by conducting discovery in a cooperative manner. The failure of counsel or the parties to litigation to cooperate in facilitating and reasonably limiting discovery requests and responses raises litigation costs and contributes to the risk of sanctions.

B. The proportionality standard set forth in Federal Rule of Civil Procedure 26(b)(2)(C) should be applied in each case when formulating a discovery plan. To further the application of the proportionality standard in discovery, requests for production of ESI and related responses should be reasonably targeted, clear, and as specific as practicable.

II. Standard for ESI Disclosures: Within 30 days after the Rule 26(f) conference, or later if the parties agree, each party shall disclose:

A. Custodians. The custodians most likely to have discoverable ESI in their possession, custody, or control. The custodians shall be identified by name, title, connection to the instant litigation, and the type of the information under his/her control.

B. Noncustodial data sources. A list of noncustodial data sources (e.g., shared drives, C. servers, etc.), if any, likely to contain discoverable ESI.

C. Third-party data sources. A list of third-party data sources, if any, likely to contain discoverable ESI (e.g., third-party email and/or mobile device providers, "cloud" storage, etc.) and for each such source, indicate the extent to which a party is (or is not) able to preserve information stored in the third-party data source.

D. Inaccessible data. A list of data sources, if any, likely to contain discoverable ESI (by type, date, custodian, electronic system, or other criteria sufficient to specifically identify the data source) that a party asserts is not reasonably accessible under Federal Rule of Civil Procedure 26(b)(2)(i). Note: Section III.C(2)(a)–(i) sets forth data sources and ESI which are not required to be preserved by the parties. Those data sources and ESI do not need to be included on this list.

III. Standard for Preservation of ESI: A party has a common law obligation to take reasonable and proportional steps to preserve discoverable information in the party's possession, custody, or control. With respect to ESI, the following provisions apply:

A. Absent a showing of good cause by the requesting party, the parties shall not be required to modify, on a going-forward basis, the procedures used by them in the ordinary course of business to back up and archive data; provided, however, that the parties shall preserve all discoverable ESI in their possession, custody, or control.

B. All parties shall supplement their disclosures in accordance with Rule 26(e) with discoverable ESI responsive to a particular discovery request or mandatory disclosure where that data is created after a disclosure or response is made (unless excluded under (C)(2) or (D)(1)–(2) below).

C. Absent a showing of good cause by the requesting party, the following categories of ESI need not be preserved:

1. Deleted, slack, fragmented, or other data only accessible by forensics.
2. Random access memory (RAM), temporary files, or other ephemeral data that are difficult to preserve without disabling the operating system.
3. Online access data such as temporary internet files, history, cache, cookies, and the like.
4. Data in metadata fields that are frequently updated automatically, such as last-opened dates. Backup data that are substantially duplicative of data that are more accessible elsewhere.
5. Server, system, or network logs.
6. Data remaining from systems no longer in use that is unintelligible on the systems in use.
7. Electronic data (e.g., email, calendars, contact data, notes, and text messages) sent to or from mobile devices (e.g., iPhone, iPad, Android, etc., devices), provided that a copy of all such electronic data is routinely saved elsewhere (such as on a server, laptop, desktop computer, or "cloud" storage).

8. The parties are to confer on any other categories of ESI that may not need to be preserved, in light of the General Principles set forth above, and determine whether the parties can agree that such categories can be added to the non-preservation list in (C)(2) above.

D. Standard for Addressing Privilege: The parties are to confer on the nature and scope of privilege logs for the case, including whether categories of information may be excluded from any logging requirements. The parties will propose an order under Federal Rule of Civil Procedure 502 for preservation of privilege.

This Protocol was derived from Model Protocol for Discovery of Electronically Stored Information in Civil Litigation, U.S. District Court, Western District of Washington, found at: https://www.wawd.uscourts.gov/sites/wawd/files/61412ModeleDiscoveryProtocol.pdf.

CHAPTER 7

Presenting ESI Evidence at Trial, Arbitration Hearings, and Mediation

Elisabeth Malsch, PhD, PE, *Author*
Leslie King O'Neal, *Contributor*

Effective advocacy requires lawyers to present the evidence supporting the client's case or defenses in a clear, concise, and persuasive manner. Construction disputes may span extended time periods, have multiple parties, and involve complex technical issues. Collecting and organizing all the facts, data, and expert opinions and making these understandable to judges, juries, and arbitrators requires counsel to synthesize facts and expert opinions into a harmonious theme for the case. To do this, advocates may use data summaries and visual aids, like schedules, timelines, diagrams, photographs, or video, to present compelling evidence to support their clients' positions.

Data summaries and visual aids are essential tools in presenting construction cases in a concise and coherent way because of the massive amounts of data involved and because structures and their components are difficult for lay people to envision solely from verbal descriptions. Demonstrative evidence focuses the trier of fact's attention in a way oral testimony alone simply cannot.[1] "Humans receive and respond to information through their senses: sight, sound, smell, touch, and taste."[2] Consequently, judges, juries, and arbitrators are more likely to understand and retain information if counsel engages more than one sense in presenting information.[3]

Fortunately, federal and state evidence rules allow demonstrative evidence and demonstrative aids to assist counsel and witnesses in their presentations,[4] subject to certain limitations and requirements. Evidence rules allow presentation of relevant photographs, video, charts, summaries, timelines, diagrams, and other demonstrative exhibits, if they are admissible evidence or if they are scientifically and accurately based on admissible evidence. In the latter case, admissibility requires providing the primary source for each item of data and a trustworthy way to support any analysis used to digest the information. Fortunately, technology can assist in the systematic creation of trial exhibits serving these needs.

A summary or model or other demonstrative exhibit demonstrates reality that could otherwise not be presented to the tribunal because the actual item or process is too bulky, too time-consuming, or no longer exists. Counsel should be prepared for objections or cross-examination about allegedly misleading aspects of the demonstrative exhibit, which, if sustained, may impeach and impact the credibility of the exhibit, the witness, and the case. For example, a timeline or summary of voluminous data may be impeached by showing inconsistencies in the underlying data set. Demonstrative exhibits must be assessed for unintended consequences; in-court demonstrations are particularly dangerous if the demonstration backfires.[5] To avoid potential courtroom fiascos, con-

---

1. Mary Quinn Cooper, *The Use of Demonstrative Evidence at Trial*, 31 Tulsa Law J. 567, 568 (1999).

2. *Id.*

3. *Id.*, citing Gail A. Jaquish & James Ware, *Adapting an Educator Habit of Mind: Modifying What It Means to "Think Like a Lawyer,"* 45 Stan. L. Rev. 1713, 1720 (1993).

4. *See* Fed. R. Evid. 611, 1006; N.Y. Ev. R. 11.03, https://nycourts.gov>evidence; Ill. R. Evid. 401, 402, 403, https://www.illinoiscourts.gove>ev.

5. *E.g.*, the infamous in-court demonstration of O.J. Simpson failing to put on the leather gloves found at the murder scene, leading to defense attorney Johnnie

sider using a pre-recorded videotape of a demonstration if the tribunal will allow it. Ideally, demonstrative exhibits should be uncomplicated, understandable, realistic, and unimpeachable.

I. Summaries of Electronically Stored Evidence

If a case involves a few relevant documents, each document is printed out and each page is numbered, foundation requirements are entered into the record, and the expert connects the evidence through testimony to support their opinions. This approach is impractical in most construction cases involving voluminous amounts of data.

As noted in previous chapters, the volume of data created in design and construction projects has grown exponentially in the past few years. Design drawing sets, for example, used to be tens of pages long. Now drawing sets contain hundreds and hundreds of pages and may be correlated to a three-dimensional model. In addition to the design and construction information, other types of automated information have increased the volume of data available for a project. Voluminous information often cannot be understood or communicated clearly without being summarized.[6] The challenge is to develop summary or timeline exhibits that synthesize the data into a coherent message unquestionably supported by relevant admissible evidence. The approach requires teamwork between trial counsel and experts to create and present suitable and admissible summaries.

Cochran's iconic phrase in his closing argument, "If it doesn't fit, you must acquit." Linda Deutsch, *O.J. Simpson Murder Trial: "If It Doesn't Fit, You Must Acquit"* (published June 10, 2014, updated June 11, 2014) https://www.nbclosangeles.com/new/local/oj-simpson-20-years-later-glove-fit-darden-dunne-mu (last accessed 3/21/23).

6. Constructed under the supervision of Skidmore, Owings & Merrill (SOM), SOM described the structural design of the John Hancock Center (Hancock Center) in Chicago in 25 full-size blueprints. The Hancock Center is 100 stories tall and was completed in 1969. Fazlur R. Khan, 5 Engr. Struct 10 (1983). Thirty years later, more than 150 drawings were produced in AutoCAD to describe the New York Times building, which is 52 stories tall and was completed in 2007. "Structural Design Challenges for the New York Times Building," Thomas Z. Scarangello, P.E.; Kyle E. Krall, P.E., and Jeffrey A. Callow, Structures Congress 2005: Metropolis and Beyond (2005).

In aggregate, processing the voluminous data developed by automated processes may result in correlations that confirm or rebut a hypothesis as to what happened and how. Examples of conditions creating extremely enormous quantities of data include surveillance data obtained with robots, jobsite cameras or drones, instrumentation data, or daily log information that may not be understandable, at least in a useful way, in its raw form.[7]

Similarly, construction managers and design teams have been employing Building Information Models (BIM) and construction specific data collection software to connect the ballooning information on their projects.[8] Similar Forensic Information Models have been developed over the past decade to aggregate, sort, explain, and identify the relevant information.[9] This often requires summarizing and compiling disparate information. To make this information admissible in court or arbitration hearing, expert witnesses must provide the foundation for the data underlying their analysis, as well as for the aggregation process, and the collection techniques.

A. Summary by Rule

The distinction between demonstrative aids, which are not admitted into evidence, and demonstrative evidence is sometimes blurred because the

---

7. Laserscan information is often collected in proprietary file formats that are not well documented. Similarly, equipment can have on board data loggers or black boxes that do not follow recognized standards when the data is collected. Black Boxes, CRANES TODAY (Oct. 9, 2002), https://www.cranestodaymagazine.com/features/black-boxes/.

8. Requests for proposal and other project specifications are beginning to include expectations about the Level of Detail (LOD) of Building Information Models (BIMs). The United BIM and BIM Forum have developed specifications. *See BIM Level of Development*, United BIM, https://www.united-bim.com/bim-level-of-development-lod-100-200-300-350-400-500/ (last visited Aug. 9, 2022); *Level of Specification Development*, BIM Forum, https://bim-international.com/wp-content/uploads/2016/03/LOD-Specification-2015.pdf (last visited Aug. 9, 2022). *See also* AIA G204-2022 and G205-2022, which provide project participants with information about LOD.

9. Forensics & Investigations | Thornton Tomasetti; F. Brando, et al., *Forensic Information Modeling: A New Forensic Tool*, 83 CIVIL ENG'G MAGAZINE 48 (Jan. 2013).

same type of information, such as a timeline[10] or a summary chart, may be used for either purpose. The distinction is that demonstrative evidence is sent back to the jury or accepted into evidence in a lawsuit; therefore, it must meet admissibility standards under the evidence rules.[11] However, demonstrative aids that merely assist the witness or counsel in presenting the case need not meet the strict foundation requirements for admissibility. Such exhibits are marked for identification to preserve the record but will not be sent back with the jury or be given the weight of evidence by arbitrators. When assessing whether a chart, summary, timeline, model, or other demonstrative exhibit should be proffered as evidence and limited as an aid, consider whether the jury would want or need access to the exhibit during deliberations and whether the higher admissibility foundation can be met.

I. Foundation Required for Demonstrative Evidence

Simply stated, the more accurate and authentic a demonstrative exhibit is, the more likely it will be admitted into evidence. The foundation for demonstrative exhibits introduced as evidence is whether the exhibit is authentic, relevant, not hearsay or subject to exception by rule, and either original or admissible secondary evidence.

Demonstrative exhibits used as "aids" to assist in a witness' testimony must be relevant and must resemble or be shown to be what it purports to be, that is, they should reasonably resemble or be substantially the same as what they represent. The proponent must explain how the exhibit will facilitate presentation of the testimony to the jury.[12] The

---

10. Timelines are addressed with specificity in Section c.

11. *See* United States v. Bray, 139 F.3d 1104, 1110 (6th Cir. 1998) for detailed discussion of the different types of demonstrative exhibits and when they may be admitted into evidence.

12. Pierce v. State, 671 So. 2d 186 (Fla. 4th DCA 1996) "In order to admit a demonstrative exhibit, illustrating an expert's opinion, such as a computer-generated animation, the proponent must establish the foundation requirements necessary to introduce the expert opinion. Specifically, (1) the opinion evidence must be helpful to the trier of fact; (2) the witness must be qualified as an expert; (3) the opinion evidence must be applied to evidence offered at trial; and (4) pursuant to section 90.403, Florida Statutes (1991), the evidence, although technically relevant, must not present a substantial danger of unfair prejudice that outweighs its probative value"

expert should testify that the exhibit will assist in presenting their testimony; some courts require a witness to testify that he or she supervised creation of a summary or exhibit to be used.[13] It is good practice to review any demonstrative exhibits with the expert witness before using them in a hearing or deposition.

An expert witness describing a sequence of events on a jobsite may use a model of the jobsite to illustrate spatial relationships or line of sight or sequence of events. In addition to the foundation questions just listed, after qualifying the witness as an expert, counsel should have the witness testify that the model was created to scale, that it accurately depicts the jobsite at the relevant time, and that the model will assist the expert in presenting testimony to the tribunal. The model and its underlying data should be available for review by opposing counsel prior to its use.

Adding to the volume of data on construction projects, contractors and subcontractors are using different tools to make the flow of the construction process more predictable and the collection of data more automatic. If received and digested properly, the data produced by these tools can provide illuminating insight into the progress of a project. Each of these collections of data could contain or itself be evidence in a case.

Online portals and proprietary software such as ProCore or Newforma are being used more frequently to help organize and choreograph the construction process. The system often logs a time stamp for who sends a document, when a document is received, when it is opened, and what comments are made on it.[14] These time stamps can be incredibly important to understanding the sequence of the construction project—especially when something does not go as planned. Similarly, time stamps can help form the foundation for or against a delay case.

---

13. U.S. v. Moon, 513 F.3d 527, 545 (6th Cir. 2008).

14. Vendors such as Procore™ offer training in the various kinds of data that are emerging at construction sites. Data in Construction Series, Procore, https://www.procore.com/data-construction-series (last visited Aug. 8, 2022). Newforma™ similarly offers a product for aggregating data. Newforma.com, Newforma, https://www.newforma.com/ (last visited Aug. 9, 2022). Translating between different kinds of aggregation software and BIM Modeling often requires even more specialized software such as Konstru™. Konstru, https://konstru.com/ (last visited Aug. 9, 2022).

Assuring that the time stamps are accurate, and have not been tampered with, is vital to the evidence's integrity. Further complicating the record, additional emails, text messages, phone and in-person conversations frequently occur outside of the proprietary system. It may be necessary to request production of strings from various communication tools—email, Slack, Zoom, texts, WhatsApp, and so on—to see a complete conversation about a topic.

Similarly, spreadsheets, models, or other methods the project team employed in real time to track the construction can be more understandable than the raw data the programs collect. For example, with radio frequency IDs (RFIDs) and barcode tagging, various software updates a model automatically when a piece of steel arrives at site.[15] The general contractor then verifies that that same piece of steel is inspected and erected. There may be multiple sources of information about a piece of steel: when it is fabricated, when the truck arrives at site, when the steel is erected—including QAQC in the factory, tickets for the trucks, and web-cam footage of the construction. Manual methods for updating or tagging models should always be correlated with secondary sources to verify that the data is reliable.

When data is collected in an automated manner with sensors or with robots, a review of the computer, controller, and circuitry may be required to verify that the information has not been tampered with. A typical source of automated information is the black box within a large piece of equipment, like a crane. Black boxes are often collected and studied from airplanes after crashes. The information log produced by this kind of source has an orderly data scheme. Each piece of information is usually time stamped. The data is collected at predetermined rates. Some equipment collects more data when the equipment is moving more quickly and less when it is moving more slowly. The setup of

15. Vela Systems developed a software that allows RFID tagged steel pieces to be logged at different stages of the construction process including during delivery and erection. *RFID Tracking for Fabricated Steel Is Expected to Save Contractors and Owners Millions*, Civil & Structural Mag. (Feb. 19, 2009), https://csengineermag.com/rfid-tracking-for-fabricated-steel-is-expected-to-save-contractors-and-owners-millions/.

the data logger is typically explained within its own data schema and associated users' manual.[16]

(a) Admissibility Foundation through Requests for Admission

The federal rules of civil procedure and most state equivalents provide a straightforward method for establishing foundation for admissibility of electronic evidence and demonstrative evidence through requests for admission.[17] Federal Rule of Civil Procedure 36(a)(1)(B) allows a party to serve on any other party a written request to admit the truth of matters relating to the genuineness of any described documents. The request must include a copy of the document unless it has been otherwise furnished or made available for inspection.[18] Because the procedure requires each matter to be admitted to be separately stated,[19] this process is suitable only for establishing the authenticity or admissibility of data underlying a demonstrative exhibit, summary, timeline, diagram, or other compilation. Requests for admission cannot establish the foundation for the demonstrative exhibit itself, which is done through expert testimony as described earlier in section 1. To determine if a particular exhibit may be used in a proceeding, counsel should obtain advance authentication and foundation for the demonstrative exhibit, summary, timeline, diagram, or other compilation either through the meet and confer and agreement with opposing counsel or through confirmation at pretrial conference.

---

16. Contract language may be needed to allow this data and black box information to be obtained from the device suppliers. Sometime suppliers are reluctant to share this information so non-disclosure and confidentiality agreements may be required. *See* discussion in Chapter 4, Section A.

17. Fed. R. Civ. P. 36. *See, e.g.*, N.J. Ct. R. 4:22; N.Y. CVP § 3123; Fla. R. Civ. P. 1.370.

18. Fed. R. Civ. P. 36(a)(2).

19. *Id.*

(b) Objections to Exhibits

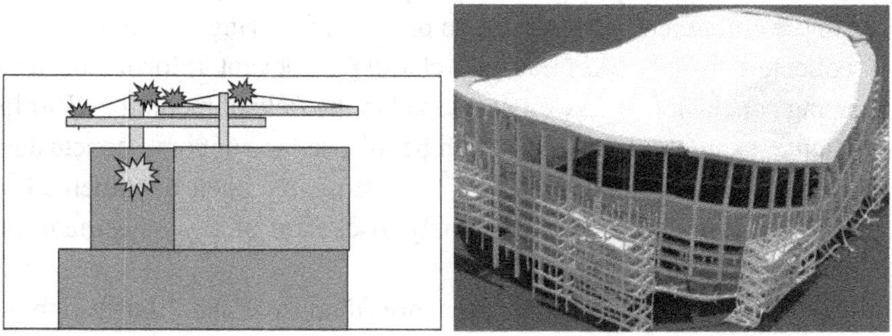

Figure 7.1: Graphic illustration of buildings and crane (left) and physics-based animation from Thornton Tomasetti (right).

When data are processed, outliers are often removed. The process and methodology for cleaning the data must be presented along with the summary information. When photos are excluded from an analysis because they are too blurry or too dark, for example, the criteria for exclusion must be presented so that any bias in the processing of the data can be reviewed and questioned. If the images are being processed by a computer, their appearance to the human eye, for example, may not be a relevant criterion. If data are modified, by cropping a photograph or by removing outliers, frank and timely disclosure of the alteration is necessary in the discovery or pretrial phase and when the exhibit is presented to the trier of fact if there is any danger of impeachment. Being the first to address an issue that requires explanation enhances counsel's and the expert's credibility with the judge, jury, or arbitrators. For example, when presenting foundation for or introducing data with outliers removed, counsel should have the expert explain how and why the data was condensed.

For processing large data, providing the foundation for any automated processing is even more critical. Bias in automated data processing such as artificial intelligence (AI) and machine learning[20] is a

20. Machine learning is a form of AI in which human input of algorithms and data teaches the computer to learn and think in an effort to improve accuracy, speed, efficiency, or ability of the device.

growing and well-documented field of research.[21] The accuracy of the output from AI is only as good as the quality of the algorithms and data fed to the computer by humans. The process of sharing information that is collected in an experiment—excluding irrelevant information and drawing conclusions—is well developed in the field of medicine. Within medicine, examples of how data can be misused to support a conclusion that does not follow the evidence have similarly been documented.[22] Again, the expert should make timely disclosure of any adjustment of a data set.

When gaps between information are filled in with an illustration or to render the foundation for any data, those assumptions must similarly be established. For example, if a collapse is the result of an explosion, and the damage that resulted from the collapse is being presented, each damage location presented in the illustration should reference a specific piece of evidence or analysis. When there is a gap in evidence between two locations, the illustration should not assume that areas that could not be seen or inspected are damaged simply because they are located between two locations that are damaged. Furthermore, using the same example, if the explosion itself is being illustrated, its size and intensity in the illustration should match the evidence regarding the best estimate for the size and intensity of the actual explosion.[23] Adding a key element to the presentation that does not reflect the evidence, for illustrative or storytelling purposes, may raise an objection and lead to exclusion of the demonstrative exhibit.

In addition to bias occasioned by faulty assumptions or data input or algorithms employed for machine learning, AI also has the regrettable potential for "deepfakes." Alteration of digital video, photographs, sound, and data has become so commonplace that applications are

21. Cynthia Weber, *Engineering Bias in AI*, 10 IEEE Pulse15 (Jan.–Feb. 2019).

22. Caroline Criado-Perez, Invisible Women: Data Bias in a World Designed for Men (Mar. 12, 2019).

23. *See* Figure 7.1. The illustration on the left is an example of what not to do. The buildings are not represented in scale with the crane. The attachment points from the crane to the building that are critical to the proceedings are not shown. The explosion is not properly scaled. Conversely, the illustration at right is physics-based, to scale with the building, and the behavior of each step of the analysis is correlated with the evidence, including the correct member and charge sizes.

readily available online to create false information on the location of a device, or spoofed text messages or email,[24] or visual or voice or sound alteration of a digital video. The internet contains examples of "fake news" created from alteration of existing video footage where political figures or celebrities are shown uttering words that have been realistically injected into the video instead of what the person actually said. Deep fakes have already made their way into evidence in legal cases.[25]

AI is a rapidly evolving scientific phenomenon, and currently there are no universally accepted scientific standards for AI processes and algorithms. Expert testimony on subjects such as enhanced photographs created from video is making its way into the courtroom, and impeachment of AI methodology creating the images can be challenging and expensive.

As deep fakes become more prevalent in the legal arena, it is hoped that technology will develop methods to uncover falsehood.[26] In the meantime, counsel must be vigilant and use all means available, such as context, metadata, uncovering of original sources, countervailing witness testimony or data, and challenges through cross-examination to discover and impeach deepfakes. Like any altered record, once a proffered deepfake is uncovered, the legal result can be game-changing for the proponent of the false evidence and devastating to any litigant, expert, or attorney involved in the deception.

---

24. To see the array of apps available for this purpose, simply go online and search for "apps to spoof texts," "apps to spoof email," or "apps to spoof location." Apps online promote their use for gags or tricks, but using an app to send or receive an email or text message that appears to come from another person's digital device can create fraudulent evidence in a legal matter.

25. *See* Paul W. Grimm, Maura R. Grossman & Gordon V. Cormack, *Artificial Intelligence as Evidence*, 19(1) Nw. J. Tech. & Intell. Prop. 71–75 (re: use of "deep fakes" in evidence), https://scholarlycommons.law.northwestern.edu/njtip/vol19/iss1/2.

26. Such technology is already being developed. One example of AI identification is chat GPTZero, which identifies language written by ChatGPT; https://www.entrepreneur.com/business-news/student-builds-chatgpt-detection-app-to-fight-ai-plagiarism/442253 (last accessed Feb. 21, 2023). Google is combating improper use of AI-generated materials with markings, labels, and "About this image." https://9to5google.com/2023/05/10/google-about-this-image/.

(c) Timelines

Timelines are a powerful demonstrative for identifying the key items in a project's history that contributed to the matter at hand. Before a structure collapses or a component fails, it is in equilibrium. For a collapse to occur, either the loads on it increased, or a component of the structure degraded over time. Similarly, for delay and scheduling claims, a project follows the anticipated schedule until something happens to push it off course. Describing the flow of construction projects over time is essential to understanding, and ultimately, to explaining, the matter in dispute.

For timeline demonstratives to be accepted at trial, the aesthetics of the timeline cannot distort the understanding of the information. To that end, keeping the time intervals in proportion is important. When the timeline becomes crowded, using a zoom technique to highlight a portion of the history is a better practice than expanding an area of the timeline for readability.[27]

Similarly, each item in the timeline should be keyed back to the supporting evidence. Adding the Bates number from the document containing the date is often helpful. Similarly, linking the timeline back to the document so that one can click on the key time and see the evidence related to it is helpful. This kind of linked demonstrative may be summarized in a PowerPoint or a PDF document that can be shared as needed without requiring specialty software or specific technical expertise.

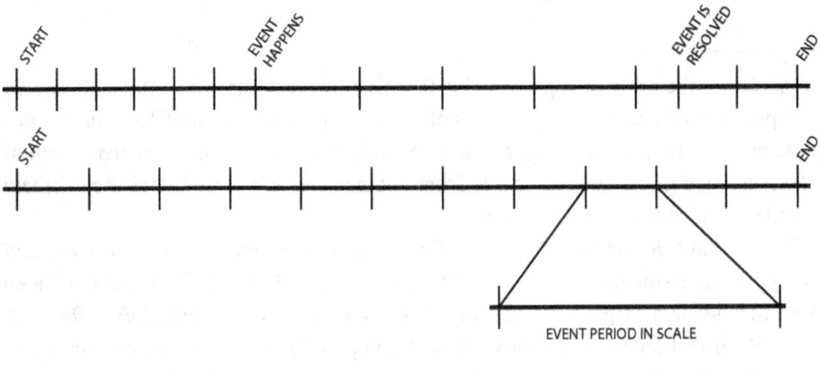

Figure 7.2: Timeline comparison.

27. See Figure 7.2. The top timeline is not to scale and suggests that the event period of interest took much longer than it did. The bottom timeline is scaled to make this distinction clear.

Another option for illustrating over a timeline is using a timeline reference at the edge of the screen and an updating model that shows how the item of interest changed over time. Webcam data of a job site may be presented efficiently with this approach. The time scales need to be verifiable and accurate for the demonstrative to be accepted. A video analysis, for example, can reveal if there are gaps in the webcam data. Any gaps must be explained.

Timelines are powerful communication tools in trial or arbitration. Plan the use of timelines to suit the story of the case from the client's perspective. Consider building a timeline as the case progresses for effective comprehension of discrete portions of the job as well as the overall story of the case. Timelines may be useful in examination and cross-examination of fact and expert witnesses. If the court or arbitration panel allows trial notebooks to be prepared for use during the trial or hearing, a timeline is an excellent reference for the trier of fact during testimony and deliberations.

(d) Graphic Demonstratives

Demonstratives that aggregate information in a manner other than a timeline similarly need to faithfully represent the underlying data they aggregate.

(e) Charts

Charts are useful for aggregating data and discerning trends. For example, looking at trends within data involves drawing a line through the information collected and using it to predict the future trend. This kind of best-fit line may suggest that a defect has been getting worse or getting better relative to a construction method or design choice. When plotting data in charts and inferring trends, the error in the underlying data must be included and considered. For example, when using a measuring tape, the error associated with any measurement would be the smallest increment on the measuring tape. In scientific journals error in the data is often represented with error bars that show the extent of the uncertainty that is contained within the data.[28] Be wary of any predictive data that does not include a depiction of the error contained in

28. *See* Figure 7.3, which does not, on its own, have enough information to make an informed prediction of the future.

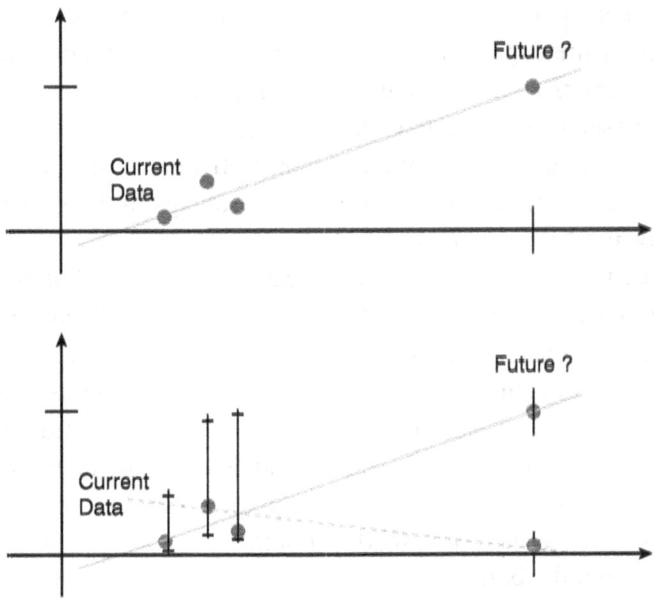

Figure 7.3: Projecting beyond the current information with and without error bars

the current data. For the purposes of a demonstrative chart the analysis underlying the chart should explain and confirm why the resolution of the data is reliable enough to draw any inferences that are represented.

Misrepresentation of data in graphs is a well-discussed topic in scientific literature. Typical approaches for misrepresenting data include axis alteration, smoothing over incomplete data, and presenting irrelevant information with conclusions that do not follow. Similarly, presenting data accurately and compellingly requires the same storytelling skills that skillful writing and oral presentation exemplify.[29]

Distorting the scale can suggest there are significant differences between different categories of information even when the differences are insignificant. Axis alteration can similarly hide or minimize significant variations. Similarly, when information is plotted in log-log

29. Nancy Duarte, Data Story: Explain Data and Inspire Action Through Story 179 (Ideapress Publishing 2019).

scale, it may appear it is correlated even though that correlation is not significant.

When including an analysis of a data set it is important to describe changes in the baseline. For example, when looking at the recovery rates in different hospitals, studies will have different results if the information was taken from the maternity ward, the ICU, or the morgue. For construction claims, noting the extent of nondamaged area helps put into context the amount of damage found. Forty concrete cracks greater than a certain width may be significant for a beam but not necessarily for a parking garage.

In each of the preceding examples, the key criterion for a chart to be effective is that it presents the significant and supportable aspects of the data underlying the summary. If the data or processing of the data or both can be impeached, then the analysis, the presenting expert witness, and the chart are all susceptible to impeachment.

(f) Diagrams and Figures

Diagrams are powerful tools for explaining the relevant science behind an expert opinion, without delving into higher-order mathematics. Since diagrams are abstractions, it may be difficult for people less familiar with the project than the expert witness is to understand what relevant components are being shown. An approach for grounding a diagram and making it understandable involves starting with the overview of a project from a map or aerial view, moving to the structure or component in question, and transitioning from photos to the diagram. This method assures the diagram is in context, that its scales are appropriate, and that it is not giving undue emphasis to a component that is not important. Exceptional examples of this kind of approach include the *New York Times*' illustrations of collapses and failures.[30]

---

30. For example, see the New York Times illustration of the cause of the Beirut Explosion. Ben Hubbard, et al., How a Massive Bomb Came Together in Beirut's Port (Sept. 9, 2020), https://www.nytimes.com/interactive/2020/09/09/world/middleeast/beirut-explosion.html; *see also* Elian Peltier, James Glanz, Weiyi Cai & Jeremy White, *Notre-Dame's Toxic Fallout* (Sept. 16, 2019), https://www.nytimes.com/interactive/2019/09/14/world/europe/notre-dame-fire-lead.html.

Like timelines and charts, diagrams allow incorporation of information beyond just the photograph or excerpt from a contract. By putting the information in context, the significant components of an investigation can be explained more clearly.[31] The wealth of information collected on construction projects makes this kind of synthesis even more important. Like charts and timelines, documenting what is included and why is almost as important as the presentation itself. Combining charts with diagrams and figures allows for the synthesis of massive amounts of information. A good diagram does not leave anything out but is not overwhelming to the observer so that the observer can discern the purpose of the diagram.[32]

(g) Analysis Models

Images, animations, and renderings produced from analysis models synthesize a large amount of analysis in a compact image form. When an expert produces the analysis, its basis should be included in the expert report. The input and output files containing all the settings for, and results of, the model should be disclosed for review. The input files should be provided so the model can be explored, and the process replicated independently on each parties' own copy of the software. In extreme cases, when truly proprietary software is being used, the parties may need to reach an agreement allowing review of the model or information in the offices of and on the equipment of the other party. When doing so, the producing party should secure safeguards against disclosure of irrelevant or proprietary information and undue time constraints on company equipment and resources that may be needed for ongoing business.

Presenting images from analysis models requires the same care as with charts. The range of information and the associated legend should be shown clearly and explained in understandable terms. If the output is

---

31. Forensics and Investigations, Thornton Tomasetti, https://www.thorntontomasetti.com/solution/forensics-investigations#:~:text=Forensic%20Information%20Modeling%20%28FIM%29%20We%20developed%20a%20better,for%20clear%2C%20persuasive%20communication%20of%20complex%20technical%20issues (last visited Aug. 9, 2022). Francesca Brando, et al. *Forensic Information Modeling: A New Forensic Tool*, 83 CIVIL ENG'G MAG. 48 (Jan. 2013).

32. EDWARD TUFTE, THE VISUAL DISPLAY OF QUANTITATIVE INFORMATION, Micro/Macro Readings, at 37, Layering and Separation, at 53 (2d Ed., Graphics Press 2001). *See also* EDWARD TUFTE, ENVISIONING INFORMATION (Graphics Press1990).

shaded with coloring from blue to red for example, care should be given to use red for the areas of issue and not use the colors in the plotting to suggest a larger issue than the evidence supports.

Analysis can similarly be used as a basis for a simulation that recreates what happened to a structure under the action of a described set of loads. These kinds of simulations must clearly explain what information is from the analysis model and what pieces are being filled in by the rendering or other illustration. The choices made in the simulation, including member sizes and configuration, must be tied back to the actual structural plans and shop drawings, and a basis for the loads and structural behavior explained.

(h) Drawings

Traditional two-dimensional design or contract drawings contain the technical information design professionals require to communicate their ideas to one another, to the owner and to the contractor for fabrication and construction. The contractors' and subcontractors' fabrication and erection drawings similarly communicate their understanding of the design drawings back to the owner and design team. Traditional two-dimensional drawings contain references to other pieces of the drawing set, including references to details and to scopes of work performed by other trades. Electronic drawings, on the other hand, can be based on three-dimensional models and include information beyond what two-dimensional paper drawings contain.

How a drawing or model is used in the construction process may also be germane to the electronic information relevant to a dispute. Some models are simply a byproduct of having used modern modeling software such as Autodesk Revit.[33] Other models can be inputted directly into a steel fabricator's computer-controlled cutting, or CNC, machines to drive the cutting and fabricating of parts.[34] The model's intended use drives the required detail. The level of detail included in three-dimensional models is often an issue laid out in contracts and

33. *Revit: BIM software for designers, builders, and doers*, Autodesk, https://www.autodesk.com/products/revit (last visited Aug. 9, 2022).

34. Accurate data for error-free automated production, Tekla, https://www.industrialcnc.com/ (last visited Aug. 9, 2022).

sometimes an item of dispute. The definition of levels of detail may differ according to contract terms.[35]

For the purposes of understanding a design and communicating it to someone outside the construction industry, a rendered three-dimensional model helps explain the context of the issue and can be tied back to photographs of the problem in the same manner as diagrams. Three-dimensional models created for the project may be used as is to explain the issues in dispute, while two-dimensional drawings usually require more explanation for a lay person.

(i) Reconstruction Video or Animation

In general, computer animations presented to enhance oral testimony are demonstrative evidence with the foundation requirement that they are a fair and accurate representation of what they purport to depict and that they are not confusing.[36] A powerful tool for explaining the progress of a construction or the collapse of a structure is a fact and analysis-based animation overlaid with the webcam still of the construction progress or the video of a collapse. Given the increasing ubiquity of videos both from security cameras, public web cameras, construction cameras, and personal devices, many building failures are documented in detail with video of the failure event.[37]

---

35. *See* U.S. General Services Administration, BIM Software Guidelines, Level of Detail, https://www.gsa.gov/real-estate/design-and-construction/3d4d-building-information-modeling/bim-software-guidelines/document-guides/level-of-detail (last visited Aug. 9, 2022); Doug Elliott, 3D BIM Modeling—BIM Level of Detail and Model Progression Specification, Trimble (Apr. 10, 2017), https://constructible.trimble.com/construction-industry/3d-bim-modeling-level-of-detail-and-model-progression-specification; and A Practical Approach to Level of Detail (LOD), United BIM, https://www.united-bim.com/practical-approach-to-level-of-detail/ (last visited Aug. 9, 2022).

36. *See* People v. McHugh, 476 N.Y.S. 2d 721, 722–23 (Sup. Ct. 1984).

37. *See* I-35 bridge collapse (actual footage), NewsFootage (Aug. 3, 2007), https://www.bing.com/videos/search?q=I-35W+Collapse+video&docid=608041771496125560&mid=609B6CD921C2E7FAF00D609B6CD921C2E7FAF00D&view=detail&FORM=VIRE. The challenges and requirements for obtaining these videos—especially from videos from personal devices is discussed in Chapter 6, Section II.C "Photos, Video and Drone Data."

Similarly, when a construction is progressing according to schedule it follows the set of assumptions that were laid forth at the start of a project—a timeline can explain what changed. Adding an animation to a timeline can help fill in the blanks in between the available video or photographic evidence. These kinds of timelines are in addition to or complement the typical CPM or critical path method schedule used by project managers and by experts evaluating delay claims.

(j) Other Demonstrative Exhibits

Beyond graphics and models that can be viewed on a computer screen and printed out on a sheet of paper, other types of demonstrative exhibits include hand-built models, three-dimensional printed models, virtual reality environments, and augmented reality views.[38] Three-dimensional computer files can be sent to specialized printers that fabricate faithful three-dimensional reproductions of the models using a process called additive manufacturing.[39] Using augmented reality tags or other model information can be overlaid on real-time camera feeds. This kind of overlay allows the integration of training, defect, or other model information.[40] If a demonstration or demonstrative exhibit is based on a scientific test, it is subject to the admissibility standards of *Daubert v. Merrill Pharmaceuticals, Inc.*[41] and Federal Rule of Evidence 702 or state court equivalents.

---

38. The wider public was exposed to augmented reality in 2016 when Niantic released the handheld video game called Pokemon Go. Pokémon GO Press Conference, YouTube (Sept. 10, 2015), https://www.youtube.com/watch?v=tU1X77BKLyY.

39. *A Powerful Additive Manufacturing Ecosystem*, Makerbot, https://pages.makerbot.com/ (last visited Aug. 9, 2022).

40. *Augmented Reality for Construction*, VisualLive, https://visuallive.com (last visited Aug. 9, 2022).

41. Daubert v. Merrill Pharmaceuticals, Inc., 509 U.S. 579, 113 S. Ct. 2786, 125 L. Ed. 469 (1993).

II. The Consultant's Role in Preparing and Authenticating ESI for Use at Trial, Arbitration, or Mediation

The subject matter experts may not have the capacity or expertise to store, sort, read, and verify the authenticity and completeness of the ESI. Database systems such as Relativity and Disco are useful for storing, tagging, and sorting documents; they are not, however, equipped for open-source files that require proprietary programs and do not always preserve the file's meta-data.[42] The tagging systems similarly do not verify the authenticity of the information. Additionally, consultants who specialize in authenticating ESI compare the data received to see how consistent it is with its own schematics and rules. The subject matter expert should parse the data themselves to verify that it is consistent with the other evidence that helps support its authenticity and applicability.[43]

The team approach among trial counsel, subject matter expert, and technical creative expert is essential to creating exhibits economically, efficiently, and effectively. Effective planning is necessary to prevent cost and time from exceeding budgetary constraints. Trial counsel, with input from the subject matter expert, confirms the purpose and strategy for presenting ESI, which is to support and communicate the case theme and story from the client's perspective. Counsel and the technical creative expert determine the information to be presented and the ability to present relevant data in summary, timeline, and/or chart forms. Trial counsel and the subject matter expert must participate in the creative process to ensure the presentation plan will result in admissible and credible evidence that will be persuasive to the tribunal.

---

42. *See Simply Powerful Software for Legal and Compliance*, RELATIVITY, https://www.relativity.com/ (last visited Aug. 9, 2022), and Raise the Bar, CSDisco, https://www.csdisco.com/ (last visited Aug. 9, 2022). See Chapter 6, Section I.A.3.b for further discussion of preservation of metadata.

43. For strategies for preserving and requesting meta data, see Chapter 6, Section I.A.3.b.

A. Planning for Use of Demonstrative Exhibits

Some exhibits have such fundamental value that with proper planning they can be used in multiple phases of a case: mediation, nonbinding arbitration, voir dire, opening statement, fact witness testimony, expert witness testimony, and/or closing argument. Planning for demonstrative evidence is too important to leave until the last minute before trial. As relevant data is collected or discovered, trial counsel and the expert should consider how and when it would best be introduced. Is it too voluminous, fragmented, or unclear in its existing form? If so, consider a demonstrative exhibit such as a chart to summarize, organize, or illustrate a collective message from the data. Using different media for various exhibits can accomplish the goal for persuasive evidence presentation while staying within the case budget.

Planning demonstrative exhibits early allows counsel to consider all paths for establishing foundation while discovery is proceeding. In early case stages, all evidentiary tools are available for securing elements for authentication and admissibility. Agreement or pretrial rulings may avoid the need for time-consuming and distracting foundation laying during the case. However, establishing the foundation for particularly important exhibits before the jury or arbitrators in persuasive fashion may be so impressive that it bolsters the credibility and importance of the exhibit as well as its underlying message.[44] Such foundation can also reinforce the credibility of the introducing expert, showing the care and proficiency involved in creating the exhibit.

Finally, planning must include consideration of whether demonstrative exhibits are overkill for a particular case or issue or the makeup of a particular jury or arbitration panel. Is an exhibit necessary to prove, reinforce, explain, or illustrate an issue in the case? Is the exhibit too complicated, too fancy, or too detached from real facts or photos? Are there so many exhibits that they become a distraction? Can the arbitrators or jury understand the evidence without a demonstrative exhibit? Although counsel or client may find a demonstrative exhibit attractive,

---

44. Some counsel stipulate that a witness is an expert to avoid the display of impressive credentials to the jury. Likewise, the opponent may stipulate to the use of a demonstrative exhibit to avoid foundation that provides the jury with information relating to the power and credibility of the exhibit.

fancy exhibits may appear contrived or manufactured to skeptical jurors who may wonder why such displays are necessary.[45]

Jury makeup may change the plan for demonstrative exhibits completely. A panel of arbitrators may be a more suitable audience for certain demonstrative exhibits than a jury. Nonetheless, our society and the technology around us increasingly exposes jurors to information delivered in technical fashion. Jurors may expect rather than reject exhibits created by sophisticated software and expert consultants. If an exhibit is important enough, consider testing acceptance by potential jurors during voir dire questioning if the jurisdiction's rules permit.[46] Also, consider whether a particularly polished or striking exhibit could have an unintended result, such as highlighting the difference in economic resources between the parties.

The team of trial counsel, subject matter expert, and technical creative expert should plan the extent and content of potential evidentiary and demonstrative exhibits. Lead trial counsel decides how, when, and if evidence will be presented in the case. Properly employed, exhibits can be a powerful communication tool, but their effective use requires foresight and planning.

B. Big Data and Use of Analytics

When the data is produced by automated systems, the challenges grow. It is no longer feasible to hand tag every piece of information. Additional expertise may be required to process the data so it is usable and can be authenticated.[47] Fortunately, there are approaches for parsing through even billion row data sets, which are used heavily in other industries and have a rigorous mathematical support.[48]

---

45. *See* James W. McElhaney, *Gizmos in the Courtroom*, 83 A.B.A.J. 74 (Nov. 1997), also found at http://www.jstor.org/stable/27840111.

46. Federal courts may limit voir dire much more than state court jurisdictions, and the potential for such inquiry and especially follow up query may be unsuited for jury selection in a federal case.

47. See Chapter 6, Section I.A.6 for discussion of use of AI and TAR in processing ESI.

48. *The R Project for Statistical Computing*, R-Project, https://www.r-project.org (last visited Aug. 9, 2022).

1. Choosing Data Subsets

In large data sets, statistical tools can be helpful for determining correlations, trends, averages, and variations. When the data is reasonably uncorrelated—that is, each piece of information is not dependent on any other piece of information in the set—robust conclusions can be drawn from a small subset of information. When data is correlated, the average of tens of pieces of information is likely equal to the average of 1,000 or 100,000 pieces—generated from the same process. Similar kinds of tools and logic form the basis for material testing procedures that require only a subset of the material be destructively tested.[49]

Furthermore, if the full set of information is available, correlations can be made and tested between different activities. Given weather and bolting data for example, one could determine if rain is correlated with a reduction or an increase in the speed at which bolts are installed at connections or whether it is wholly unrelated. Determining whether rain is causal to bolts being installed, or bolts are causal to rain occurring, needs analysis beyond the correlations shown in the data. When choosing subsets of data identifying what part of the project is similar and uncorrelated is an important decision to make and defend.

2. Machine Learning and AI for Data Processing

As computer systems and storage increase in speed and magnitude, machine learning and AI are becoming more user friendly. With machine learning one can teach a computer how to identify patterns within similar kinds of data. This is especially helpful in the construction industry, where thousands, if not millions, of photos are produced for every project.[50] Open-source machine learning platforms such as TensorFlow contain huge databases of existing patterns and information that help filter out the relevant portions of an image, like a beam versus

---

49. *See, e.g.*, ASTM E105-16 Standard Practice for Probability Sampling of Materials, ASTM E122-17 Standard Practice for Calculating Sample Size to Estimate, With Specified Precision, the Average for a Characteristic of a Lot or Process, and other standards published by the ASTM Standards under the Jurisdiction of Committee E11 on Quality and Statistics.

50. See Chapter 6, Section I.A.6 for further discussion of AI use in reviewing data.

a chair or a wall versus a plant.[51] Once the walls are identified, features in the wall such as cracks can be identified as well. AI technology based on machine learning is already being used to process drone footage and identify cracks in masonry structures.[52] On future claims, rather than having an engineering intern or a paralegal sort through all the photos in the file, AI may be able to automate that search.

The AI itself is not equivalent to an expert, and any information that it highlights will need to be reviewed by an expert witness to ensure it is reliable and relevant. Similarly, the AI approach does not guarantee that every defect will be pattern matched and identified. As with any other automated processing, it is important to verify whether the AI is identifying relevant information. How the AI is set up, what features it is trained to identify, the algorithms it is based on, the training set, the evaluation criteria for performance precision, and testing and cross validation should be provided along with any other elements used to develop or alter the process.[53] AI is merely a means to focus attention on the appropriate data, and the expert must be available and informed to provide the foundation for admissibility and the suitability of the derived data for the purposes trial counsel identifies in planning the case presentation.

AI can also be used to determine patterns within conversations. AI could be used to track email and other project conversations and provide alerts if the response times seem to be changing, the group of people copied on the conversations appears to be increasing or decreasing, or even if the tone of the conversation is becoming adversarial.[54] AI is already being used to tie together disparate information at a job site such that the related documents to a note on a drawing are correlated with

---

51. *An End-to-End Open-Source Machine Learning Platform*, TensorFlow, https://www.tensorflow.org (last visited Aug. 9, 2022)

52. *Continuous AI-Driven Monitoring to Fix Little Problems before They Turn into Big Headaches*, T2D2, https://www.t2d2.ai/ (last visited Aug. 9, 2022).

53. Martin Zinkevich, *Rules of Machine Learning: Best Practices for ML Engineering*, Developers.Google, https://developers.google.com/machine-learning/guides/rules-of-ml (last visited Aug. 9, 2022).

54. *Azure Cognitive Service for Language documentation*, Microsoft, https://docs.microsoft.com/en-us/azure/cognitive-services/language-service/ (last visited Aug. 9, 2022).

one another in an automated way.[55] When this kind of AI processing is incorporated into the construction process, it may itself become the subject of an ESI assessment. In addition to its use as an investigative tool, AI may help expedite or make the document review process more thorough especially when navigating unsorted digital data.

C. Developing Demonstrative and Evidentiary Exhibits

Demonstrative and evidentiary exhibits pull together the building blocks outlined in the preceding sections to present the facts and analysis in an understandable way without overshadowing or misstating any of the underlying data. Construction claims have the benefit of being about something tangible and understandable. Everyone can picture a building and the construction process. Buildings, structures, and systems are part of our lives. If the issue cannot be explained clearly it is usually because the answer is not clear yet.

All construction projects are located in space. They have an address and a breadth. Each demonstrative exhibit should put the evidence in the context of the location of the project and within the structure or system. Models can be helpful for filling the gap between where a project is located and a smaller detail being discussed, focusing the attention of the trier of fact, avoiding distraction, and distilling the message to an understandable amount of information. Data processed from automatic sources usually has location information in it as well and can be displayed on the model either as a rendering or diagrammatically. Identification can also be useful in separating discrete messaging or issues by location for later summary by the witness or by counsel in closing argument. A key may be prepared as an incorporated or separate exhibit as suitable for the case. If a trial notebook is used, information needed for later reference may be included in the notebook.

For demonstrative and evidentiary exhibits each modeling choice needs to be based on evidence or the choice clearly explained if it is not. The focus of a demonstrative exhibit should be the issue at hand and not simply a review of all the available material. The balance between

55. *Futuristic Technology, Years in the Making*, OpenSpace, https://www.openspace.ai/the-tech/ (last visited Aug. 9, 2022). See Chapter 8, Section I for discussion of tools available for reviewing patterns in email strings.

presenting the information clearly and without bias is balanced with not adding too much information into a document. A series of exhibits may be summarized in a separate exhibit identifying the exhibits and placing them in sequence of importance or time or by location.

1. *Foundational Testimony*

The expert must testify the basis for his or her reliance on the data. If AI was used, that process should be referenced, and the data analyst should provide foundational testimony. For every choice made in the demonstrative, the expert should be able to testify why those choices were made and their foundation. Any uncertainties with the validity or source of the information similarly should be clearly disclosed.

(a) Expert Opinions

Expert opinions based on ESI are not fundamentally different than expert opinions based on information collected more conventionally. The chain of custody, parsing of information, and preparation of demonstrative evidence may require expertise beyond what the subject matter expert can provide. Regardless of the other parties involved, the subject matter expert should be able to explain and evaluate that the demonstratives are consistent with the underlying evidence, that the choices made in the representation are consistent with their opinions, and the impact of any filtering or other automated data processing. ESI specific experts may be required for verifying that the data was properly collected and data received was not tampered with. They should be able to verify that the collection of the data, and associated data conversion, did not alter the data in any significant way.[56]

2. *Using AI in Decision-Making*

AI technology excels in finding patterns and it compares in what way two situations are similar or different to one another. As more and more information is digitized, the amount of past information that the AI is trained on related to construction disputes and costs increases. When the

56. See Chapter 6, Section I.A for discussion about the role of the eDiscovery expert regarding testimony about how ESI was collected, organized, and processed.

background data is sufficient, the AI can be used to present informed conclusions and inform decision-making.

(a) Early Case Assessment

Whenever predictive patterns exist, AI can be used to evaluate how a new case is like the ones that came before. In the future, AI may help evaluate the strength of a contract, the completeness of contract drawings, and the reliability of a construction plan. AI trained on many projects may be able to quantify what the professional standard of care is for a particular design and provide backup for the weights it calculates. AI can assist lawyers in providing case evaluations to clients. "In today's practice, effective litigation managers can supplement their legal training and years of practice with enhanced insight from strategic and proactive use of quantitative predictions derived from statistical patterns and practices uncovered by data analytics and AI,"[57] to provide case evaluation and cost prediction for clients.

(b) Algorithmic Dispute Resolution

For many construction cases, the fact patterns of a dispute are similar across different cases. The key documents, including the contract, rate of RFI response, number of nonconformances, and the speed of responses, may be well correlated with findings of fault and ultimately predictive of whether a case will settle quickly, may be drawn out, and even what the result may be. Artificial intelligence is currently being used in dispute resolution proceedings in commercial and judicial settings. As in other areas, AI's use in dispute resolution continues to evolve as technology improves, and its use spurs debate among scholars and practitioners about AI's proper role as a tool in dispute resolution.[58]

---

57. Nan L. Grube, *Data Analytics and Artificial Intelligence in Litigation,* 78(1) J. Mo. Bar. (Jan.–Feb. 2022), https://news.mobar.org/data-analytics-and-artificial-intelligence-in-litigation/ (last accessed 3-24-23).

58. *See* Hibah Alessa, *The Role of Artificial Intelligence in Online Dispute Resolution: A Brief and Critical Overview*, 31 Inf. & Comm. Tech. Law 319 (June 2022), https://doi.org/10.1080/13600834.2022.2088060; Orna Rabinovich-Einy & Ethan Katsh, *Artificial Intelligence and the Future of Dispute Resolution*, ch. 17 in Online Dispute Resolution: Theory and Practice (Mohamed Abdel Wahab, Daniel

AI is necessarily challenged when patterns are not followed. Currently there is no scientifically accepted agreement on AI algorithms or processes available for case-by-case impeachment, and the preference of one set of AI algorithms and data application over another may be a matter of opinion. Competing experts base their approach or algorithms on their own knowledge, experience, and qualifications. Traditional impeachment of an AI process advanced by an expert against universally accepted scientific standards is not prevalent. Experts and professionals still need to evaluate the outlier cases, and the boundary between a usual and an unusual situation will surely be a topic in future disputes.

III. Conclusion

The explosion of data sources and data types in construction expands the need for partnership between construction attorneys and construction experts to review, organize, and manage the information to assist experts in rendering their opinions and to assist counsel in presenting supporting evidence persuasively.

Rainey & Ethan Katsh, eds., Eleven International Publishing, 2021), https://papers.ssrn.com/sol3/papers.cfm?abstract_id=3830033 (last accessed 3/22/23).

CHAPTER 8

Technology Tools for the Construction Litigator

Joseph T. Imperiale, John J. Gazzola, and Chris G. Haley, CISSP, *Authors*

One of the most significant challenges in construction litigation is the need to present complex concepts in a clear, concise, and persuasive manner. Construction litigators need to utilize technology to achieve this end. Technology allows attorneys to leverage their experience and resources to deliver better results—at lower costs—for their clients. Whether the result is a compelling presentation at a mediation, an effective argument at an arbitration hearing, or a persuasive closing at trial, technological tools are available each and every step of the way to straddle efficiency and effective advocacy.

Technology will certainly continue to advance and develop. New platforms, programs, and tools will hit the shelves before this book. But the key purposes for which lawyers use technology will remain. These include:

- Developing winning themes;
- Efficiently identifying key evidence amongst large quantities of data;
- Presenting complex projects and technical concepts in easily digestible ways; and
- Effectively preparing and presenting a case.

This chapter identifies certain technological tools available to achieve these ends. It also describes legal technology expected to become more prevalent soon and outlines recommendations for using technology in legal practice.

I. Using Artificial Intelligence to Identify the Sentiment Behind Written Records

Several applications made specifically for document review offer features to identify and analyze the sentiment of various word strings within documents. One such application is Reveal | Brainspace ("Reveal").[1] Once Reveal identifies and collects sentiments from the universe of documents, it generates summaries that show hot topics, the individuals discussing those topics, the sentiments apparent in those discussions, and the frequency of the discussions.

Sentiment analysis employs artificial intelligence to target the following sentiments:

- Intent: Identify someone's intention or purpose.
- Opportunity: Identify circumstances making it possible for someone to do something.
- Pressure: Identify attempts to persuade, influence, or intimidate.
- Rationalization: Identify attempts to explain or justify.
- Sentiment Alternation: Identify fluctuations in how people speak, detecting discomfort and tone changes, mainly to detect dishonesty.
- Positivity: Identify content that tends to be positive and optimistic, such as compliments or emojis.
- Negativity: Identify content that tends to be pessimistic, such as complaints or profanity.

---

1. This chapter references various platforms, tools, and applications that can be used for various functions. References to specific products are not endorsements of those products, or an indication that a named product is the only product designed to fulfill the purpose described. Rather, the products are referenced as examples to assist the reader.

Sentiment analysis is particularly helpful in developing a winning theme because it can identify the reasons or motivations behind key decisions. For example, we can use sentiment analysis in matters involving the following types of issues and disputes.

- In matters involving disputed change orders, correspondence regarding the necessity of an addition or change in work scope can be critical to proving entitlement. In such a case, the sentiments of pressure, rationalization, or alternation may assist in probing the necessity of the changes.
- In matters involving allegations of defective work, correspondence regarding the quality of the work is critical. Claimants seek to identify and highlight deficiencies in the work. On the other hand, defendants try to demonstrate that the work complied with the applicable requirements and the claims are exaggerated and unsubstantiated. In either case, the sentiments of positivity or negativity may identify contemporaneous project correspondence that accurately reflect the quality of the work.
- In matters involving allegations of delay or loss of productivity, correspondence regarding the availability of work fronts, mobilizations and demobilizations, and work interruptions is critical. In these cases, sentiments of opportunity and pressure may help to assess the availability of work and the reasons behind work interruptions.

In addition to assisting in the selection of a winning theme, sentiment analysis can also support witness selection and preparation. Sentiment analysis indicates the witness's propensity for certain emotions and a preview of their testimony. For example, targeting sentiments such as negativity can indicate a witness's disposition and how they may respond under pressure. Identifying sentiment alternation can indicate a witness's propensity to waffle during difficult questioning.

Additionally, sentiment analysis can help to identify "hot" documents in internal correspondence, such as communications illustrating internal strife or disagreement. This is critical when selecting exhibits for cross-examination. Simply put, sentiment analysis attaches emotion to text. Its uses are limited only by our own creativity.

II. Extraction Tools That Compile Data from a Large Volume of Documents

All construction lawyers know that construction projects are document and data intensive. Some of the most important details in a case consist of the data in invoices, change orders, schedules, and daily reports.

On large projects with hundreds of contractors, subcontractors, consultants, and suppliers, organizing and distilling the data from these forms is labor intensive. This expensive effort is necessary to prove or disprove liability and the extent of damages incurred.

Technology can accomplish this feat at a significantly reduced cost. Tools such as DocParser, Amazon Textract, and Microsoft Form Recognizer facilitate efficient data extraction from Word documents, PDFs, and image files and send it to more user-friendly formats, like Excel. Some tools can also extract handwriting. Extraction tools allow users to tailor the system's parsing system for specific purposes. In other words, the user can introduce a particular form to the system and teach it how to extract relevant data from that form. This additional flexibility makes parsing tools a key aspect of any case, regardless of how intricate or unique our client's forms may be.

Once the data is compiled in Excel, attorneys, clients, and expert witnesses can synthesize the data to support their analysis. For example, this tool can extract the following information from the face of a change order form: (1) contractor, subcontractor, and supplier names; (2) change order numbers; (3) submission dates; (4) work descriptions; (5) units of additional materials or supplies; and (6) claimed costs. This data is then sent to Excel where it can be compiled, tallied, and analyzed. Similarly, applying these tools to collections of invoices or shipping manifests allows the extraction of key data, such as (1) invoice numbers, (2) departure dates, (3) arrival dates, (4) item descriptions, (5) quantities, and (6) costs.

Patterns are more easily and quickly detectable when these details are extracted, compiled, and tallied. For example, routine change order requests can indicate significant changes in the scope of work performed. By compiling descriptions of the work reflected in change order requests, the dates the change order requests were submitted, and the associated costs, contractors can illustrate the magnitude of changes over the course of a project. These types of details are critical when the case involves cost overruns, delay claims, or even assertions of abandonment or cardinal change.

Similarly, daily reports can tell a variety of stories based on commentary by those with "boots on the ground." For instance, in prosecuting a loss of productivity claim, details from daily reports illustrating unavailable work fronts, demobilizations, remobilizations, and the associated hours are probative facts that can make or break the claim. Teaching a platform like DocParser how to syphon these details from daily reports can be invaluable. The entire story of a project can live in these reports; if the details are compiled in a streamlined format, they will be very convincing evidence.

Using such platforms allows tasks that would typically take attorneys days of document review and drafting chronology reports to be accomplished in an afternoon, saving the legal team hundreds of hours of fact investigation.

III. Depicting Complex Projects and Technical Concepts in Easily Digestible Ways

Visual depictions that allow a judge, arbitrator, and/or jury to understand the circumstances and conditions giving rise to a claim are a key aspect of every proceeding. Depending on the size of the project at issue, project files can contain tens of thousands of photographs and videos of the work performed, the conditions in which it is performed, the equipment used to perform the work, and the workers in action.

The magnitude of available information presents two challenges: (1) identifying photographs and videos that are *relevant* to your dispute, and (2) identifying photographs and videos that are *critical to winning* your dispute. Due to the lack of recognizable text in these files, the typical document screening tools cannot be used to identify relevant or critical photographs and videos. As a result, identifying the key videos and photographs in project files is often a "needle in the haystack" exercise. While it can be done, it demands countless hours of review and is an expensive undertaking.

Technology is available, however, to sift quickly through the mountains of data and target the necessary files. Indeed, artificial intelligence can be used to derive information from digital images and videos.

For example, the tool Reveal can identify, classify, and review images in a near native manner. This capability enables the program to survey photographs of a construction site and identify building materials, equipment, and other aspects of the depicted work.

Tools such as Reveal not only sift through thousands of JPGs to identify relevant or responsive documents, but they also can target the critical photographs and videos needed to explain projects and issues in a compelling, understandable way.

Reveal is equipped with the following capabilities and functions:

- Image Detection: Determine if an image is present in a collection.
- Image Classification: Classify images into specified categories.
- Object Detection: Detect specific objects within an image.
- Object Tracking: Follow an object's path as it moves through a video.
- Semantic Segmentation: Break down an image to the pixel level to differentiate between objects.
- Instance Segmentation: Categorize different varieties of similar objects.
- Image Recognition: Identify when an image is present.
- Image Categorization: Identify a category in which an image fits.

These functions present several advantages in construction cases. For example, this technology can categorize photographs and the images in them. This allows collection and organization of photographs of various aspects of the work. Showing the work at each phase displays, describes, and explains a project's development. The better the audience understands the life cycle of a project, the better they will understand the issues in dispute and the more likely they will be to make an accurate, informed decision.

These functions can also depict the types of equipment used on projects and the extent to which they are used. Many years ago, the authors represented a subcontractor in a dispute arising from the construction of a major metro rail system. Delay and lost productivity were key issues in the case. Questions arose regarding whether the client used a certain type of excavator on the project and, if so, how often and where. The legal team searched through thousands of project photographs for evidence to illustrate the client's use of the equipment. While the manual search eventually revealed the evidence needed, the process could have benefited significantly from a resource like Reveal. By finding a single photograph of the excavator, a platform such as Reveal could learn to identify other photographs depicting the excavator and videos of it in use, saving significant time and expense.

While photographs and videos are mainstays on construction matters, new technology is providing new vantage points. For example, many contractors use time lapse photographs and videos to show the development of a project over time. Time lapse depictions are particularly compelling for vertical construction projects such as skyscrapers, where the sequence and progression of the work is clearly visible over time. Similarly, when projects span several seasons, these depictions help the audience to appreciate the challenges the client may have faced throughout the life of the project.

Aerial photographs and videos are much more available with the advent and accessibility of drones. Drones offer excellent perspectives on large projects and can show the breadth and extent of linear projects. A single drone flight can illustrate the length of a pipeline and the conditions through which it passes. *Seeing* that a pipeline traverses 100 miles of wooded terrain has a much greater effect to an arbitrator, mediator, judge, or jury than merely *hearing* it. This is particularly advantageous when a project's location makes it inaccessible.

IV. Effectively Preparing and Presenting the Case[2]

Technology has become expected in legal proceedings. Slide decks, video evidence, and graphics have taken the place of foam boards. Many judges and arbitrators expect, and even request, thumb drives containing electronic exhibits before hearings rather than exhibit binders (and boxes upon boxes thereof). And a growing number of arbitrators use iPads with preloaded exhibits, so they can annotate the exhibits in real time.

Newer technology offers much more than these bare-bones capabilities. Indeed, recent technological developments allow attorneys to engage with judges, arbitrators, jurors, and even legal teams more deeply.

2. See also Chapter 7, Presenting ESI Evidence at Trial, Arbitration Hearings, and Mediation.

For example, for many attorneys, tablets or iPads have taken the place of legal pads. Attorneys can use their tablets during mediations, arguments, hearings, and even trials to present an organized and persuasive case. Moreover, applications such as TrialPad, Oncue, and TrialDirector 360 offer a range of litigation-focused capabilities. Attorneys can use these applications to deliver presentations; introduce, mark, and annotate exhibits; highlight particular portions of transcripts; and even present, pause, and emphasize videos. The size and convenience of tablets allow attorneys to use them on their feet, throughout trial, and in front of the judge and jury or arbitration panel. Attorneys are no longer constrained by laptops or power cords. With thousands of exhibits, transcripts, photographs, and work papers at one's fingertips, these platforms make for a much more efficient recollection and presentation of evidence.

Additionally, platforms that combine audio, video, screen-sharing, and conferencing capabilities are now common and useful litigation tools. Over the last three years, most clients and lawyers have become comfortable with remote proceedings and the platforms making them possible. New technology, however, offers expanded capabilities for in-person and remote proceedings. For example, LiveLitigation allows users to follow and search transcripts in real time; to import, annotate, and stamp exhibits; and even to chat privately with members of their legal team in nondiscoverable chat rooms. These platforms may give legal teams an edge throughout trial, whether remote or in person.

Mastering these tools and their capabilities separates the technologically advanced from the technologically competent. Seamlessly working through exhibits, transcripts, and videos—whether in person or remotely—gives attorneys an impressive presence. An efficient, effective, and smooth examination will make witnesses more comfortable and presentations more compelling.

V. Litigation Technology on the Horizon—What's to Come?

The goal to deliver better, faster, and more cost-effective results to clients will drive invention, development, and use of technology in law practices. So, how can attorneys stay on the cutting edge of technology? Pay attention to social media and popular culture because they often drive innovation. Technologies with the potential to automate routine tasks, anticipate and satisfy needs and preferences, analyze large volumes of data, secure data and personal information, and allow for a more connected culture will always have an impact on communities. As new and different technologies are used in our everyday lives, legal technology needed to collect, compile, synthesize, and present the associated data will undoubtedly follow.

Similarly, as attorneys become more accustomed to new technology outside the workplace, they will be more likely to use it in the courtroom. For example, with the advent of improved and accessible virtual reality software, there is a movement to make use of it in legal proceedings. Recreating project sites and providing the arbitrator, judge, or jury with a firsthand view of the environment from which a claim arose can be a compelling aspect of a case. If the setting is an important aspect of a claim or defense making a site visit necessary, virtual reality can reduce the time and expense associated with transporting a dozen jurors to a construction site.

The pace of change and the introduction of new technology is increasing exponentially. Staying informed of these rapid developments can be daunting. Meet this challenge by making legal technology and the developments within it a routine aspect of your practice. Free resources such as articles, blog posts, podcasts, webinars, and CLEs are a great way to stay informed of new legal technology and current trends. Once you have identified a new technology that you would like to use in your practice, dedicate the time necessary to become comfortable with it. Ask vendors for demonstrations. Speak to colleagues who use it. Practice using the tools during your down time. Attorneys who stay informed about technology and its developments will certainly have an advantage in the future.

VI. Recommendations and Best Practices

The tools and platforms outlined here are just a few of the many available to construction litigators. Regardless of the tools chosen, keep in mind the following recommendations and best practices for employing technology in your construction litigation practice.

- ***Litigation technology is not a one-size-fits-all approach.*** Tailor the technological tools for each case. Ensure that the tools used will be effective for a specific matter or issue.
- ***Do your homework.*** Before selecting the tools to use, make sure that they are permitted (and welcome) in the courts and jurisdictions where the matter is pending. Research the judge's, mediator's, or arbitrator's rules and operating procedures before attempting to use these tools in a hearing.
- ***Develop protocols for the use of technology accordingly.*** When planning to use certain trial technologies, negotiate protocols with opposing counsel allowing for their use during proceedings. For example, if planning to submit exhibits to the arbitrator or judge on an iPad, make sure that procedure is included in a joint status report, discovery protocol, or terms of reference.
- ***Practice, practice, practice.*** Be prepared to use the tools selected. If planning to use technology tools during trial or hearings, make sure that you are comfortable using them and knowledgeable of their capabilities. Do dry runs. Consult with your firm's IT team. Have IT on standby to assist if issues arise. Speak with attorneys who have used the tools to identify any nuances or quirks that may arise.
- ***Be ready to play defense.*** Be prepared to defend the propriety of the technological tools to be employed. Just recently, the propriety of technology was a key issue during a highly public criminal trial. Counsel argued over whether the "pinch to zoom" feature of an iPad distorted the image to be displayed. The court placed the burden on the prosecution—who intended to use the video feature during cross-examination of the defendant—to prove that zooming in on a video with an iPad does not alter or manipulate the footage. Anticipate challenges to selected technology and be prepared to overcome them at trial.
- ***Use technology to complement traditional trial work.*** Use technology to capitalize on work and preparation, not to cut

corners. Nothing can take the place of effective direct or cross-examination; however, technology tools can enhance the presentation.

Make technology a routine part of your practice. The more attorneys know about legal technology, the more likely they are to use it and to explore new and different tools hitting the market. Read blog posts, attend CLEs, and discuss trends with colleagues and industry associates. Ask colleagues and friends about the technology they have used, and what they have seen their adversaries use. Be open and curious about technology and willing to try new applications, platforms, and products.

V. Conclusion

Just as technology provides new opportunities for designers, contractors, subcontractors, and suppliers, it also provides new opportunities for construction lawyers to find relevant facts more easily and to present evidence in compelling ways for clients. Becoming proficient in using technology can make construction lawyers more efficient as well as being better advocates.